Misunderstanding, Nationalism, or Legalism

Misunderstanding, Nationalism, or Legalism

Identifying Israel's Chief Error
with Reference to the Law in Romans 9:30—10:13

RICHARD WELLONS WINSTON

WIPF & STOCK · Eugene, Oregon

MISUNDERSTANDING, NATIONALISM, OR LEGALISM
Identifying Israel's Chief Error with Reference to the Law in Romans 9:30—10:13

Copyright © 2020 Richard Wellons Winston. All rights reserved. Except for brief quotations in critical publications or reviews, no part of this book may be reproduced in any manner without prior written permission from the publisher. Write: Permissions, Wipf and Stock Publishers, 199 W. 8th Ave., Suite 3, Eugene, OR 97401.

Wipf & Stock
An Imprint of Wipf and Stock Publishers
199 W. 8th Ave., Suite 3
Eugene, OR 97401

www.wipfandstock.com

PAPERBACK ISBN: 978-1-7252-7605-5
HARDCOVER ISBN: 978-1-7252-7606-2
EBOOK ISBN: 978-1-7252-7607-9

Manufactured in the U.S.A.   09/03/20

I dedicate this dissertation to Beth,
with thanks for your constant encouragement.

Contents

Permissions ix

Preface xi

Abbreviations xiii

Abstract xv

Chapter 1   Introduction   1

Chapter 2   Romans 9:30–33   23

Chapter 3   Romans 10:1–4   46

Chapter 4   Romans 10:5   81

Chapter 5   Romans 10:6–8   109

Chapter 6   Romans 10:9–13   139

Chapter 7   Conclusion   160

Bibliography 165

Permissions

Scripture quotations marked RSV are from the Revised Standard Version of the Bible, copyright © 1946, 1952, and 1971 National Council of the Churches of Christ in the United States of America. Used by permission. All rights reserved worldwide.

Scripture quotations marked NRSV are from the New Revised Standard Version Bible, copyright © 1989 National Council of the Churches of Christ in the United States of America. Used by permission. All rights reserved worldwide.

Scripture quotations marked NIV taken from the Holy Bible, New International Version®, NIV®. Copyright © 1973, 1978, 1984, 2011 by Biblica, Inc.™ Used by permission of Zondervan. All rights reserved worldwide. www.zondervan.com. The "NIV" and "New International Version" are trademarks registered in the United States Patent and Trademark Office by Biblica, Inc.™

Scripture quotations marked NIV84 taken from the Holy Bible, New International Version®, NIV®. Copyright © 1973, 1978, 1984 by Biblica, Inc.™ Used by permission of Zondervan. All rights reserved worldwide. www.zondervan.com The "NIV" and "New International Version" are trademarks registered in the United States Patent and Trademark Office by Biblica, Inc.™

Scripture quotations taken from the New American Standard Bible® (NASB), Copyright © 1960, 1962, 1963, 1968, 1971, 1972, 1973, 1975, 1977, 1995 by The Lockman Foundation. Used by permission. www.Lockman.org.

Scripture quotations marked are from the ESV® Bible (The Holy Bible, English Standard Version®), copyright © 2001 by Crossway Bibles, a publishing ministry of Good News Publishers. Used by permission. All rights reserved.

Scripture quotations marked HCSB are taken from the Holman Christian Standard Bible®, Used by Permission HCSB ©1999, 2000, 2002, 2003,

2009 Holman Bible Publishers. Holman Christian Standard Bible®, Holman CSB®, and HCSB® are federally registered trademarks of Holman Bible Publishers.

Preface

Many deserve special thanks for contributing to this project. Aaron Burk encouraged me years ago to attend seminary, and this dissertation is the culmination of those studies. Greg Stiekes and Dr. Michael Barrett were instrumental in directing me towards Central Baptist Theological Seminary, and in challenging me to think deeply and seriously about Scripture. My interest in Paul and the law began in Dr. Jon Pratt's class on the same topic, and I appreciate his patience in reading many of my papers on this topic and now finally a dissertation. Special thanks also go to the faculty and students of Central Baptist Theological Seminary for encouragement and challenge throughout the doctoral program. I am grateful for my brothers and sisters in Christ at Faith Free Presbyterian Church for their constant interest, encouragement, and prayers for my studies. Your labor was not in vain! I am also grateful to Dr. Charles Barrett and Geneva Reformed Seminary for the opportunity to finish this dissertation while employed as a member of the Resident Faculty. I do not know how I would have finished it otherwise. Special thanks are due to my parents for taking me to church, and introducing me to the things of God. Finally, immense gratitude is due to my wife, Beth, and my children, Ben and Grace. Your patience, encouragement, and support have meant to the world to me.

    Richard Wellons Winston
    Greenville, South Carolina
    May, 2015

Abbreviations

BDAG	Walter Bauer, Frederick W. Danker, W. F. Arndt, and F. W. Ginrgich. *A Greek-English Lexicon of the New Testament and Other Early Christian Literature.* 3rd ed. Chicago: University of Chicago Press, 2000.
HALOT	Ludwig Koehler and Walter Bumgartner. *The Hebrew and Aramaic Lexicon of the Old Testament.* New York: Brill, 1994–2000.
MT	Masoretic Text
NA^{28}	*Novum Testamentum Graece,* 28th edition
UBS^3	United Bible Societies *Greek New Testament,* 3rd edition
UBS^4	United Bible Societies *Greek New Testament,* 4th edition

Abstract

Richard Wellons Winston, PhD
Central Baptist Theological Seminary, 2015
Committee Chair: Dr. Jonathan Pratt

This dissertation examines Paul's exegetical and theological argument in Rom 9:30–10:13, with special attention to his use of the Old Testament. It argues that Paul criticizes Israel for pursuing a right standing with God by obeying the Mosaic law when they should have discerned within their own Scriptures both humanity's inability to keep the Mosaic law and the necessity of salvation by faith alone. It proves this thesis in two ways. First, by exegeting key phrases throughout Rom 9:30–10:13, and showing that their meaning best accords with a law-gospel approach to Paul. Second, by showing that Paul uses the OT to argue that the law's demands for perfect obedience must be read in light of the salvation-historical priority of salvation by faith. This work also argues against the ideas that the Mosaic law primarily commands faith and that Israel was guilty of a nationalistic approach to righteousness.

Chapter 1

Introduction

THESIS

This dissertation examines Paul's exegetical and theological argument in Rom 9:30—10:13, with special attention to his use of the Old Testament. Paul declares at the beginning of Romans that the gospel is the power of God unto salvation for all who believe (Rom 1:16). His confidence in the gospel's power to save is based upon the fact that it reveals the righteousness of God which is obtained by faith (Rom 1:17a). The OT itself teaches that the righteous live by faith (Rom 1:17b citing Hab 2:4). Together, Rom 1:16-17 announce the theme of Romans: the gospel which reveals the righteousness of God for all who believe.[1]

Paul develops this theme throughout the major sections of Romans: 1:18—3:20 establish humanity's need of righteousness; 3:21—4:25 develop the provision of justifying righteousness by Christ for all who believe; 5:1—8:39 explain the reality of sanctifying righteousness for all who have

---

1. Based on Moo who identifies the theme or main topic of Romans simply as "the gospel" (*Epistle to the Romans*, 29–30), and Stuhlmacher who elaborates the theme as follows: "*according to Romans 1:1–17 this theme must be the gospel carried by Paul, i.e., the gospel of the divine righteousness in and through Christ, by virtue of which those who believe from among the Jews and Gentiles (according to the promise from Hab. 2:4) obtain life*" ("Theme of Romans," 335, emphasis original). While not disputing 1:16-17 as the theme of the epistle, Wright argues that the Christological theme of 1:3-4 gives coherence to Paul's argument in Romans ("Messiah").

believed, and 12:1—15:13 give practical exhortations that illustrate the nature of the sanctified life.² Interpreters, however, dispute the role that 9:1—11:36 play in the overall argument of Romans.³

C. H. Dodd famously argued that these chapters were the remnants of an old sermon on Israel's rejection that Paul carried around with him and inserted here in order to fully answer questions raised in 3:1–9.⁴ Rom 9–11 does address questions raised in 3:1–9,⁵ but it does not logically follow that the material contained therein was merely inserted into the flow of an otherwise tightly constructed letter. Rom 9–11 flows directly from 8:31–39.⁶ Since Paul promises that God's people suffer no condemnation in Christ and cannot be separated from the love of God in Christ, what are they to make of God's OT people, Israel, who are presently accursed and separated from Christ (implied in 9:3)?⁷

On the opposite side of the equation, some argue that Rom 9–11 constitute the climax of Paul's theological argument in Rom 1–11.⁸ While this

---

2. This approach to Romans reflects a traditional Lutheran approach to Paul, and is well-defended by Gathercole, "Justified by Faith," 147–84; Moo, "Israel and the Law," 185–216; Moo, *Epistle to the Romans*, 548–52; Schreiner, *Romans*; Seifrid, *Christ, Our Righteousness*, 35–76; Seifrid, "Unrighteous By Faith," 105–45; Westerholm, *Perspectives*, 384–401. Key sources that reflect the New Perspective on Paul's approach to Romans include Dunn, "Letter to the Romans," 842–50; Dunn, *Romans*; Wright, *Justification*, 177–248; Wright, *Romans*. For an overview of the major literature on the topic of Paul and the law, see Moo, "Paul and the Law," 287–307; Toews, "Law," 3–104; Westerholm, "New Perspective at Twenty-Five," 1–38.

3. Wright observes, "Many have given it [Rom 9–11] up as a bad job, leaving Romans as a book with eight chapters of 'gospel' at the beginning, four of 'application' at the end, and three of puzzle in the middle" (*Climax*, 231). For a dated but still very useful summary of the history of interpretation of Rom 9–11, see Sanday and Headlam, *Romans*, 269–75.

4. Dodd, *Romans*, 148–50. Sanday and Headlam argue that Paul finishes his main argument at the end of chapter 8, but they also highlight the importance of chapters 9–11 in defending God's justice in the light of Israel's present exclusion from salvation (*Romans*, 225).

5. Schreiner, *Romans*, 469.

6. Calvin, *Romans*, 332–33.

7. Longenecker finds Dodds proposal "highly likely," but still admits "it must always remain largely conjectural" (*Romans*, 831–32).

8. Wright, *Climax*, 234; Fitzmyer, *Romans*, 541. In his most recent assessment of Rom 9–11, Wright puts forth a similar argument, viewing the section as Paul's explanation of how God has redefined the elect people of God around the Messiah in fulfillment of his promise to Abraham to create a worldwide family of faith (*Paul*, 1156–257). Dunn claims that viewing Rom 9–11 "as the real climax of Paul's attempt to understand the place of Jew and Gentile within the purpose of God" is the dominant view (*Theology*, 501).

approach gives coherence to Rom 1–11 (and anticipates 14:1—15:13),[9] Rom 9–11 has a different emphasis than Rom 1–8. Rom 1–8 develops the righteousness of God; Rom 9–11 focuses on those who have received and on those who have rejected the righteousness of God (esp. 9:30–10:21). Rom 4:1–25 highlights continuity in God's means of crediting righteousness to his people; Rom 9–11 focuses on the recipients of this righteousness (esp. 9:1–29 and 11:1–33). The more sound approach is that Rom 9–11 addresses an integral part of the overall theme of the letter, but not its climax.[10]

Paul uses Rom 9–11 to answer the potential objection that Israel's present exclusion from salvation means that Paul's gospel may not be the power of God unto salvation for all who believe.[11] If the Christian gospel is that power, and if it is the fulfillment of the OT promises, then what does Israel's exclusion imply about God's power and promises? Have they in some way failed Israel? And if they have failed Israel, will they fail Christians (cf. 8:31–39)? The purpose of Rom 9–11 is to demonstrate that the word of God has not failed (9:6a).[12] The gospel really is the power of God unto salvation for all who believe.[13]

---

9. Wright, *Climax*, 235.

10. Moo, *Epistle to the Romans*, 547; Naselli, "Paul's Use," 225.

11. Aune, "Romans," 159; Byrne, *Romans*, 307; Cranfield, *Romans*, 446–47; Longenecker and Still, *Thinking Through Paul*, 186; Marshall, *New Testament Theology*, 323–25; Moo, "Israel and the Law," 196–98; Moo, *Epistle to the Romans*, 547–49; Osborne, *Romans*, 259–60; Piper, *Justification of God*, 19, 46; Schreiner, *Romans*, 470–71; Thielman, *Law*, 28. For an overview of the argument of Rom 9–11, see Westerholm, "Paul and the Law," 215–37.

12. Piper, *Justification of God*, 19; Southall, *Rediscovering Righteousness*, 152–53.

13. On the unity of Paul's argument in Rom 9–11, see Johnson, "Romans 9–11," 211–39; Moo, "Theology," 240–58; Theobald, "Unterschiedliche Gottesbilder," 135–77; Thielman, "Unexpected Mercy," 169–81. Our assessment of Paul's argument is as follows: 9:1–5: Paul's anguish over Israel's present separation from Christ; 9:6–18: defense of God's faithfulness on the grounds that God never promised to save every ethnic Israelite, but has the sovereign right to elect whomever he wills to salvation (and this is in continuity with Israel's Scriptures); 9:19–29: defense of God's faithfulness on the grounds that he has elected many gentiles to salvation and a remnant of Israelites (and this is in continuity with Israel's Scriptures); 9:30–10:21: defense of God's faithfulness on the grounds that whereas gentiles have sought righteousness by faith, Israel has failed to keep the terms of God's covenant with them (and this is in continuity with Israel's Scriptures); 11:1–32: defense of God's faithfulness on the grounds that God has not rejected his people; all Israel will be saved (and this is in continuity with Israel's Scriptures); 11:33–36: concluding doxology extolling the wisdom and knowledge of God. For a similar assessment, see Schreiner, *Romans*, 472–75. Aletti highlights the similarity of progression in thought between Rom 9–11 and the prayer of Azariah in the Greek additions to Daniel: (1) the supremacy of God's works, (2) human condition the result of human sin, and (3) the faithfulness of God to save his people ("Romans," 1589).

Paul uses a two-pronged approach throughout Rom 9–11 to prove God's faithfulness to his word. In 9:6b–29, Paul attributes Israel's lack of salvation (9:1–5) to the sovereignty of God to save whomever he wishes to save. God's promises have not failed (9:6a) because God never promised to save every ethnic Israelite (9:6b–13). In fact, God has even purposed to save many gentiles (9:14–29). This sovereign purpose is one reason many gentiles have obtained a right standing with God whereas many Jews have not.

However, this is not the only reason, and in 9:30—10:13 Paul addresses from the human standpoint[14] why Israel has not obtained a right standing with God.[15] Paul gives two reasons: (1) their lack of faith in Jesus as Messiah (9:30, 32b–33; 10:4, 9–13), and (2) their error with reference to the law (9:31–32a; 10:2–3, 5–8). For the most part, interpreters of Paul do not dispute the reality or seriousness of the first reason (Israel's lack of faith in Jesus as Messiah).[16] The more disputed question concerns the identification of Israel's error with reference to the law.[17] Does Paul criticize Jewish misunderstanding of the true message of the law (they failed to see that the law ultimately demands faith), a nationalistic approach to righteousness (salvation is only available within the confines of Israel and the law), or a legalistic attempt to earn a right standing with God through obedience to the law? What is Israel's chief error with reference to the law in Rom 9:30—10:13? This dissertation argues that Paul criticizes Israel for pursuing a right standing with God by obeying the Mosaic law when they should have discerned within their own Scriptures both humanity's inability to keep the Mosaic law and the necessity of salvation by faith alone.

---

14. While Rom 9–11 is more than a doctrinal treatise on predestination and human responsibility, such themes are an integral part of Paul's explanation of why many gentiles are experiencing salvation while many Israelites are not.

15. Southall, *Rediscovering Righteousness*, 159; Wilckens, *Römer*, 2:210.

16. Some exceptions exist. Gaston writes, "Romans 9 is not about the unbelief of Israel nor the rejection of Israel. Paul does refer elsewhere to Israel's lack of understanding (10:3, 19), to Israel's disobedience (10:21; 11:11–12, 31) and to Israel's lack of faithfulness (3:3; 11:20), all with respect to the Gentile mission. In Rom 2:17–24 Paul refers bitterly to Israel's task of being a light to the Gentiles, a task in which they have failed in his opinion. But he really does not, in Romans 9–11 or elsewhere, charge Israel with a lack of faith or a concept of works-righteousness" (*Paul and the Torah*, 99). Likewise, Stendahl admits that non-Christian Jews do not believe in Messiah but does not think this is a problem to Paul: "Paul does not say that when the time of God's kingdom, the consummation, comes Israel will accept Jesus as the Messiah. He says only that the time will come when 'all Israel will be saved' (11:26)" (*Paul Among Jews*, 4). We address these arguments in our discussion of Rom 10:1.

17. Schreiner writes, "Locating the precise reason why the Jews failed to obtain righteousness via the law is the most controversial issue in Rom 9:30–10:3" ("Israel's Failure," 209).

Introduction

JUSTIFICATION OF THE STUDY

Paul begins Rom 9:30—10:13 with a question: "What therefore should we say?" (Τί οὖν ἐροῦμεν). Rather than bringing 9:6b–29 to a conclusion,[18] Paul's language indicates that he is now beginning a new paragraph, and therefore introducing the next stage in the discussion of God's faithfulness.[19] He identifies the limits of this next section by beginning and ending the passage with a reference to the gentiles (9:30; 10:11, 13), as well as a citation of Isa 28:16 (9:33; 10:12).[20] Paul also resumes the familiar language of righteousness, law, faith, and works.[21]

The passage develops a threefold contrast between righteousness by works and righteousness by faith (9:30–33; 10:1–4, 5–13).[22] The first paragraph (9:30–33) states the thesis, and the rest of the passage (10:1–13) develops it.[23] While Paul begins by highlighting gentile inclusion in God's

---

18. As argued by Haacker, *Römer*, 223; Hendriksen, *Romans*, 333; and Lambrecht, "Caesura," 141–47.

19. Paul uses the phrase Τί οὖν ἐροῦμεν five other times in Romans, and in each occurrence it opens a new paragraph (4:1; 8:31; 6:1; 7:7; 9:14). Grieb, *Romans*, 97; Kruse, *Romans*, 393; Longenecker, *Romans*, 829–30. Mohrmann, "Semantic Collisions," 206n803, also observes that 9:30–33 focuses more on the present than on the past, indicating that it belongs more with 10:1–13 than 9:6b–29.

20. Moo, *Epistle to the Romans*, 619–20. Grieb observes that Paul also uses an *inclusio* to mark off the previous section: the reference to "seed" (σπέρμα) in 9:7, 29 (*Romans*, 97). Commentators rightly recognize that Paul continues to discuss themes raised in 9:30—10:13 in 10:14–21 (e.g., Longenecker and Moo treat Rom 9:30—10:21 as one section [*Romans*, 827, and *Epistle to the Romans*, 616, respectively]). Longenecker even notes that the quotation of Isa 65:1–2 in 10:20–21 functions to close the subsection 9:30—10:21 just as the citation of Isa 10:22–23 and 1:9 earlier in 9:27–29 functioned to close the subsection 9:6–29 (*Romans*, 834). However, the πῶς οὖν which begins 10:14 shifts the focus from the necessity of calling upon Christ for salvation (9:30—10:13, particularly 10:9–13) to the means of doing so (10:14–17). Furthermore, 9:30—10:13 is held together by several occurences of γάρ and ὅτι, whereas 10:14 features οὖν, just as 9:30 (the beginning of the new subsection) does.

21. Dunn, *Romans*, 2:577; Moo, *Epistle to the Romans*, 618; Toews, *Romans*, 258.

22. Dunn, *Romans*, 2:577; Moo, *Epistle to the Romans*, 619; Toews, *Romans*, 258. Several interpreters argue that the OT citations in 10:5–8 are complementary rather than contrastive, but do not dispute the overall contrast throughout the passage.

23. Badenas, *End of the Law*, 101; Barth, *Dogmatics*, 242; Barrett, *Romans*, 192; Cranfield, *Romans*, 2:505; Dunn, *Romans*, 2:579; Käsemann, *Romans*, 276; Longenecker, *Romans*, 831; Stuhlmacher, *Romans*, 152; Toews, "Law," 106. Other commentators such as Dodd, Fitzmyer, and Wilckens view 9:30–33 as transitional to the main argument in 10:1–13 (*Romans*, 160; *Romans*, 576; and *Römer*, 2:211, respectively). However, two factors warrant against this. First, since 9:30–33 contains the same contrast one finds in 10:1–13, one would expect the latter paragraphs to develop what is stated in the first. Second, the occurrence of μέν without other particles indicates that μέν functions in 10:1 as a marker of continuation (BDAG, 630). Paul begins his argument in 9:30–33 and continues

saving purposes (9:30), the reference to gentile inclusion does not establish the main theme of the passage.[24] Rather, the reference to gentile inclusion flows from the conclusion to the previous section (9:24–29), and provides the necessary foil for unbelieving Israel (9:31—10:13). Paul focuses in 9:30—10:13 on Israel's plight (9:30—10:3) and its solution (10:4–13).[25]

Rom 9:30—10:13 carries a weight in Pauline studies out of proportion to its length. The amount of secondary literature on the passage is enormous. This abundance of literature raises the question of the necessity of another study on the passage. The following factors justify the addition of a full-length research project to the library of studies on Rom 9:30—10:13.

First, the content of Rom 9:30—10:13 indicates its own importance with reference to discussions on the relationship between the law and faith, righteousness and the law, Moses and Christ, and the Old and New Testaments. Consider the following: 9:30 refers to the righteousness which is from faith; 9:31 refers to Israel pursuing a law of righteousness and not attaining the law; 9:32 refers to pursuing the law not by faith but as if from works; 10:1 refers to salvation; 10:2 refers to zeal for God; 10:3 refers to Israel's ignorance of the righteousness of God, their attempt to establish their own righteousness, and their failure to submit to the righteousness of God; 10:4 refers to Christ as the τέλος of the law, and righteousness for all who believe; 10:5 refers to the righteousness which comes from the law and the life that comes to those who do it; 10:6–8 refers to the righteousness of faith; 10:9 refers to faith and salvation; 10:10 refers to believing unto righteousness and confessing unto salvation; 10:11 refers to whoever believes; 10:12 refers to all who call upon God; 10:13 refers to salvation. The interaction of all these topics in this short passage testifies to the importance of understanding this passage in order to understand the larger topic of Paul and the law.

---

it in 10:1–13. The content of 9:30–33 is foundational and essential, not just transitional.

24. As argued by Barth, *People of God*, 39–40; Gaston, *Paul and the Torah*, 99, 142; Wright, *Paul*, 1166; Wright, *Romans*, 646–47. For the argument that the theme of gentile inclusion receives equal emphasis with the explanation of Israel's failure, see Kaylor, *Paul's Covenant Community*, 166; Mohrmann, "Semantic Collisions," 268; Toews, *Romans*, 257; Watson, *Beyond the New Perspective*, 322–33.

25. Aquinas, *Romans*, 277–78; Black, *Romans*, 136; Byrne, *Romans*, 307; Calvin, *Romans*, 376; Dumbrell, *Romans*, 102; Dunn, *Romans*, 2:576–77; Fitzmyer, *Romans*, 576; Hultgren, *Romans*, 376–77; Johnson, *Romans*, 166–68; Käsemann, *Romans*, 276; Keck, *Romans*, 242; Kruse, *Romans*, 392–93; Moo, *Epistle to the Romans*, 617–18; Mounce, *Romans*, 205; Nygren, *Romans*, 376–77; Osborne, *Romans*, 259–61; Sanday and Headlam, *Romans*, 301; Schreiner, *Romans*, 531; Seifrid, "Romans," 650; Stowers, *Romans*, 302–3; Stuhlmacher, *Romans*, 151; Thielman, *Theology*, 368–69; Witherington, *Romans*, 249–51.

Second, Paul's heavy use of the OT indicates the passage's importance with reference to the relationship between the Old and New Testaments. Paul cites the OT eight times throughout these sixteen verses: Isa 8:14; 28:16 in 9:33; Lev 18:5 in 10:5; Deut 8:17a; 9:4a; 30:12–14 in 10:6–8; Isa 28:16 in 10:11; and Joel 2:32 in 10:13.[26] Paul believes that his argument is in continuity with the OT and can be proven by frequent appeal to it.[27] Therefore, a right understanding of the passage plays a large role in understanding how the NT uses the OT.

Third, students of Paul and the law highlight the central significance of the passage in understanding Paul and the law. As early as 1977, John Toews observed the growing importance of Rom 8–10 in discussions on Paul and the law.[28] Jason Meyer calls it "one of the most hotly contested passages in all of Paul."[29] In addition, advocates of different theological approaches to Paul and the law usually appeal to this passage to justify their approach. For example, William Dumbrell uses this passage to illustrate how "a salvation-history approach to biblical theology provides an understanding of what was at stake in Paul's continuing clash with Jewish Christianity." He chooses this section "because, in a relatively small context, major questions of Pauline approach to Israel, law and covenant are present." The passage addresses "the macrodynamics of Pauline theology."[30]

Fourth, students of Paul and the law often highlight Paul's seemingly contradictory statements about the law.[31] Since this passage contains both positive (9:32a) and negative (10:4) statements about the law, it gives a clue to how both perspectives work together. Paul even cites the law as a witness to the righteousness of faith (10:6–8). Some degree of coherence must hold these statements together.

Fifth, the amount of secondary literature on the passage testifies to its own importance. Articles, essays, and commentaries often address the question of Israel's chief error with reference to the law in Rom 9:30—10:13. However, whereas articles, essays, and commentaries are limited in how much attention they can give to this passage, a full-length research project

26. While we are confining our inquiry to Rom 9:30–10:21, Longenecker notes that Paul uses more OT quotations, biblical allusions, and proverbial materials based on OT Scripture in Rom 9:30—10:21 than he does in 9:6–29 (*Romans*, 830).

27. Moo, *Epistle to the Romans*, 618. Pattee observes, "looking at the wider parameters of Romans 9 and 10, the influence of the OT is clearly discernable at almost every juncture" ("Stumbling Stone," 155).

28. Toews, "Law," 101.

29. Meyer, *End*, 210.

30. Dumbrell, "Paul," 286.

31. Hübner, *Law*; Hultgren, "Paul," 205–6; Moyise, *Paul*, 60; Räisänen, *Paul*, 1:29.

can probe the relevant issues in depth. Furthermore, the way the different paragraphs within the passage reinforce one another necessitates a project that can study the entire passage in depth.

Sixth, although three dissertations have been written on this passage,[32] this dissertation takes a different approach. The main differences include the meaning Paul discerns in the OT passages he cites, the relationship between faith and the law, the validity of the new perspective on Paul, and the identification of Paul's main critique of Israel.

Romans 9:30—10:13 is central to discussions on Paul and the law. Many have addressed the passage, but there exists still the need to explore the section in depth in order to understand Paul's critique of Israel and his proposed solution. Attention must be given to the exegesis of the passage, Paul's use of the Old Testament, rival interpretations of Paul's critique, and the overall theological point that Paul is making.

PREVIOUS LITERATURE

The following survey highlights major studies on Rom 9:30—10:13 as a whole (or significant portions of the passage).[33] In 1971, Ragnar Bring published "Paul and the Old Testament: A Study of the Ideas of Faith, Election, and Law in Paul, with Special Reference to Rom. 9:30-10:13."[34] Bring authored the first extensive study that pioneered a new approach to the relationship between law and faith in Paul. For Paul, law refers to revelation.[35] Many misinterpret Paul's view on the law because they confuse the law with its misuse.[36] Both the OT and the NT teach that God elects his people, and expects from them the response of faith.[37] The law exists to demonstrate the faith and faithfulness God demands from his covenant people, and to bring them back to the right path when they stray.[38] Humans err when they try to keep the law and glory in their obedience.[39] In Rom 9:30—10:13, Paul faults Israel for zealously trying to keep the law because their zeal is based on

---

32. Mohrmann, "Semantic Collisions"; Pattee, "Stumbling Stone"; Toews, "Law."

33. This literature review focuses on articles, essays and monographs. We interact with the commentary literature in the exegesis.

34. Bring, "Paul," 21–60.

35. Bring, "Paul," 22.

36. Bring, "Paul," 25.

37. Bring, "Paul," 26.

38. Bring, "Paul," 26–27.

39. Bring, "Paul," 27.

false assumptions about how to obtain God's promised blessing.[40] "Works" refers to following the law with the wrong intent.[41] Law and faith are not opposites, for faith is the fulfillment of the law.[42]

In 1975, C. E. B. Cranfield published "Some Notes on Romans 9:30–33."[43] Cranfield previously addressed the issue of Paul and the law in "St. Paul and the Law,"[44] but failed to discuss Rom 9:30–33.[45] For Cranfield, the νόμον δικαιοσύνης (9:31) refers to the law which promises a status of righteousness before God.[46] The law was given to show Israel the way to a righteous status before God, but they have failed "to grasp its real meaning and to render it true obedience."[47] Paul criticizes Israel not for pursuing the law, but for the way they have pursued it.[48] Israel should have responded to the claim to faith which God makes through the law.[49]

In 1977, C. K. Barrett published "Romans 9.30–10.21: Fall and Responsibility of Israel."[50] Barrett follows the trajectory established by Bring and Cranfield. Israel tried to keep the law and to achieve the righteousness it required, but failed to do so.[51] The reason for their failure was that they misunderstood the law, thinking that it required works, when the obedience it truly demanded was faith.[52] Israel was scandalized by this true meaning of the Law,[53] but Paul uses Lev 18:5 and Deut 30:11–14 to show that there is a right and wrong response to the law.[54]

John Toews's dissertation constitutes the first academic full-length examination of Rom 9:30—10:13.[55] Toews first gives a history of biblical

---

40. Bring, "Paul," 44.
41. Bring, "Paul," 44.
42. Bring, "Paul," 48.
43. Cranfield, "Some Notes," 35–43.
44. Cranfield, "St. Paul," 43–68. Now Cranfield, "St. Paul and the Law," 148–72.
45. A failure Cranfield identifies as "a reprehensible omission" ("Some Notes," 40n10).
46. Cranfield, "Some Notes," 37.
47. Cranfield, "Some Notes," 38.
48. Cranfield, "Some Notes," 39.
49. Cranfield, "Some Notes," 40.
50. Barrett, "Romans 9.30–10.21," 99–121. Now Barrett, "Fall and Responsibility of Israel," 132–53.
51. Barrett, "Fall and Responsibility of Israel," 140.
52. Barrett, "Fall and Responsibility of Israel," 141.
53. Barrett, "Fall and Responsibility of Israel," 144.
54. Barrett, "Fall and Responsibility of Israel," 147–48.
55. Toews, "Law."

scholarship on the law in Paul,[56] and then examines Rom 9:30—10:13 in order to test his hypothesis on the direction of Paul's law-theology in Romans. He argues that "Rom. 9.30–10.13 read as a unit affirms the fulfillability of the law in faith, affirms the law accepted in faith as a way to righteousness for the Jews, while at the same time declaring that Christ has fulfilled the law."[57] The passage "asserts two ways to righteousness, faith in God via the law and faith in God via Jesus Christ."[58]

In 1981, C. Thomas Rhyne published *Faith Establishes the Law*.[59] The bulk of Rhyne's monograph focuses on Rom 3:21—4:25, but includes a chapter on 9:30—10:21 because the central concepts of the earlier passage reappear here.[60] Attaining the law is the same thing as receiving righteousness by faith.[61] Israel did not understand that the law promises righteousness to those who believe.[62] Instead, they used it as a tool of personal achievement.[63] All who believe in Christ receive God's righteousness and achieve the goal of the law.[64] Rhyne writes, "the heart of Israel's failure lies in their refusal to believe."[65] Paul cites Lev 18:5 to represent Israel's mistaken notion of the way to righteousness.[66]

In 1985, Sanders addressed Rom 9:30—10:13 in *Paul, the Law, and the Jewish People*.[67] Building on his new approach to Paul and the law in *Paul and Palestinian Judaism*,[68] in this work Sanders devotes eight pages to a discussion of Rom 9:30—10:13.[69] While he credits Cranfield with coming close to rightly understanding the passage, he disagrees with Cranfield's assessment that Israel pursued the law in a legalistic manner.[70] Instead, Sanders argues, "Israel's failure is not that they do not obey the law in the correct

---

56. Toews, "Law," 3–104.
57. Toews, "Law," 106.
58. Toews, "Law," 106.
59. Rhyne, *Faith*.
60. Rhyne, *Faith*, 95–115, 165–73. This chapter reappears in Rhyne, "Nomos Dikaiosynēs," 486–99.
61. Rhyne, *Faith*, 100–101.
62. Rhyne, *Faith*, 101.
63. Rhyne, *Faith*, 101.
64. Rhyne, *Faith*, 103–4.
65. Rhyne, *Faith*, 111.
66. Rhyne, *Faith*, 106.
67. Sanders, *Paul*, 36–43.
68. Sanders, *Paul and Palestinian Judaism*.
69. There is no sustained discussion of the passage in Sanders, *Paul and Palestinian Judaism*.
70. Sanders, *Paul*, 36–37.

way, but that they do not have faith in Christ."[71] They are preoccupied with the righteousness that Jews exclusively possess because they possess the law, and they stumble over the fact that God in Christ has now ended the law and provided righteousness for all believe.[72] Israel's greatest error is that they did not believe in Christ.[73]

The same year saw Robert Badenas publish *Christ the End of the Law: Romans 10.4 in Pauline Perspective*. As part of Badenas's study of the meaning of τέλος in Rom 10:4, Badenas offers a detailed exposition of Rom 9:30—10:13.[74] Badenas defines νόμος generally as divine revelation.[75] Israel has not attained the goal of Torah, and they have not attained righteousness by faith because they have looked at Torah as a legal code rather than a record of God's saving interactions with his people.[76] Israel's failure to attain the law is their failure to recognize from Scripture Jesus Christ as the promised Messiah.[77] Their refusal to submit to the righteousness of God is their refusal to submit to the Christ-event.[78] In Christ is manifested the righteousness to which the law witnessed.[79]

James Dunn contributed to the discussion in 1988 with "'Righteousness from the Law' and 'Righteousness from Faith': Paul's Interpretation of Scripture in Romans 10:1–10."[80] Dunn locates himself within the New Perspective on Paul, yet approaches the passage differently from Sanders. Dunn argues that Israel is zealous to protect their distinctives, the covenant righteousness which is theirs because they are the chosen people of God.[81] Christ has ended the era during which righteousness was focused on ethnic Israel.[82] This attitude towards righteousness as belonging only to Israel is summed up in Lev 18:5, which Paul now regards as *passé*.[83] God, not Israel, establishes the covenant, and he does this in response to faith, as Deut

---

71. Sanders, *Paul*, 37.
72. Sanders, *Paul*, 37–38.
73. Sanders, *Paul*, 42.
74. Badenas, *Christ*, 101–44.
75. Badenas, *Christ*, 103.
76. Badenas, *Christ*, 104–5.
77. Badenas, *Christ*, 107.
78. Badenas, *Christ*, 110.
79. Badenas, *Christ*, 118.
80. Dunn, "Righteousness," 216–28.
81. Dunn, "Righteousness," 221–22.
82. Dunn, "Righteousness," 222.
83. Dunn, "Righteousness," 223.

30:12–14 demonstrates.[84] The contrast between the two texts is essentially salvation-historical.[85]

Frank Thielman surveys Rom 9:30—10:8 in *From Plight to Solution: A Jewish Framework for Understanding Paul's View of the Law in Galatians and Romans*.[86] Thielman surveys the major interpretations of the passage and argues that the simplest explanation is the correct one: Israel tried to keep the precepts of the law but failed to do so, and exists under the curse of the law.[87] Paul's criticism of Israel's own righteousness is a criticism of their insufficient righteousness (9:32; 10:3 echoing Deut 9:4—10:10) and a failure to submit to God's gracious provision for solving her plight.[88]

In 1990, Glenn Davies published *Faith and Obedience in Romans: A Study in Romans 1–4*.[89] Like Byrne, Davies's monograph focuses on an earlier section of Romans yet addresses 9:30—10:13 at the end since that section revisits the main topics of the earlier part of Romans.[90] With a growing tide of interpreters, Davies argues that Israel failed to read the law properly and thought they could follow it in their own strength rather than by faith.[91] They did not realize that the righteousness the law requires consists in trusting and believing.[92] Christ accomplished the righteousness promised in the law to those who believe.[93] The obedience which Lev 18:5 and Deut 30:11–14 command is that which flows from faith.[94]

In 1991, Stephen Bowser Pattee wrote "Stumbling Stone or Cornerstone? The Structure and Meaning of Paul's Argument in Romans 9:30-10:13."[95] Pattee studies Paul's use of the OT in 9:30—10:13, and makes much application to the theology of the passage. He argues that the nature of Israel's error is that they have misunderstood the law's fundamental goal and requirement. The law's goal was to save all people, Jew and gentile alike. Its most fundamental requirement, therefore, was that Israel love the gentiles as they loved themselves and grant them the same privileges that they

---

84. Dunn, "Righteousness," 224.
85. Dunn, "Righteousness," 225.
86. Thielman, *Plight*, 111–15.
87. Thielman, *Plight*, 111–12.
88. Thielman, *Plight*, 113.
89. Davies, *Faith*.
90. Davies, *Faith*, 177–204.
91. Davies, *Faith*, 181–82.
92. Davies, *Faith*, 183.
93. Davies, *Faith*, 188.
94. Davies, *Faith*, 192–201.
95. Pattee, "Stumbling Stone."

themselves enjoyed under the law. Israel, in her pride and hypocrisy, failed to do this, and thus by misunderstanding the law, the law has become her downfall. Christ, however, accomplished the goal of the law in his death on the cross, and all may be saved by faith in Christ.

In 1991, Thomas Schreiner published "Israel's Failure to Attain Righteousness in Romans 9.30–10.3."[96] Schreiner's essay describes Rom 9:30—10:8 as a "pivotal text for understanding Paul's theology of law."[97] He identifies Israel's failure to achieve righteousness via the law as the most controversial issue in 9:30—10:3.[98] Schreiner argues that Israel pursued the law in order to obtain a right standing before God, but they did not obtain that right standing with reference to the law.[99] Israel failed to obtain this right standing because they did not perform the requirements of the law.[100] The OT law, in the sense of both commandments and revelation, points to Christ.[101] If Israel had pursued the law by faith, they would have believed in Christ, for the law points to him.[102] Paul thus faults Israel both for legalism (thinking they could gain righteousness by their works) and for inability to obey the law (οὐκ ἔφθασεν [9:31]).[103] Righteousness by works is a wrong pursuit of the law because no one can obey law perfectly.[104]

In 1994, Steven Richard Bechtler wrote "Christ, the Τέλος of the Law: The Goal of Romans 10:4."[105] Bechtler argues that Israel imagined they could disregard Christ and attain righteousness by observing the law, but that is to misunderstand both God's act in Christ and the nature of the law itself. Such a mistaken pursuit of the law results in failure to obtain the law and its righteousness.[106] More specifically, Israel's "zealous commitment to its exclusivistic view of the covenant precludes the possibility of God's offer of salvation to Gentiles outside the covenant."[107] Thus Israel excludes themselves from the grace God offers in Christ.[108] They are ignorant of the fact

---

96. Schreiner, "Israel's Failure."
97. Schreiner, "Israel's Failure," 209.
98. Schreiner, "Israel's Failure," 209.
99. Schreiner, "Israel's Failure," 213.
100. Schreiner, "Israel's Failure," 214.
101. Schreiner, "Israel's Failure," 215.
102. Schreiner, "Israel's Failure," 215.
103. Schreiner, "Israel's Failure," 219–20.
104. Schreiner, "Israel's Failure," 220.
105. Bechtler, "Christ," 288–308.
106. Bechtler, "Christ," 295.
107. Bechtler, "Christ," 298.
108. Bechtler, "Christ," 298.

that God's righteousness is eschatologically manifested in Christ, not the law.[109] Paul uses Lev 18:5 to represent Israel's nationalistic misunderstanding of the law, and Deut 9:4; 30:12–14 to demonstrate that the locus of God's righteousness is not the law but Christ.[110] Paul concludes his argument by underscoring the universality of salvation, not primarily the means to it.[111] Bechtler believes that the true contrast in this passage is between universal and limited salvation.

In "YHWH and His Messiah: Pauline Exegesis and the Divine Christ,"[112] David Capes examines the passage as a whole and especially Paul's use of the OT. He argues that Israel is zealously trying to gain saving righteousness by works of the law, but they are missing the right way to righteousness before God. The essence of the law has always been righteousness through faith not performance. God makes this clear in Christ.[113] Capes argues that Lev 18:5 depicts "a negative assessment of the outcome of a performance-based righteousness derived from the Law."[114]

In 1999, Edith Humphrey wrote "Why Bring the Word Down? The Rhetoric of Demonstration and Disclosure in Romans 9:30–10:21."[115] Humphrey's essay focuses on the rhetorical effect of Rom 10:6–8 yet relates those verses to Paul's larger argument in Rom 9:30—10:21. She argues that Israel has erred by trying to establish their unique covenant membership by observing the Mosaic Covenant's boundary makers.[116] This mistaken pursuit errs on two fronts: (1) the Mosaic Covenant was to be pursued by faith and not boundary markers, and (2) God has ended the era of the Mosaic Covenant by demonstrating righteousness in Christ.[117] Paul uses the OT to show that the righteousness witnessed to by the law and the prophets (Lev 18:5) is the righteousness of faith (Deut 30:12–14).[118]

In *Paul, the Law, and the Covenant*, A. Andrew Das devotes a chapter to Rom 9:30—10:8.[119] He first surveys the New Perspective reading of this passage and offers a critique of the New Perspective's understanding of "works

---

109. Bechtler, "Christ," 302.
110. Bechtler, "Christ," 304–6.
111. Bechtler, "Christ," 306.
112. Capes, "YHWH," 121–43.
113. Capes, "YHWH," 125.
114. Capes, "YHWH," 125.
115. Humphrey, "Rhetoric," 129–48.
116. Humphrey, "Rhetoric," 141.
117. Humphrey, "Rhetoric," 141–42.
118. Humphrey, "Rhetoric," 142.
119. Das, *Paul*, 234–67.

of the law" and Paul's polemic against human effort. He then offers his own reading of the passage which argues that Israel mistakenly pursued the law by works and did not recognize the law's witness to righteousness by faith.[120] Christ empties the law of its gracious significance; he reconstructs Judaism's gracious framework around himself.[121] Lev 18:5 represents how Paul now views the law (as empty obligations) apart from Judaism's gracious context.[122] Deut 30:12–14 proves that the law bears witness to righteousness by faith in Christ.[123] The two citations express antithetical perspectives on the law.[124]

The same year John Paul Heil published "Christ, the Termination of the Law (Romans 9:30–10:8)."[125] Heil investigates Rom 9:30—10:8 in order to prove his interpretation of Rom 10:4 that Christ terminates the law as the way of attaining righteousness before God by obeying its works.[126] He explains from 9:30–33 that Israel has committed two errors: they sought the impossible goal of righteousness through obedience to the law (impossible due to human sinfulness), and they failed to believe in Christ.[127] From 10:1–4, he explains that Christ has ended Israel's futile attempt to gain righteousness through obedience to the law.[128] He then uses the OT citations in 10:5–8 to contrast works-based attempts to fulfill the law with God's way of righteousness through faith.[129]

In 2001, Douglas Carl Mohrmann wrote "Semantic Collisions at the Intertextual Crossroads: A Diachronic and Synchronic Study of Romans 9:30–10:13."[130] Mohrmann argues that Israel's problem is not their approach to the law. For Paul, the works of the law are a matter of indifference until they become essential for salvation.[131] Rather, Israel has failed to realize that Christ stands at the center of God's administration of righteousness in the present age.[132] Paul emphasizes typological patterns between the OT Scriptures and his universal gospel in order to demonstrate continuity between

---

120. Das, *Paul*, 245.
121. Das, *Paul*, 251.
122. Das, *Paul*, 255.
123. Das, *Paul*, 258.
124. Das, *Paul*, 262.
125. Heil, "Christ," 484–98.
126. Heil, "Christ," 486.
127. Heil, "Christ," 487–88.
128. Heil, "Christ," 489–90.
129. Heil, "Christ," 490.
130. Mohrmann, "Semantic Collisions."
131. Mohrmann, "Semantic Collisions," 209–16.
132. Mohrmann, "Semantic Collisions," 267.

the two, but he also opens up these same scriptural references to new meanings.[133] He utilizes this latter strategy "to redefine Isaiah's stumbling stone and Israel's test of faith, to supplant the law with Christ in God's administration of righteousness, to challenge Jewish presumptive boasting over the law and their historical relationship with God, and to invite all humanity to a new confession of faith in God in Christ."[134]

In 2004, William Dumbrell published "Paul and Salvation History in Romans 9:30–10:4."[135] Dumbrell uses Rom 9:30—10:4 to illustrate his salvation history approach to biblical theology.[136] He argues that Paul criticizes Israel for continuing to obey the Jewish law when the Mosaic Covenant's validity ceased with the death of Christ.[137] Although Israel followed a law that was designed to express covenant membership, they did not obtain membership in the new covenant.[138] The Mosaic Covenant was a legitimate means of expressing the obedience of faith before the cross; Israel was supposed to pursue the law of righteousness (the law which demonstrated the maintenance of the covenant).[139] Israel's problem is that they are "seeking to keep the Sinai covenant by law-based conduct not prompted by faith in Christ at a time when the Sinai covenant itself had been replaced by the new covenant inaugurated by the death of Christ."[140]

In 2007, Francis Watson published a revised edition of his earlier *Paul, Judaism and the Gentiles* (1986), with the new subtitle, *Beyond the New Perspective*.[141] Watson argues that Paul is not concerned in this passage to identify Israel's fault. Rather, in 9:30—10:21 Paul articulates a scripturally based hope for the future transformation of Israel "in which the apparent rigidity of the image of the potter (9:19–21) gives way to a more dynamic account of the relation between the vessels of mercy and the vessels of wrath."[142] He argues that Israel is presently rejected "on account of their zealous pursuit of righteousness as defined by the law—a righteousness that God chooses

---

133. Mohrmann, "Semantic Collisions," 268.
134. Mohrmann, "Semantic Collisions," 268.
135. Dumbrell, "Paul."
136. Dumbrell, "Paul," 286–312.
137. Dumbrell, "Paul," 286.
138. Dumbrell, "Paul," 307.
139. Dumbrell, "Paul," 308.
140. Dumbrell, "Paul," 308.
141. Watson addresses Rom 9:30—10:13 on pp. 322–33. References are from the 2007 edition.
142. Watson, *Beyond the New Perspective*, 333.

not to accept *in order that* another way of righteousness may be opened up to the hopelessly unrighteous Gentiles."[143]

In 2009, Jason Meyer published *The End of the Law: Mosaic Covenant in Pauline Theology*.[144] Meyer joins those interpreters who argue that the law demands faith.[145] Paul faults Israel for not understanding the law of righteousness rightly.[146] They were right to pursue the law, but they pursued it by works instead of by faith.[147] This mistaken pursuit caused them to stumble over Christ.[148] They did not recognize God's provision of righteousness in Christ, and that the law pointed to him as its culmination all along.[149] Leviticus 18:5 represents Israel's misguided pursuit of the law, and Deut 30:11–14 represents the pursuit of the law by faith.[150]

Finally, in 2013, N. T. Wright again addressed Rom 9:30—10:13 in *Paul and the Faithfulness of God*.[151] Wright argues that Israel sought the law of righteousness in the wrong way: they used particular nationalistic works (sabbath, food-laws, circumcision) as a way of establishing themselves exclusively as God's people and keeping everyone else at bay.[152] The true keeping of the Torah that God was aiming at all along was the universal confession of Jesus as Lord, and faith that God raised him from the dead.[153] The person who does this will live; this is the fulfillment of the Torah now made possible for all nations in Christ.[154]

TAXONOMY OF VIEWS

The literature review reveals three major positions on Israel's chief error with reference to the law in Rom 9:30—10:13.

---

143. Watson, *Beyond the New Perspective*, 333, emphasis original.
144. Meyer, *End*.
145. Meyer, *End*, 207–29.
146. Meyer, *End*, 211.
147. Meyer, *End*, 211.
148. Meyer, *End*, 211.
149. Meyer, *End*, 212.
150. Meyer, *End*, 212.
151. Wright, *Paul*, 1156–257. Previous assessments include Wright, *Climax*, 231-57; Wright, *Romans*, 620–26; and Wright, *Justification*, 240–48.
152. Wright, *Paul*, 1177–78.
153. Wright, *Paul*, 1179.
154. Wright, *Paul*, 1173.

Misunderstanding

First, some argue that Israel essentially misunderstood the true demand of the law and sought to fulfill it in the wrong way. At its core, the law actually demands faith. The Jews misunderstood this fundamental requirement of the law, and thus rejected Christ because they were preoccupied with lesser forms of obedience.[155]

N. T. Wright summarizes this view with these words: "To confess Jesus as lord and to believe that God raised him from the dead is to 'attain the Torah', the *nomos dikaiosynēs*, the 'law of covenant membership', the point towards which the whole Pentateuch was heading. Conversely, to reject the Messiah is to fail to attain Torah, to stumble over the stone."[156] Similarly, John Toews writes, "Israel perceived the law as a demand for human performance instead of a call to faith."[157] Charles Cranfield asks, "What then is this pursuit of the law ἐκ πίστεως? The answer must be, surely, that it is to respond to the claim to faith which God makes through the law."[158]

Nationalism

Second, Israel limited the expression of righteousness to their nationalistic symbols. The Jews think that righteousness is available only for Jews. The work of Christ which makes righteousness available to all is a stumbling-block to them.[159]

---

155. Achtemeier, *Romans*, 167–71; Badenas, *Christ*, 107; Barrett, *Romans*, 192–200; Barrett, "Romans 9.30–10:21," 141–43; Barth, *Shorter Commentary on Romans*, 124; Bell, *Provoked*, 187–88; Boor, *Römer*, 239; Bring, "Paul and the Old Testament," 21–60; Cranfield, *Romans*, 2:505, 510; Das, *Paul and the Jews*, 90; Das, *Paul*, 246–47; Davies, *Faith*, 181–82; Fuller, *Gospel*, 65–88; Käsemann, *Romans*, 277–81; Keener, *Romans*, 124–27; Lohse, *Römer*, 287–88; Meyer, *End*, 210–15; Rhyne, "*Nomos Dikaiosynēs*," 490; Toews, *Romans*, 258; Toews, "Law," 143, 245, 332–39; Wright, *Climax*, 240; Wright, *Justification*, 245; Wright, *Paul*, 1173–79; Wright, *Romans*, 649.

This list of advocates shows that this dissertation's specific question unites and divides interpreters in a way that they may not otherwise be united or divided. For example, James Dunn and N. T. Wright agree that Israel was guilty of nationalistic righteousness and not works righteousness, but they disagree on the chief error Paul highlights in Rom 9:30—10:13. On the other hand, Jason Meyer opposes the New Perspective's interpretation of works of the law, but agrees with Wright that Israel's chief error is that they misunderstood the law's call for faith.

156. Wright, *Paul*, 1179.

157. Toews, "Law," 143.

158. Cranfield, *Romans*, 2:510.

159. Barnett, *Romans*, 217–22; Bryan, *Romans*, 165–67; Dumbrell, "Paul," 308–9; Dumbrell, *Romans*, 102–3; Dunn, *Romans*, 2:576–77; Gaston, *Paul and the Torah*,

James Dunn articulates this view well: "The trouble with Israel is that they have confused the law and the righteousness it speaks of with works like circumcision which serve to make righteousness a function of Jewish identity rather than of God's gracious outreach to and through faith. This failure came to eschatological expression and climax in their refusal to recognize Christ as Messiah."[160] Stephen Pattee summarizes his approach with these words:

> Rom 10:5 is actually an interpretive paraphrase of Lev 18:5, in which Paul uses Lev 19:18 to assist in articulating the true meaning of "the righteousness of the law." Because of this connection, Paul was able to conclude that the demand of Lev 18:5 to keep the entire law was met when the impartial love described in Lev 19:18 is practiced. The significance of this conclusion is that it enabled Paul to define precisely the nature of Jewish hypocrisy. By their failure to grant gentiles co-equal status before God, the Jews had violated the most succinct summation of the law's requirements.[161]

141–42; Humphrey, "Rhetoric," 141–42; Jewett, *Romans*, 611, 618; Johnson, *Romans*, 167–69; Keck, *Romans*, 247; Longenecker, *Eschatology*, 216–17; Mohrmann, "Semantic Collisions," 209–16, 267–68; Pattee, "Stumbling Stone," 317–18; Sanders, *Paul*, 37–38; Stowers, *Romans*, 302–3; Witherington, *Romans*, 259–61.

At first glance, Sanders sounds like he views Israel's chief error as lack of faith in Christ rather than preoccupation with their own righteousness (this would be consistent with his solution-to-plight view of Paul [*Paul*, 37]). However, his full discussion reveals that he views Israel's lack of faith in Christ as at least bound up with their preoccupation with their own righteousness. Therefore, he is categorized here rather than under a separate category. Interestingly, Moo argues that Israel's chief error in Rom 9:30—10:13 is a failure to perceive the salvation-historical shift that has come about in Christ, a view that sounds similar to Sanders (*Epistle to the Romans*, 619). However, he also argues that their failure to perceive this shift is bound up with their legalism, and perhaps even caused by their legalism. Therefore, he properly belongs to the category of interpreters who argue that Israel's chief error is their inability to achieve righteousness by obeying the law. Bryan is like Sanders in that he indicates that Israel's chief error is lack of faith of Christ, but he also argues that their lack of faith is bound up with their preoccupation with their own righteousness (*Romans*, 165–67). Finally, Jewett initially appears to disagree with this position, but later reveals that he properly belongs here (*Romans*, 611). On p. 618, he interprets "their own righteousness" as a reference to Israel's ethnic and sectarian righteousness. On p. 611, he argues that Jewish ethnocentrism is not yet in view in Paul's reference to seeking the law by works (9:32a), but still asserts that Israel erroneously believes that righteousness can be reached by performing the works of the law.

160. Dunn, *Romans*, 2:576–77.
161. Pattee, "Stumbling Stone," 317–18.

Doug Mohrmann argues that Paul aimed "to supplant the law with Christ in God's administration of righteousness, to challenge Jewish presumptive boasting over the law and their historical relationship with God, and to invite all humanity to a new confession of faith in God in Christ."[162]

Legalism

Third, Israel tried to keep the law in order to attain righteousness by works instead of by faith. However, sinful humans cannot adequately perform the law's righteous demands, and exist under the curse of the law. Because of their preoccupation with their own works, Israel rejected Christ's gift of righteousness.[163]

Thomas Schreiner summarizes this view in the conclusion to his article on Rom 9:30—10:3:

> The Jews pursued the law in order to obtain right standing with God, but they failed to attain that righteousness with reference to the law because they did not obey the law perfectly. Why is

---

162. Mohrmann, "Semantic Collisions," 268.

163. Aquinas, *Romans*, 273–79; Barth, *People of God*, 40–41; Black, *Romans*, 136; Bruce, *Romans*, 186–87; Byrne, *Romans*, 307–11; Calvin, *Romans*, 377; Dodd, *Romans*, 164–66; Edwards, *Romans*, 245–47; Fitzmyer, *Romans*, 576–78; Heil, "Christ," 485–86; Heil, *Paul's Letter to the Romans*, 110; Heil, *Romans*, 70–71; Hendriksen, *Romans*, 334; Hodge, *Romans*, 298; Huby, *Romains*, 361; Hultgren, *Romans*, 377; Kaylor, *Paul's Covenant Community*, 177–78; Kuss, *Römerbrief*, 744; Kruse, *Romans*, 393–95; Lange and Fay, *Romans*, 325–26; Luther, *Commentary*, 144–48; Luther, *Lectures on Romans*, 86–91, 405–10; Michel, *Römer*, 322; Moo, *Romans*, 326; Moo, *Epistle to the Romans*, 619; Mounce, *Romans*, 205–6; Morris, *Romans*, 375; Munck, *Christ*, 84; Murray, *Romans*, 2:43; Nygren, *Romans*, 377–79; Origen, *Romans*, 135–36; Osborne, *Romans*, 89–90, 261–62; Pelagius, *Romans*, 121–22; Pesch, *Römerbrief*, 81; Royster, *Romans*, 257–59; Sanday and Headlam, *Romans*, 275–76; Schlatter, *Romans*, 210–12; Schreiner, "Israel's Failure," 220; Schreiner, *Romans*, 533; Seifrid, *Christ*, 120–23; Seifrid, "Romans," 650; Stuhlmacher, *Romans*, 152; Thielman, *Plight*, 111–15; Thielman, *Paul*, 205–7; Thielman, *Law*, 29–30; Thielman, *Theology*, 368–69; Westerholm, *Justification*, 21; Wilckens, *Römer*, 2:220.

Dodd belongs here more than in the other two positions, but he attributes Israel's inability to keep the law to the ceremonial and mechanical nature of the Law of Holiness and Priestly Code contained in Leviticus (*Romans*, 164–66). Dodd congratulates Paul on recognizing in Deuteronomy (and this "without the aid of modern criticism") a stratum that goes deeper than the legalism of Leviticus "and comes very near in spirit to Christianity" (166). Bring, "Paul," 21–60, speaks of unbelief as disobedience to the law, and faith as the true fulfillment of the law, but he also defines the law as the Old Testament, arguing that the Old Testament as a whole witnesses to righteousness by faith, and that the law is given to reveal humanity's sinfulness and direct their attention to Christ in order to be justified by faith. That accords more with this third view than the first.

it that Israel did not obtain righteousness by pursuing the law? It is not because pursuing the law, properly understood, is evil or misguided, but because the law was pursued "as from works" instead of by faith. To pursue the law from works is to use the law as a means of establishing one's own righteousness, but employing the law to establish one's own righteousness is a delusive enterprise precisely because no one can obey the law perfectly. To pursue the law in faith is to recognize that the law cannot be obeyed sufficiently to obtain salvation, and that salvation can only be obtained by believing in Christ.[164]

Similarly, John Calvin writes, "they sought to be justified by works, and thus laboured for what no man could attain to; and still further, they stumbled at Christ, through whom alone a way is open to the attainment of righteousness."[165] Peter Stuhlmacher also observes, "Instead of living before God on the basis of faith, Israel stands before the Law and attempts to follow the path which is—as Paul already indicated in 3:20 (cf. Gal. 2:16)—condemned by God to fail, namely, to be justified on the basis of works."[166]

This dissertation argues the third view: Paul criticizes Israel for pursuing a right standing with God by obeying the Mosaic law when they should have discerned within their own Scriptures both humanity's inability to keep the law and the necessity of salvation by faith alone. Throughout the passage, Paul contrasts righteousness by faith with righteousness by works, and uses the OT to prove his theological argument. The result is a dense argument against the folly of works-righteousness based on the law and the necessity of salvation by faith alone as witnessed by the OT as a whole.

STRUCTURE OF THE ARGUMENT

Successive chapters study Rom 9:30—10:13 section by section. Chapter 2 examines the foundational paragraph of 9:30-33 and Paul's use of Isa 8:14; 28:16 in Rom 9:33. Special attention is given to interpreting the phrase νόμον δικαιοσύνης (9:31), and Paul's statement that Israel pursued the law by works instead of by faith (9:31-32a). Since Paul concludes each paragraph in 9:30—10:13 with an OT citation to prove his argument, special attention is given throughout to Paul's use of the OT.[167] All OT citations are

164. Schreiner, "Israel's Failure," 220.
165. Calvin, *Romans*, 377.
166. Stuhlmacher, *Romans*, 152.
167. Pattee observes, "Nowhere in Paul's writings does he refer to the OT more frequently than in Romans, and nowhere in Romans are OT citations and allusions

studied under the following methodology: the original OT context; the use of the OT passage in Jewish literature; textual factors; Paul's hermeneutics and theological point.[168]

Chapter 3 examines the second stage of Paul's argument in 10:1–4. This paragraph echoes 9:30–33 but develops the main idea further. Special attention is given to the interpretation of Rom 10:4.

The OT citations in 10:5–8 flow out of the argument in 10:1–4 but are too complex to address in a single chapter. Therefore, chapter 4 examines Paul's use of Lev 18:5 in Rom 10:5, and chapter 5 examines Paul's use of Deut 8:17a; 9:4a; 30:12–14 in Rom 10:6–8. The two citations contrast the differing approaches to righteousness offered by the law and the gospel.

Chapter 6 concludes the exegesis of the passage by examining Rom 10:9–13 and Paul's use of Isa 28:16 in Rom 10:11 and Joel 2:32 in Rom 10:13. Here Paul moves from criticism to cure as he articulates the proper response to the gospel. Chapter 7 concludes the study and offers areas of further research.

We offer this dissertation with the goal of demonstrating that a traditional Law-Gospel (Lutheran) approach to Paul is defensible within one of Paul's most important discussions of the law. In addition, it is consistent with the Old Testament's approach to the issues of faith and righteousness. No full length-study has attempted to prove that point by focusing on this particular passage; this dissertation meets that need.

---

found as often as in chapters 9–11" ("Romans 9:30–10:13," 106).

168. Based on Beale and Carson, *Commentary*, xxiv–xxvi. Sometimes the order of analysis varies, or multiple aspects are addressed at once, but the basic process is the same throughout.

Chapter 2

Romans 9:30–33

INTRODUCTION

Paul's concern for Israel is evident throughout Romans 9–11. In 9:2, he states that he has "great pain and unceasing distress" in his heart.[1] In 9:3, he says, "I could almost wish myself to be accursed from Christ for the sake of my brothers and sisters."[2] He desires and prays for Israel's salvation (10:1). These statements capture Paul's assessment of Israel's condition: they are separated from Christ, and in need of salvation. When he comes to Rom 9:30—10:13, he explains what Israel has done (and failed to do) that has generated this plight.

Paul uses three contrasts throughout Romans 9:30—10:13 to explain Israel's plight.[3] In 9:30-33, Paul contrasts gentiles who were not pursuing righteousness and yet have obtained it (ἔθνη τὰ μὴ διώκοντα δικαιοσύνην κατέλαβεν δικαιοσύνην, v. 30) with Israel who was pursuing the law of righteousness and yet did not obtain it (Ἰσραὴλ δὲ διώκων νόμον δικαιοσύνης εἰς νόμον οὐκ ἔφθασεν, v. 31). That contrast is restated in 10:1-4, where Paul

---

1. Unless otherwise indicated, all translations of primary source materials are our own.
2. Wallace identifies the imperfect verb ηὐχόμην as an example of the voluntative/tendential imperfect. It describes an action that was almost desired to be made (*Greek Grammar*, 551–52).
3. Dunn, *Romans*, 2:577; Moo, *Epistle to the Romans*, 619; Toews, *Romans*, 258.

contrasts submitting to the righteousness of God with seeking to establish one's own righteousness (10:3). Finally, 10:5–13 contrast the righteousness which is from the law (τὴν δικαιοσύνην τὴν ἐκ [τοῦ] νόμου, v. 5) with the righteousness which is from faith (ἡ ἐκ πίστεως δικαιοσύνη, v. 6).[4]

In this first paragraph (9:30–33), Paul establishes the main idea that he develops in the subsequent verses (10:1–13).[5] He argues that Israel was trying to keep the law in order to obtain a right standing with God, but due to human inability they fell short of their goal (9:31–32a). Blinded by such a pursuit, they rejected Jesus as Messiah and the salvation he offers (9:32b–33). This explanation of Israel's error depends on three elements in 9:30–33: (1) the nature of Israel's pursuit, captured in the phrases "law of righteousness" (νόμον δικαιοσύνης, 9:31) and "did not attain unto law" (εἰς νόμον οὐκ ἔφθασεν, 9:31); (2) the reason for Israel's failure, captured in "because not from faith but as from works" (οὐκ ἐκ πίστεως ἀλλ' ὡς ἐξ ἔργων, 9:32); and (3) the meaning and purpose of Paul's citation of Isa 8:14; 28:16 (9:33).

THE NATURE OF ISRAEL'S PURSUIT

Paul's opening statements in 9:30–31 summarize the discussion of 9:6b–29. Due to God's sovereign decree, many gentiles are experiencing salvation whereas many Israelites are not. Paul states in verse 30, "Gentiles, who were not pursuing[6] righteousness, have obtained righteousness, even the righteousness of faith." As a class, gentiles[7] were not seeking a right standing[8]

4. Even if one interprets the OT citations in 10:5–8 as complementary, one cannot deny the difference in wording between the righteousness of 10:5 and that of 10:6–8.

5. Paul opens with the transitory question, "What therefore shall we say to these things" (Τί οὖν ἐροῦμεν), in order to shift the argument from the discussion of God's role in Israel's current plight to the explanation of the human behavior that has generated that plight. Longenecker also notes that the opening question Τί οὖν ἐροῦμεν does not respond to an objection, but is a rhetorical question used to highlight the discussion that follows (*Romans*, 833). This is consistent with Paul's other uses of Τί οὖν ἐροῦμεν throughtout Romans (4:1; 8:31; 6:1; 7:7; 9:14).

6. "Pursuing" translates διώκοντα, the first of several athletic terms used throughout 9:30—10:13. Badenas highlights the following: "διώκων (for denoting the earnest pursuit of a goal), κατέλαβεν (for describing the attaining of the goal), οὐκ ἔφθασεν (for the stumbling over an obstacle), καταισχύνω (for the disappointment and shame of the defeat), and τέλος (for the goal, winning post, or finishing line itself)" (*Christ*, 101). The combination of διώκοντα and δικαιοσύνην may echo LXX Isa 51:1, οἱ διώκοντες τὸ δίκαιον. See Toews, "Law," 207–9; Wagner, *Heralds*, 122.

7. The absence of the definite article highlights the qualitative aspect of ἔθνη (Wallace, *Greek Grammar*, 244–45).

8. Interpreters continue to debate whether δικαιοσύνη refers to a legal standing or a

with the one true and living God (ἔθνη τὰ μὴ διώκοντα δικαιοσύνην).⁹ Because of the sovereign mercy of God (9:14–29), gentiles have heard the gospel message and believed it (κατέλαβεν δικαιοσύνην), thus obtaining a right standing with God by means of faith (δικαιοσύνην δὲ τὴν ἐκ πίστεως).¹⁰

relational status. I argue that throughout 9:30—10:31 δικαιοσύνη communicates a legal idea, "right standing with God," as opposed to "covenant membership" (for the latter in translation, see Wright, *Kingdom New Testament*, 327). Seifrid argues that "a standard or norm is generally associated with the צדק word-group," an idea underscored by the requirement that balances, weights, and measures be "righteous" (Lev 19:36; Ezek 45:10 ["Righteousness Language," 420]). Dunn and Wright, however, limit that norm to God's covenant with Abraham and Israel, and identifies God's righteousness as God's faithfulness to that covenant, expressed in the salvation of his people (*Romans*, 1:41, and *Paul*, 799, respectively). Seifrid argues that this is an illegitimate reduction, and points out that "Only rarely do ברית and צדק terms appear in any proximity to one another, despite their considerable frequency in the Hebrew Scriptures" ("Righteousness Language," 423). Seifrid also observes that the LXX does not translate צדק- terms with the σωτ- root ("Paul's Use," 51). One should not limit δικαιοσύνη to covenantal and salvific ideas (*contra* Badenas who states that δικαιοσύνη primarily describes a relationship and is particularly used to denote God's saving activity [*Christ*, 102]). While Isa 51:6 uses righteousness and salvation in parallel statements, such parallelism does not rule out a right status that results from God's saving (justifying) activity (so Moo, *Epistle to the Romans*, 74). Westerholm helpfully notes that "'righteousness' does not *mean* 'covenant faithfulness'; but keeping one's promises, covenantal or otherwise, is one *example* of righteousness" (*Justification*, 71, emphasis original).

In his discussion of δικαιοσύνη θεοῦ in Rom 1:17, Schreiner argues that the language of faith being reckoned (λογίζειν) as righteousness "suggests a status that is ascribed to one because of faith" (Rom 4:3, 5–6, 9, 11 [*Romans*, 64]). He also argues that τῆς δωρεᾶς τῆς δικαιοσύνης (Rom 5:17) must refer to a gift that is granted to a person. The occurrences of δικαιοσύνη in Rom 9:30—10:13 fit within this trajectory. Gentiles have obtained the right standing that comes by faith (9:30). Israel pursued the law in order to obtain a right standing with God (9:31). Because they are ignorant of the right standing that comes from God, and are seeking to establish their own, they do not submit to the right standing that comes from God (10:3). Christ ends the law, and the result is a right standing for all who believe (10:4). Moses describes the right standing based on the law in terms of performance (10:5), whereas the right standing that comes from faith is described in terms of belief (10:6–8, 10). For more exegesis of the relevant occurrences of δικαιοσύνη throughout Romans, see the discussion of 10:3.

Two other explanations of δικαιοσύνη are worth noting. Fitzmyer defines δικαιοσύνη as "uprightness" and "rectitude," indicating moral righteousness (*Romans*, 577). Southall argues that "personified Righteousness becomes a character invention and takes on the role ordinarily played by Christ himself" (*Rediscovering Righteousness*, 151). The arguments articulated above for the legal interpretation of δικαιοσύνη would also warrant against these interpretations.

9. Paul's statement about gentile non-seeking in 9:30 depends on his argument in 1:18–32. Although the moral actions of many gentiles bear witness to the law of God written on the heart (2:14–15), in general they do not seek a right standing with God as defined by Torah.

10. Building on the subjective genitive understanding of πίστεως Ἰησοῦ Χριστοῦ in Rom 3:22, Dunn and Southall interpret ἐκ πίστεως here as a reference to God's

The experience of the Jews is quite different: although they pursued the law of righteousness, they did not attain the law (Ἰσραὴλ δὲ διώκων νόμον δικαιοσύνης εἰς νόμον οὐκ ἔφθασεν, v. 31).[11] Paul does two things with this statement. On the one hand, he completes his summary of the previous section: many gentiles have attained salvation, whereas most Jews have not. On the other hand, this statement initiates his critique of Israel: although Israel pursued the law of righteousness, they did not attain the law. They fell short of their goal. In order to assess the nature of their failure, one must identify the object of their pursuit: what is the "law of righteousness" (νόμον δικαιοσύνης) which Israel pursued, and what did they fail to attain (εἰς νόμον οὐκ ἔφθασεν)?

Israel Pursued the Law of Righteousness

The phrase νόμον δικαιοσύνης does not occur elsewhere in the NT, and only once in intertestamental literature (Wis 2:11).[12] The immediate context of Wis 2:11 discusses the oppression of the weak, and the phrase communicates the idea of "might makes right."[13] The meaning of the phrase in Wisdom of Solomon does not fit the context of Rom 9:30–33 and is therefore of little value in interpreting Rom 9:31.[14] Rather, the larger context of Rom 9:30—10:13 provides the best clues for interpreting the enigmatic phrase.

Five interpretations of νόμον δικαιοσύνης emerge in the literature. First, some translate the genitive adjectivally, "the righteous law."[15] While this parallels Paul's statements in Rom 7:12,[16] it requires an interpretation

---

faithfulness (*Romans*, 2:580, and *Rediscovering Righteousness*, 189, respectively). We read πίστεως Ἰησοῦ Χριστοῦ in Rom 3:22 as objective: Christ is the object of faith (the focus of faith) for all who believe (the scope of faith). Paul knows how to emphasize the faithfulness of Jesus (so Phil 2:5–11), but in Romans 3:21–26, God the Father is the active agent (3:25: ὃν προέθετο ὁ θεὸς, "whom *God* set forth"). For the history and contour of the debate, see Bird and Sprinkle, *Faith of Jesus Christ*; Campbell, *Rhetoric*, 58–60; Carson, "Atonement," 125n20; Davies, *Faith*, 107n1; Jewett, *Romans*, 277n75; Moo, *Epistle to the Romans*, 224n25; Wright, *Romans*, 467n103.

11. The participle διώκων communicates a concessive force.

12. Readers of Paul are more familiar with the concept of "the righteousness of the law" (e.g., Rom 10:5, τὴν δικαιοσύνην τὴν ἐκ [τοῦ] νόμου) than "the law of righteousness."

13. The NRSV reads, "But let our might be our law of right [νόμος τῆς δικαιοσύνης]."

14. Toews, "Law," 131–32.

15. Barrett, "Romans 9.30–10.21," 140; Johnson, *Romans*, 166; Luther, *Lectures on Romans*, 86n29; Toews, "Law," 131–36 (Toews's explanation appears to fit here, though he identifies the genitive as a subjective genitive); Westerholm, "Paul," 232.

16. Barrett, "Romans 9:30–10:21," 140.

of δικαιοσύνη ("righteous") that differs from its other occurrences in 9:30—10:13 ("right standing").[17] It also mutes the contribution of the word δικαιοσύνη to Paul's argument. To identify the law as righteous is a truism for Paul at this point in the argument of Romans (Rom 7:7–12). Rather, Paul is contrasting the gentiles who did not pursue righteousness with the Jews who pursued the law of righteousness. The word δικαιοσύνη calls for more significance than simply modifying νόμον.[18]

Second, some interpret the phrase as the law which gives righteousness when one keeps it. Different nuances include a law that demands righteousness,[19] the law which promises righteousness,[20] or a rule of life which would produce righteousness.[21] Although these explanations have theological legitimacy (e.g., Lev 18:5; Deut 6:25), they require much more information than the context supplies.[22] The best explanation of an obscure phrase will be that which adds the least information to the meaning.[23]

Third, advocates of the new perspective on Paul see here a reference to the Torah,[24] and thus more specifically to the boundary markers that demarcate Israel from the nations.[25] This explanation suffers from the same weakness as the previous one: it assumes information (in this case, a particular definition of "works of the law") which cannot be sustained from this context. Rom 9:12 contrasts works with God's call (οὐκ ἐξ ἔργων ἀλλ᾽ ἐκ τοῦ καλοῦντος), indicating that works are something humans do whereas mercy is something God distributes (cf. Rom 11:6). The reference to works in 9:32 gives no indication that it is referring to more specific works such as circumcision, food laws, and the Sabbath. Like 9:6–29, this section contrasts God's mercy with human achievement, and the antithesis between faith and works hearkens back to Paul's critique of the law in 3:27–4:8.[26] Even if Paul

---

17. Schreiner, *Romans*, 537.

18. Technically, the attributed genitive is also possible ("legal righteousness"), but no interpreter argues for this.

19. Hultgren, *Romans*, 378; Porter, *Romans*, 194; Westerholm, *Perspectives*, 310.

20. Cranfield, *Romans*, 2:508n1; Leitzmann, *Römer*, 94; Lohse, *Römer*, 287; Michel, *Römer*, 321n5; Wilckens, *Römer*, 212n944.

21. Barth, *Romans*, 124; Sanday and Headlam, *Romans*, 279.

22. Schreiner, *Romans*, 537.

23. Schreiner, *Romans*, 537; Silva, *Biblical Words*, 150–51.

24. Dunn interprets the grammatical aspect of the phrase like the previous position: the law which requires righteousness. He differs on the identification of those demands (*Romans*, 2:581).

25. Dumbrell, "Paul," 307; Dumbrell, *Romans*, 102; Dunn, *Romans*, 2:581; Lodge, *Romans*, 105; Wright, *Climax*, 240.

26. Das, *Paul*, 238, 240.

had a specific referent for works in mind (such as boundary markers), it would not exclude a focus on human performance. Phil 3:1–14 defines works done to maintain national identity as an attempt to establish one's own righteousness rather than submitting to the righteousness of faith.[27]

Fourth, some explanations focus on the second word in the phrase and highlight "righteousness" in their explanation. Calvin, for example, saw this as an occurrence of *hypallage* and read the phrase as "the righteousness of the law."[28] Although this transposition creates a clean parallel with 9:30, it raises the question of why Paul put νόμον as the object of εἰς in 9:31 and not δικαιοσύνην. Also, why would Paul use the obscure expression "law of righteousness" if he meant "righteousness of the law," a phrase he is more than capable of writing (cf. Rom 10:5; Phil 3:6, 9)?[29] Interpreters must not rewrite the text to make it say what we think Paul should have said.

Others arrive at this position not by rewriting the text but by interpreting νόμον metaphorically. They thus interpret νόμον δικαιοσύνης as a principle of righteousness.[30] While νόμος can communicate a metaphorical meaning, it does not happen as frequently as other meanings, and many of the occurrences are disputed.[31] One should first search for a more concrete meaning before choosing the metaphorical interpretation.[32] The metaphorical reading here would produce a meaning of νόμος that is inconsistent with the other occurrences of the word in the immediate context (9:31; 10:4–5).

The fifth explanation sees a general relationship between the two words. Some build on a particular explanation of νόμου πίστεως in Rom 3:27 and see a reference in 9:31 to the law as a witness to righteousness.[33] However, that explanation of Rom 3:27 is by no means certain,[34] and the distance between 3:27 and 9:31 raises questions about whether the two phrases interpret one another.

Instead, we favor the objective genitive, "the law whose object is righteousness."[35] This reading satisfies the desire to make sense of the phrase

27. Das, *Paul*, 241.

28. Calvin, *Romans*, 378. The RSV and NRSV read "the righteousness based on (the) law."

29. Cranfield, *Romans*, 2:507n4.

30. Murray, *Romans*, 2:43; Snodgrass, "Christological Stone Testimonia," 260n37; Witherington, *Romans*, 259.

31. See the chart in Moo, "Law," 76.

32. Winger suggests that νόμος in compound expressions (usually νόμος plus a noun in the genitive) specify a definite νόμος (*By What Law?*, 86).

33. Das, *Paul*, 245; Käsemann, *Romans*, 277.

34. See Schreiner, *Romans*, 201.

35. Fitzmyer, *Romans*, 578; Harrison, "Romans," 109; Jewett, *Romans*, 610; Moo,

without reading too much information into it. The phrase communicates the idea that law and righteousness are inseparable; a person is supposed to do the law and thus obtain righteousness (Rom 10:5). Israel pursued the law for this very purpose (v. 31a),[36] but as we will see in the next section, they did not attain their goal. One advantage of this reading is that it allows one to emphasize both words in the phrase (νόμον and δικαιοσύνης) without reading νόμον metaphorically or reversing the order of the words.[37] To pursue the law is to pursue righteousness, for the very purpose of pursuing the law is in order to gain a right standing with God.[38]

This interpretation of νόμον δικαιοσύνης indicates that Paul does not fault Israel for pursuing the law. By its very nature, the law demands obedience (Rom 10:5; Gal 3:12). YHWH demanded obedience when he initiated the Mosaic covenant (Exod 19:5-6), and Israel consented to give it (Exod 19:8).[39] Furthermore, the law promises righteousness to those who keep it (Lev 18:5). It was not wrong for Israel to seek to obey the law. However, as Paul argues in Rom 4:1-25, obedience to the law cannot be the basis of one's relationship with God and his righteousness. While the law is inseparably bound up with righteousness, it is not the way that righteousness is obtained by fallen human beings (Rom 7:7-25).

Epistle to the Romans, 625; Ortlund, "Zeal," 241n26; Refoulé, "Romains IX, 30-33." 175-77; Schreiner, "Israel's Failure," 212-13; Schreiner, *Romans*, 537. See also HCSB, "the law for righteousness"; ESV, "a law that would lead to righteousness"; and NIV, "the law as the way of righteousness."

36. As Schreiner writes, "Israel was seeking the law 'for righteousness,' for a right relationship with God" (*Romans*, 537). Longenecker describes νόμον δικαιοσύνης as a periphrastic expression that would connote the concept of a 'legalistic' or 'nomistic form of righteousness'" (*Romans*, 836).

37. Nor are we reaching for δικαιοσύνην when Paul has written νόμον, as Dunn alleges (*Romans*, 2:582). Bechtler writes, "Paul's preoccupation with 'righteousness' in the surrounding veres indicates that it is the genitive (δικαιοσύνη) no less than the accusative (νόμον) with which he is concerned" ("Christ," 294). The concept of νόμος is inseparably joined to δικαιοσύνη.

38. Mohrmann posits a genitive of source for νόμον δικαιοσύνης ("the law derived from righteousness"), but can still write, "Israel did not attain the law *and most importantly the righteousness*, modeled by Abraham, at the foundation of their law" ("Semantic Collisions," 212-213, emphasis added). Southall favors the objective genitive construction while interpreting the phrase as a personified reference to Christ (*Rediscovering Righteousness*, 193-200).

39. Toews depicts Israel's attitude at Sinai as one of surrender and trust in God's gracious salvation (Exod 3:15; 6:3f; 20:2 ["Law," 138]). While we do not deny that the Mosaic Covenant is a gracious administration of God enjoyed by faith, the law contained therein is characterized by works, not grace and faith.

Israel Did Not Attain Unto Law

Despite the appropriateness of Israel's goal, they did not attain it (εἰς νόμον οὐκ ἔφθασεν, 9:31b). The verb φθάνω means "come up to," "reach," "attain something."[40] The verb communicates racetrack imagery and indicates that what Israel pursued they failed to attain.[41] They did not reach their goal; they did not attain unto the law.[42]

Thomas Schreiner supplies δικαιοσύνην as the object of ἔφθασεν, and interprets εἰς νόμον as an adverbial accusative of general reference ("Israel did not attain righteousness with reference to the law").[43] Although Israel pursued the law for righteousness, they did not attain righteousness with reference to the law.[44] But it is not necessary to supply δικαιοσύνην in order to make sense of Paul's logic in 9:31b. Since Paul identifies the object of Israel's pursuit as νόμον in 9:31a, he is not likely to change objects a few words later in 9:31b. The preposition εἰς often identifies the goal of a pursuit, and that meaning works quite naturally here.[45] Israel did not attain unto the law.

However, the concept of righteousness has not dropped out of Paul's discussion. When Paul repeats νόμον in 9:31b, it functions as shorthand for the full phrase just used, νόμον δικαιοσύνης.[46] Israel pursued the law in order to obtain a right standing with God, but they did not obtain the law *and that right standing*. As noted earlier, Dunn criticizes this approach as reaching for δικαιοσύνην when Paul has written νόμον,[47] but the reach is not far: εἰς νόμον immediately follows νόμον δικαιοσύνης. Even Toews, who maintains a sharp distinction between the gentiles pursuing righteousness and Israel pursuing the law,[48] still writes, "Israel's goal was to live in harmony with the law because the law was righteous and showed the people how they might be righteous before God."[49] The law and righteousness are inseparably bound up with

---

40. BDAG, 1053.
41. Toews, "Law," 134.
42. Badenas, *Christ*, 104.
43. Schreiner, "Israel's Failure," 213.
44. Schreiner, "Israel's Failure," 213.
45. BDAG, 288–89.
46. Early scribes recognized this and appended δικαιοσύνης here to match the previous occurrence of the phrase (ℵ² F Ψ 1881 *Byz* lat sy). P. Schmiedel conjectures replacing νόμον with δικαιοσύνην, but there is no textual evidence to support this.
47. Dunn, *Romans*, 2:582.
48. Toews, "Law," 132–34.
49. Toews, "Law," 133.

one another.⁵⁰ To pursue the law is to pursue it for righteousness; to fail to obtain the law is to fail to obtain the righteousness it requires.

THE REASON FOR ISRAEL'S FAILURE

Paul now supplies the reason for Israel's failure. He opens 9:32 with the question, διὰ τί ("Why?").⁵¹ Why did Israel fail to attain the law and its righteousness? His terse answer contains no verb: ὅτι οὐκ ἐκ πίστεως⁵² ἀλλ' ὡς ἐξ ἔργων⁵³ ("because not by faith but as by works," 9:32a). However, the preceding verse supplies the missing information: Israel pursued the law of righteousness (διώκων νόμον δικαιοσύνης) not by faith but as if it could be attained (εἰς νόμον οὐκ ἔφθασεν) by works.⁵⁴ The ὡς identifies the perspective from which Israel operated in their pursuit of the law.⁵⁵ They imagined that they could attain the law and its righteousness by works, but they should have pursued the law and its righteousness by faith.

Those who argue that Israel misunderstood the true demand of the law (faith) and sought to fulfill it in the wrong way (works) seize on Paul's language here. They point out that Paul does not criticize Israel for pursuing the

---

50. As noted earlier, even Dunn identifies νόμον δικαιοσύνης as the law which requires righteousness (*Romans*, 2:581).

51. BDAG, 225.

52. Toews observes the contrast between the gentiles obtaining righteousness "from faith" (ἐκ πίστεως, 9:30) with Paul's description of Israel as "not from faith" (οὐκ ἐκ πίστεως ["Law," 138]).

53. Several reputable mss append νόμου to ἔργων (ℵ² D Ψ 33 Byz vg^ms sy), but others omit it (ℵ* A B F G 6. 629. 630. 1739. 1881. *pc* lat co). Cranfield and Metzger interpret the addition as assimilation to Rom 3:20, 29; Gal 2:16; 3:2, 5, 10 (*Romans*, 2:509 and *Textual Commentary*, 462–63, respectively). Porter notes that ἔργων and ἔργων νόμου essentially mean the same thing (*Romans*, 194).

54. Schreiner, *Romans*, 538. Gordon argues that the elliptical phrase modifies νόμος and not διώκω ("Israel," 163–66). Paul's statement refers to the nature of the Mosaic Covenant and not Israel's pursuit: "Because the Sinai Covenant [νόμος] is not identified/characterized by faith" (163). Das observes that Gordon does not account for the presence of ὡς, which emphasizes the subjective aspect, and suggests a misunderstanding of the Jews approach to the law and not a statement about the law itself (*Paul*, 243n41; also Leitzmann, *Römer*, 94). Southall also argues that ἐκ πίστεως (referring to Christ's faithfulness) modifies νόμον δικαιοσύνης, arguing that Israel "failed to pursue the personified runner Νόμος Δικαιοσύνης ἐκ πίστεως" (*Rediscovering Righteousness*, 203). Das' criticism also applies to Southall's reading.

55. BDAG, 1104. Sanday and Headlam write, "St. Paul wishes to guard himself from asserting definitely that ἐξ ἔργων was a method by which νόμον δικαιοσύνης might be pursued. He therefore represents it as an idea of the Jews, as a way by which they thought they could gain it" (*Romans*, 280).

law, but for pursuing it in the wrong way. They then deduce that what the law really demands is faith, not works.⁵⁶ But this deduction clashes with Paul's contrasts between faith and the law. According to Rom 3:21, the law bears witness to the righteousness of God,⁵⁷ but the law is not the vehicle by which righteousness is manifested (χωρὶς νόμου δικαιοσύνη θεοῦ πεφανέρωται). Rather, righteousness comes through faith in Jesus Christ. In Rom 4:13, Paul states that the promise is not mediated through (obedience to) the law but through faith. Rom 4:14 states that if the promise comes to those of the law then faith is nullified. Rom 4:15 provides the overarching explanation: the law brings wrath (not righteousness). Rom 7:7-10 describes the law in terms of lifestyle demands, not calls for faith. For Paul, there is a contrast between the nature of the law itself and faith.⁵⁸

Furthermore, Paul depicts humanity as unable to perform the law's demands. In Rom 3:20, Paul states that no human being can be justified by the law because the law brings knowledge of sin, not righteousness (cf. Rom 5:13). In fact, human sinfulness uses the law to produce disobedience and death (Rom 7:11-25).⁵⁹ Throughout Romans, Paul depicts humans as disobedient to God's moral demands as expressed in the law (1:18-3:20; 7:1-25); he does not depict them as disobedient to the call for faith in the gospel. Paul contrasts faith in the gospel with the works of the law, and presents the obedience of faith as the solution to the problem of humanity's disobedience to God and his law (Rom 1:5, 16-17; 3:21-31).

Since the law demands obedience, and no human can fulfill its demands, justification can come only by faith. Paul states this clearly in Rom 3:21-31, and he goes on to argue that the OT supports his assertion (4:1-25). Abraham's justification by faith, which took place prior to the giving of the law, demonstrates that the Scriptures as a whole teach salvation by faith (Rom 4:1-12). However, that does not mean that the law commands

---

56. Badenas, *Christ*, 107; Barrett, "Romans 9:30-10:21," 141-43; Barth, *Shorter Commentary on Romans*, 124; Boor, *Römer*, 239; Bring, "Paul," 21-60; Cranfield, *Romans*, 2:510; Das, *Paul*, 247; Meyer, *End*, 211-13; Wright, *Romans*, 649. Wright argues that Paul develops this idea throughout Romans in 2:25-29; 3:27-31; 8:4-8; 9:32a; and especially 10:6-9.

57. Though the occurrence of νόμος in the phrase τοῦ νόμου καὶ τῶν προφητῶν indicates that Paul uses νόμος there in the sense of Scripture.

58. *Contra* Bring who claims that Paul's negative statements are against Jewish misunderstandings of the law ("Paul," 22, 45-46). Paul's statements describe the law itself, not one's approach to it.

59. Toews claims that to depict the law as unfulfillable allows the perspective of Galatians to interpret Romans ("Law," 136). Yet the verses examined here show that Paul makes the same argument in Romans as well. The law cannot be fulfilled by sinful human beings.

faith, as Paul explains in Rom 4:13–15. The law brings wrath (Rom 4:15), and is given to magnify transgression (Rom 3:20; 5:13), thus revealing faith as the means of salvation.[60] Israel should have discerned this within their Scriptures.[61]

When Paul comes to Rom 9:31–32a, he builds on these prior arguments. According to 9:31, Israel was not merely pursuing the law, but the law and its righteousness (νόμον δικαιοσύνης). They erred not by pursuing the law and its righteousness, but by pursuing the law and its righteousness by works (9:32a). They did not misunderstand what the law was demanding, for the law truly demands works (Rom 7:7–10).[62] However, they overestimated their ability to fulfill the law (Rom 7:11–25).[63] They should have pursued the law and its righteousness by faith because the law brings wrath to those who cannot obey it (Rom 3:20; 4:14–15). The righteous standing which the law offers comes through faith alone (Rom 3:21–22; 4:13; 9:30).[64]

---

60. Gutbrod, "νόμος," 1072; Westerholm, "Paul," 234. Paul makes a similar argument in Gal 3:1–29. For a nice summary of Paul's salvation-historical argument there, see Carson, "Mystery," 411–12.

61. Westerholm writes, "In the NT, *law* refers primarily to the sum of commandments given to Israel through Moses on Mount Sinai, or to the part of Scripture—the Pentateuch (the first five books of the OT)—that contain them. Occasionally the term is extended to include the whole of the Jewish sacred Scriptures (see John 10:34; 12:34; 15:25; Rom 3:19; 1 Cor 14:21)" ("Law," 594). Westerholm's distinctions help alleviate some of the terminological confusion attending discussions on the relationship between faith and the law. The law in the first sense does not set forth faith as the way of salvation. Rather, it promises life in exchange for obedience (Rom 10:5). The Mosaic covenant and its commands tie blessing to obedience; the law is not characterized by faith but by obedience (Gal 3:12). In the latter sense, however, the law does teach salvation by faith. The OT Scriptures as a whole set forth faith as the way of salvation (e.g., Gen 15:6; Isa 7:9). The law in the first sense (the Mosaic Covenant and its commandments) does not change God's way of justifying sinners (Gal 3:15–18). However, it does emphasize obedience and highlight transgressions, thus making it antithetical to justification by faith (Rom 4:13–15; Gal 3:19–22). The two different emphases are able to work together in that the law's work of revealing transgressions drives sinners to trust God for their righteous standing and not their own works (Rom 3:21–31). This is what Paul expected Israel to understand from their Scriptures, and this is what he criticizes them for missing.

62. Ridderbos writes, "he who strives after the righteousness that is by the law is then bound to the word of Moses, that is, to do what the law demands"; "he who seeks righteousness in the law faces, as appears from the law itself, the requirement of doing" (*Paul*, 156).

63. Huby, *Romains*, 361.

64. Mohrmann argues for a similar position, but insists that one must hear the echo of Isa 51:1–8 and Gen 15:6 (or Rom 4) in this passage in order to understand that the law ultimately calls for faith in Christ ("Semantic Collisions," 213). We think a better approach is to set the law in its proper salvation-historical location (after the salvation of Abraham by faith alone), and to recognize that while the law commands obedience,

Those who argue that Israel's chief error was the pursuit of nationalistic righteousness also accuse Israel of misunderstanding the law, yet in a different manner. For these interpreters, Israel misunderstood the law when they defined it in terms of requirements which mark off Jews from gentiles. Instead, they should have understood it in terms of faith, an obedience which even gentiles can render.[65] However, like the New Perspective explanation of νόμον δικαιοσύνης, this interpretation gives a more specific nuance to ἔργων than the context justifies. Paul gives no indication in 9:30—10:13 that he has such specific works in mind.[66] He does not even mention practices such as circumcision, Sabbath, and food laws in Rom 9–11.[67] The two other occurrences of ἔργων in Rom 9–11 are set in opposition to doing good and evil (9:11–12) and in opposition to grace (11:6).[68] Furthermore, the connection between righteousness and law in this passage (captured by νόμον δικαιοσύνης) indicates that Torah is more than a matter of religious and ethnic identity; it is a way of life that will lead to righteousness before God if one perfectly obeys it (cf. 10:5).[69]

Additionally, the nationalistic explanation of Israel's error weakens the nature of Paul's contrast. Jewish ethnocentrism does not logically contrast exercising faith. Even Dunn indicates a change of subject when he contrasts the two: "on the one hand, the law defining righteousness understood too narrowly in terms of the requirements of the law which mark off Jew from gentile; on the other hand, the law defining righteousness understood in terms of the obedience of faith which a Gentile can offer *as Gentile*."[70] Notice that in the first clause, Israel misunderstands the law's requirements, but in the second clause gentiles render the obedience of faith. However, if pursuing the law by works is rejecting the inclusion of the gentiles, then pursuing it by faith is granting them inclusion. Yet Paul's suggested remedy says nothing about granting gentiles inclusion in the people of God.[71] Rather, he

---

the Scriptures as a whole recognize that one cannot keep such commands, and that one must obtain righteousness through faith alone.

65. Dunn, *Romans*, 2:582–83.

66. For this understanding of "works" and "works of the law" in Paul, see Cranfield, "Works," 89–101; Gutbrod, "νόμος," 4:1069–71; Moo, "Law," 73–110; Schreiner, "Works," 217–44; and Westerholm, *Perspectives*, 297–340.

67. Schreiner, "Paul's View," 116.

68. Ortlund, "Zeal," 243.

69. Toews observes that references to works in Romans are much more general and ambiguous than those in Galatians ("Law," 141–43). In Romans, "'works' continue to denote the demand for human performance as a contrast to faith" (143).

70. Dunn, *Romans*, 2:582–83, emphasis original.

71. Schreiner writes, "the Jews are not specifically reproved for being too exclusive

admonishes them to abandon their reliance on works and put their faith in Christ (Rom 10:9–13).[72]

The traditional explanation of Israel's error with reference to the law coheres well with Paul's language in 9:31–32a, and also with his prior arguments in Romans: Israel tried to keep the law and to attain righteousness by works instead of by faith, but sinful humans cannot adequately perform the law's righteous demands.[73] They failed to attain the law and its righteousness because they did not obey the law's requirements perfectly.[74] Sinful humans cannot obtain righteousness by obeying the law, but by exercising faith in Christ.

THE MEANING AND PURPOSE OF PAUL'S CITATION OF ISA 8:14; 28:16

Paul argues in Rom 9:31–32a that Israel tried to keep the law in order to obtain a right standing with God (9:31). Due to human inability, they fell short of their goal (9:32a). The proper approach to gaining a right standing with God is faith in Christ (9:32b). Now Paul uses the OT to prove that Israel should have discerned that truth from their Scriptures (9:33).

Paul leads into his OT citation by juxtaposing his description of Israel's pursuit (v. 32a) with a declaration of Israel's stumbling (v. 32b). After describing their pursuit of the law as "not from faith but as if from works" (οὐκ ἐκ πίστεως ἀλλ' ὡς ἐξ ἔργων), Paul announces, "they stumbled over the stumbling stone" (προσέκοψαν τῷ λίθῳ τοῦ προσκόμματος).[75] Since the original manuscripts contain no punctuation, one can either start a new sentence with "they stumbled,"[76] or deduce a cause and effect relationship between the two clauses ("because seeking it not by faith, but as from works, they stumbled").[77] A full cause and effect relationship deduces more than the grammar allows: there is no connective between the two clauses outside

---

in Rom 9:30–10:8. Instead, they are censured for failing to obey the law and for legalism" ("Paul's View," 117).

72. Perhaps Dunn indicates what he sees as the proper contrast when he writes that misguided zeal (Rom 10:2) defends Israel's prerogative by killing rather than fulfilling the law by loving one's neighbor (Rom 13:8 [*Romans*, 2:587]). But Paul never cites the command to love one's neighbor in discussions of justification.

73. Thielman, *Plight*, 112.

74. Schreiner, "Israel's Failure," 212–13, 220.

75. τοῦ προσκόμματος is a genitive of product: the stone that produces (causes) stumbling (see Wallace, *Greek Grammar*, 104–06).

76. Favored by Cranfield, "Some Notes," 38–39, and most commentators.

77. Favored by Mounce, *Romans*, 206n38.

of the Byzantine tradition, and there is no verb in 9:32a (it is supplied in English to make sense of the passage). However, it is difficult to read this sentence without detecting some kind of subordination between the two clauses. Schreiner argues that there is probably an implicit "therefore" joining vv. 32a and 32b.[78] The flow of Paul's argument supports this deduction. Paul first addresses Israel's reliance on works before addressing their lack of faith, implying that the latter flows out of the former.[79] Also, the hostility expressed towards Jesus and his approach to the law in the Gospels implies that it was mistaken ideas about Torah that caused the Jews to stumble over Jesus' claims (Matt 5:17; Luke 24:44; John 5:45–47; 7:19; 9:28–29). Israel pursued the law by works instead of by faith; therefore, they stumbled over the stone of stumbling.[80]

Paul concludes this paragraph in 9:33 by citing Isa 8:14 and 28:16. Paul uses καθώς to introduce the citation and to connect it with 9:32b: "they stumbled over the stumbling stone, just as (καθώς) it is written: 'Behold, I lay in Zion a stone of stumbling and a rock of offence, and the one who believes in him/it (ἐπ' αὐτῷ) will not be disappointed.'" Paul employs this citation because it highlights the folly of trusting in human resources. Just as Israel in Isaiah's day relied on human alliances to deliver them, so Israel in Paul's day trusts in their own efforts to obtain righteousness and deliver them from eschatological judgment.[81] To prove this, we consider the original context of Isaiah, the source of Paul's citation, and whether Paul sees a fulfillment of these verses in his day, or argues analogically.

The Original Contexts of Isa 8:14; 28:16

The theme of trust unites Isa 7–39. Faced with foreign invaders, Israel must decide whether they will trust YHWH to deliver them from their enemies or whether they will depend on alliances with foreign nations.[82] Motyer even claims that "Isaiah is the Paul of the Old Testament in his teaching that

---

78. Schreiner, *Romans*, 540.

79. Schreiner writes, "the failure to discern the significance of salvation history is rooted in anthropology. It is precisely because they desired to achieve their own righteousness that they failed to believe in Christ, for believing in Christ gives all the glory to God while observing the law means that glory and praise accrue to human beings" (*Romans*, 541–42).

80. Meyer, *End*, 211. Cranfield argues that the asyndeton adds a special solemnity to the statement (*Romans*, 2:510).

81. Käsemann and Schreiner note that καταισχύνω refers to vindication in the final judgment (*Romans*, 279, and *Romans*, 541, respectively).

82. Oswalt, *Isaiah, Chapters 1–39*, 193–94.

faith in God's promises is the single most important reality for the Lord's people: this is the heart of chapters 1–37."[83]

Isaiah introduces this theme in Isa 7:9. When King Ahaz is troubled over the threat of the Pekah-Rezin alliance, Isaiah admonishes him to stand firm in his faith: "If you do not stand firm in your faith, you will not stand at all" (NIV). This theme continues in chapter 8. Although Judah rejoices in their temporary deliverance through their alliance with Assyria, eventually Assyria herself will invade Judah (8:5–10). The people must trust YHWH to be their deliverer (8:13).[84] In 8:14, Isaiah highlights the two different experiences the people will have of YHWH, depending on whether or not they trust him instead of Assyria.[85] Together, 8:13–14 read:

> The Lord Almighty is the one you are to regard as holy, he is the one you are to fear, he is the one you are to dread, and he will be a sanctuary;[86] but for both houses of Israel he will be a stone that causes men to stumble and a rock that makes them fall. And for the people of Jerusalem he will be a trap and a snare (NIV84).[87]

To those who sanctify YHWH and put their trust in him, he is a sanctuary and refuge. To those who reject him and trust instead in Assyria, he is a stone that causes stumbling and a rock that makes people fall (he is a source of destruction).[88]

The same theme occurs in Isa 28:16. The historical situation is quite similar: faced now with the realized threat of Assyrian invasion, Judah is considering an alliance with Egypt to deliver them (Isa 30:1–7; 31:1–5).[89] Chapters 28–33 demonstrate the foolishness of trusting the nations instead

---

83. Motyer, *Isaiah*, 21.

84. Webb, *Isaiah*, 64–66.

85. Oswalt, *Isaiah 1–39*, 234. First Pet 2:4–10, which also cites Isa 8:14; 28:16, especially highlights this dual experience of the Lord.

86. Watts proposes substituting למקשיר ("conspiracy") for למקדש ("sanctuary"), indicating that the Lord will be the cause of trouble or difficulty for Israel (*Isaiah 1–33*, 156). Snodgrass surveys suggested emendations and concludes, "The text as it is preserved in the MT should be preferred since it is the more difficult reading and since it is also supported by 1QIsa. The differences of the LXX and targums [sic] are an attempt to explain away the judgment of Yahweh" ("Stone Testimonia," 24).

87. We cite the 1984 edition of the NIV here because it reflects the contrast between the first line of verse 14 and the rest of the verse (so also Keil and Delitzsch, *Commentary*, 7:154, and Snodrass, "Stone Testimonia," 26). Paul cites the middle lines of v. 14: "a stone that causes people to stumble and a rock that makes them fall" (NIV).

88. Grogan, "Isaiah," 181; Motyer, *Isaiah*, 97; Ortlund, "Insanity of Faith," 273; Oswalt, *Isaiah 1–39*, 234; Smith, *Isaiah 1–39*, 227; Snodgrass, "Stone Testimonia," 26; Webb, *Isaiah*, 66; Young, *Isaiah*, 1:312.

89. Webb, *Isaiah*, 116.

of the Lord.⁹⁰ The judgment promised in Isa 8:6, 8, 14 for trusting the nations (the Assyrian invasion) will soon take place, and Judah is again considering an earthly alliance to rescue them.⁹¹

Therefore, Isaiah admonishes the people to put their trust in God, expressed in Isa 28:16 under the imagery of the stone: "See, I lay⁹² a stone in Zion,⁹³ a tested stone, a precious cornerstone for a sure foundation; the one who relies on it will never be stricken with panic" (NIV). As in Isa 8:14, faith determines which aspect of God one experiences. Those who trust YHWH will have peace;⁹⁴ those who do not will waver and shake.⁹⁵

Together, Isa 8:14 and 28:16 echo the "Isaian core" first expressed in Isa 7:9.⁹⁶ Joseph Blenkinsopp summarizes this core as follows: "political action is not religiously and morally autonomous; it must be based on trust in God, not on the self-interested assistance of foreign powers."⁹⁷ The Israel of Isaiah's day was foolishly trusting human resources to deliver them from death when they should have trusted YHWH. This theme is consistent with Paul's argument in Rom 9:30–33 regarding Israel's trust in their own resources to secure their righteousness when they should have believed in Christ.

---

90. Oswalt, *Isaiah 1–39*, 504.

91. Oswalt, *Isaiah 1–39*, 504. Snodgrass also notes verbal parallels between 8:8 and 28:15, 18, and 8:15 and 28:13 ("Stone Testimonia," 33).

92. The הנני יסד construction which begins the sentence is unusual. Several versions and commentators emend the text (1QIsᵃ reads מיסד; IQIsᵇ reads יוסד; MT apparatus suggests יסד). Roberts argues that the "preterite orientation" of Isa 14:32 has influenced Isa 28:16 because of the similar theology between the passages, and that in this instance the *lectio difficilior* is not to be preferred ("Yahweh's Foundation," 28). Snodgrass favors the participial reading, "I am founding" ("Stone Testimonia," 28–29). Beuken observes the uniqueness of the construction, but retains the reading because it is the *lectio difficilior* (*Isaiah*, 14–15). He translates the phrase as "Behold me who have laid for a foundation" (cf. Kautzsch, *Gesenius' Hebrew Grammar*, 486–87). Dunn and Käsemann argue that the active "I lay" continues the predestinarian emphasis of 9:18–22 (*Romans*, 2:584 and *Romans*, 279, respectively).

93. Roberts argues that ב is used locatively: "I am about to lay in Zion a foundation stone" ("Yahweh's Foundation," 29).

94. We address the identification of the stone in our discussion of Paul's hermeneutics.

95. Beuken translates יחיש as "to waver, shake, quake" (*Isaiah 28–39*, 15). Calvin observes, "the design of the Prophet is, to extol faith on account of this invaluable result, that by means of it we enjoy settled peace and composure. Hence it follows that, till we possess faith, we must have continual perplexity and distress; for there is but one harbor on which we can safely rely, namely, the truth of the Lord, which alone will give us peace and serenity of mind" (*Isaiah*, 290).

96. Blenkinsopp, *Isaiah 1–39*, 394.

97. Blenkinsopp, *Isaiah 1–39*, 394.

The Textual History of Isa 8:14; 28:16

A large amount of the discussion of Paul's use of Isa 8:14; 28:16 in Rom 9:33 focuses on the source of Paul's citation.[98] The text form that Paul uses does not correspond perfectly to any extant text. It resembles the MT and Aquila, Symmachus, and Theoditian more than the LXX,[99] yet with noticeable differences.[100] Also, the question arises of whether the combined citation of Isa 8:14 and 28:16 originated with Paul or previously existed in a testimony book linking such stone passages with Christ.[101]

Paul's citation is a partial citation of Isa 28:16 with a line from Isa 8:14 spliced into the middle. Paul introduces the citation with the formula καθὼς γέγραπται, "just as it is written," and then cites Isa 28:16a: ἰδοὺ τίθημι ἐν Σιὼν λίθον, "Behold, I place in Zion a stone." The LXX reads Ἰδοὺ ἐγὼ ἐμβαλῶ εἰς τὰ θεμέλια Σιων λίθον, "Behold, I establish as a foundation in Zion a stone." The MT's reading is shorter: הנני יסד בציון אבן, "Behold, I place in Zion a stone." Paul's citation of this line is closer to the MT than the LXX.[102]

The word λίθον links Isa 28:16 with Isa 8:14.[103] Paul describes the stone which God appoints in Zion as a λίθον προσκόμματος καὶ πέτραν σκανδάλου, "a stone of stumbling and a rock of offense."[104] Here the citation differs greatly from the LXX. The LXX attempts to bring out the conditional nature of the description of YHWH as either a God who blesses or a God who judges based on one's response to him (a legitimate inference based on the exegesis of Isa 8:14). The full verse reads, καὶ ἐὰν ἐπ' αὐτῷ πεποιθὼς ᾖς, ἔσται σοι εἰς ἁγίασμα, καὶ οὐχ ὡς λίθου προσκόμματι συναντήσεσθε αὐτῷ οὐδὲ ὡς πέτρας πτώματι, "and if you will be persuaded, he will be to you a sanctuary, and not as a stone of stumbling happening to him, nor as a rock of offense." Paul simply cites the references to

---

98. The same is true for Peter's use of these verses in 1 Pet 2:6, 8. Mohrmann also sees an allusion to Isa 8:14 in Luke 20:18 and 1 Cor 1:23 (the latter reference a very loose allusion), and an allusion to Isa 28:16 in Eph 2:20 ("Semantic Collisions," 52–55, 83–84).

99. Koch, *Die Schrift*, 60.

100. Schreiner, *Romans*, 540.

101. Dodd argues "both Paul and the author of 1 Peter made use of a twofold *testimonium* already current in the pre-canonical tradition in a version different somewhat from the LXX" (*According*, 43; also Ellis, *Paul's Use*, 89, and Stanley, *Paul*, 122).

102. Targum Jonathan reads האנא ממני בציון מלך תקיף גיבר ואימתן מלך, "Behold, I appoint a king in Zion; a King mighty, powerful, and terrible" (Pauli, *Chaldee Paraphrase*, 89); the Vulgate reads "Ecce ego mittam in fundamentis Sion lapidem," "I lay a stone in the foundations of Zion."

103. Pattee, "Stumbling Stone," 110.

104. The citations overlap: the last word of the citation of Isa 28:16a is also the first word in the citation of Isa 8:14.

the stone and the rock with their genitive modifiers, which again closely resemble the MT (ולאבן נגף ולצור מכשול, "a stone of stumbling and a rock of offense").

The citation concludes with the final line of Isa 28:16: καὶ ὁ πιστεύων ἐπ' αὐτῷ οὐ καταισχυνθήσεται, "and the one who believes in him/it will not be disappointed." Here Paul's citation matches the LXX almost exactly.[105] It differs from the MT in that καταισχύνω is never used to translate חוש in the LXX except for here. The two concepts, however, are not opposed: those who trust God are not in haste but rather have peace (MT); they are not disappointed because they have put their trust in God (LXX). Isaiah 28:16 describes the stone as "a tested stone" and "a precious cornerstone for a sure foundation" (NIV). Perhaps those descriptions influenced the LXX translator to choose a word that conveyed the idea that those who trusted this reliable stone would not be disappointed with their choice. Perhaps Paul cites the LXX here instead of the MT in order to make use of that idea in his argument.

The textual history of these two verses and their use in intertestamental Jewish literature display a diversity of approaches.[106] We have already noted the protasis added to 8:14 (καὶ ἐάν ἐπ' αὐτῷ πεποιθὼς ᾖς), perhaps in an effort to match the emphasis on faith in 28:16.[107] The LXX increases that emphasis in 28:16 with the addition of ἐπ' αὐτῷ. The Targum reads באלין ("in these things"), indicating that ἐπ' αὐτῷ is original to the LXX and not added because of Rom 9:33.[108] Targum Isa 8:14 also leads with a protasis.[109]

The members of the Qumran community may have thought of themselves as the agents of destruction or salvation in Isa 8:14, but they could also use the image in a derogatory sense of others.[110] Some references perhaps allusively refer the stumbling-stone to the end time.[111] The Rule of the Community (1QS 8:7b) identifies the Qumran community as the precious cornerstone of Isa 28:16,[112] though 1QS 8:7b reads תומת instead of אבן.[113]

---

105. The LXX reads οὐ μὴ καταισχυνθῇ. Paul omits the μὴ and uses a future passive construction instead of the aorist passive of the LXX. The differences are negligible. D F G read μὴ καταισχυνθῇ in line with the LXX.

106. In addition to the use of Isa 8:14; 28:16 in intertestamental literature, Mohrmann suggests that Ezek 11:16 alludes to Isa 8:14 ("Semantic Collisions," 48–49).

107. Snodgrass, "Stone Testimonia," 52–53.

108. Snodgrass, "Stone Testimonia," 51–52.

109. Snodgrass, "Stone Testimonia," 75.

110. Snodgrass, "Stone Testimonia," 60.

111. Seifrid, "Romans," 652.

112. Wise et al., *Dead Sea Scrolls*, 129.

113. Shum, *Paul's Use*, 108.

Similar language occurs in 1QH 14:26f; 15:9.[114] In the rabbinical literature, a story in b. Sanh. 38a (third century) interprets Isa 8:14 messianically.[115] Isaiah 28:16 is used rarely; the verse functions as proof that the exiles will return or that the temple will be rebuilt.[116]

At times Paul's citation matches the MT; in the last line it resembles the LXX. Paul could have been making his own translation of the MT until the final line when he decided to cite the LXX. Perhaps he cited a Greek MS that is not available to us. At this point, it is not immediately clear exactly how Paul obtained these citations or how they fit into the textual history.[117] Enough differences exist between Paul's use of Isa 8:14; 28:16 and Peter's to argue that they did not cite from a common source.[118] Paul put these verses together himself.[119] We can conclude that Paul intended to cite Isaiah and use these citations to advance his argument regarding Israel's plight.

Paul's Hermeneutics

The question of Paul's hermeneutics concerns whether Paul uses Isa 8:14; 28:16 analogically or whether he views the Isaiah passages as actually predicting Israel's rejection of Christ. Seifrid defends the latter position and writes, "in Isa. 8:14 and Isa. 28:16 Paul finds in the pattern of God's dealing with Israel in judgment and salvation a pattern (type) that has come to fulfillment in his eschatological dealings with them in Christ."[120] Likewise, Snodgrass argues that "the mixed citation serves as literal fulfillment of the

---

114. Shum, *Paul's Use*, 153–56.

115. Ortlund, "Insanity," 277–78; Snodgrass, "Stone Testimonia," 75–76.

116. Snodgrass, "Stone Testimonia," 80. See Strack and Billerbeck, *Kommentar*, 3:276 for references. Mohrmann also suggests an allusion to Isa 8:14 in *Sibylline Oracles* 3:289–90 ("Semantic Collisions," 50).

117. Snodgrass, "Stone Testimonia," 251; Wagner, *Heralds*, 134. Toews suggests a text in flux based on the fact that it is never cited the same way ("Law," 156). Toews also uses this flux to argue against the idea of a stone testimonia ("Law," 161–68).

118. Hultgren, *Romans*, 380. We note the following differences: (1) Peter repeats the reference to the stone; (2) Peter uses πέτρα whereas Paul uses πέτραν; and (3) Peter uses οὐ μὴ καταισχυνθῇ. Shum, *Paul's Use*, 213–16, gives the following as evidence that Paul was responsible for the citation and fusion of Isa 8:14 and 28:16 in Rom 9:33, and that he cited directly from Isaiah: (1) Paul knew the OT; (2) 1 Pet 2:6, 8 could be dependent on the OT and Rom 9:33; (3) no evidence for a pre-Pauline tradition that interpreted the stone as a reference to Jesus; (4) the ancient practice of notebooks does not prove a pre-Pauline stone-Jesus tradition; and (5) Paul may have had access to the OT through certain Corinthian Christians.

119. Wilckens, *Römer*, 214.

120. Seifrid, "Romans," 652.

rejection of Christ by the Jews and as a further proof of salvation by faith."[121] However, the lack of prophetic language both in Isaiah 8:14; 28:16 and Paul's citation formula argues against this. Isaiah 8:14; 28:16 anticipates judgment or salvation for the Israel of Isaiah's day based on whether or not they will trust YHWH and forsake their sinful alliances. This in and of itself does not rule out the possibility of a typological pattern, but Paul's lack of fulfillment language in his citation formula makes fulfillment difficult to prove. Paul states that the Israel of his day has stumbled over the stumbling stone (9:32), but he amplifies his statement in 9:33 ("just as it is written") without claiming that a supposed prophecy or type has been fulfilled.

We conclude then that the similarity between the contexts of Isaiah and Romans enables Paul to compare the Israel of Isaiah's day and his analogically. Toews writes, "Just as Israel refused to trust the word of God in the face of the Assyrian threat (Isa. 28), so now she stumbles over the law in faith."[122] Paul uses Isaiah's language to describe his contemporaries who commit the same mistake: they rely on human resources instead of trusting God's promises.[123]

This assessment of Paul's usage helps answer the question of the identification of the stone. There are many interpretive options present in the literature, including God and his promises,[124] divine security,[125] the law,[126]

---

121. Snodgrass, "Stone Testimonia," 262–63. See also Dunn, *Romans*, 2:594; Jewett, *Romans*, 613–14, and Moo, *Epistle to the Romans*, 630.

122. Toews, *Romans*, 261. Also Wagner, *Heralds*, 150, 154–55, 157. We cite Toews and Wagner because they describe Paul's use of Isaiah in analogical terms. We disagree with their identification of the stone as the law, and their argument that Israel was not guilty of using the law to obtain righteousness by works.

123. Oss, "Interpretation," 195. Ortlund, "Zeal," 248, also shows how this reading of Isa 8:14; 28:16 argues against a nationalistic understanding of Israel's error with reference to the law: "the alternative to faith in Isaiah 8 and 28 is not social presumptuousness rooted in racial lineage and sustained by observance of ethnically distinguishing badges, but rather self-resourced deliverance: looking to one's might, one's own or that of other nations, for security."

124. Smith, *Isaiah 1–39*, 487.

125. Ortlund, "Insanity," 276, emphasis original.

126. Barrett, "Romans 9.30–10.21," 144; Pattee, "Romans 9:30–10:13," 136–38, 317–18. Pattee builds his case for identifying the stone as the law by arguing that Paul not only cites Isa 8:14; 28:16 in Rom 9:33, but also alludes to Ps 119:165 and Sir 32:15, texts which present the law as something positive that prevents stumbling when one believers in it ("Romans 9:30–10:13," 115–34). Pattee argues that these latter two texts reconcile the tension between Isa 8:14; 28:16, which supposedly present the law as something both negative and positive. We disagree with Pattee's approach because he allows the two texts that Paul does not directly cite to exert influence over the meaning of the two texts that he does cite. The foundation of Pattee's whole argument is tenuous.

the law not accepted in faith,[127] faith,[128] the temple,[129] YHWH's election of Zion,[130] the Messiah,[131] a divinely-controlled government,[132] the true seed of David,[133] a complex of ideas,[134] and Christ.[135] Within the Isaiah passages, the best candidate for the immediate referent is YHWH himself. In Isa 8:13, Isaiah commands the people to regard YHWH as holy and to fear and dread him. YHWH is the only possible antecedent in 8:14 for the phrase "he will be a stone that causes people to stumble and a rock that makes them fall" (NIV). This admonition to trust YHWH echoes the key admonition to trust the Lord in 7:9. In 28:16, YHWH is the one who establishes the stone, but

127. Toews, "Law," 146, 198–99, 202–3. While the law is a prominent factor in the context of Rom 9:30–33, the exegesis of 9:31–32a warrants against viewing the law as the object of Israel's faith. Grieb also observes that a reference to the law seems unlikely in view of all that Paul has said in Rom 7 about the inability of the law to oppose sin (*Romans*, 98).

128. Porter, *Romans*, 195.

129. Watts, *Isaiah 1–33*, 437.

130. Beuken, *Isaiah*, 49.

131. Grogan, "Isaiah," 181–82.

132. Snodgrass, "Stone Testimonia," 34.

133. Keil and Delitzsch, *Commentary*, 7:306.

134. Oswalt writes, "The cornerstone may be the whole complex of ideas relating to the Lord's revelation of his faithfulness and the call to reciprocate with the same kind of faithfulness toward him. That entire message would one day be summed up in Jesus Christ. The issue remains the same today as then: upon what shall we build our lives, human schemes or divine trustworthiness?" (*Isaiah 1–39*, 518) Humphrey and Southall interpret the stone as both Torah and Christ ("Rhetoric," 141, and *Rediscovering Righteousness*, 210, respectively).

135. Aageson, "Typology," 61; Aquinas, *Romans*, 274; Barth, *Romans*, 369; Byrne, *Romans*, 310; Calvin, *Isaiah*, 291; Das, *Paul*, 100n16; Dumbrell, *Romans*, 103; Gignac, "Christ," 75; Harrison, "Romans," 110; Heil, *Paul's Letter to the Romans*, 111; Kaylor, *Paul's Covenant Community*, 166; Leitzmann, *Römer*, 94; Lohse, *Römer*, 288; Longenecker, *Romans*, 837; Luther, *Isaiah*, 229; Meyer, *Law*, 214n130; Moo, *Epistle to the Romans*, 630; Morris, *Romans*, 376; Murray, *Romans*, 2:44; Nygren, *Romans*, 377–78; Pesch, *Römerbrief*, 81; Räisänen, *Paul*, 174–75; Royster, *Romans*, 252; Sanday and Headlam, *Romans*, 280; Sanders, *Paul*, 37; Schreiner, *Romans*, 541; Snodgrass, "Stone Testimonia," 263; Wagner, *Heralds*, 157; Westerholm, *Perspectives*, 310; Westerholm, "Paul," 231; Wright, *Romans*, 650.

Mohrmann argues that in Isaiah the stone refers to something positive (a just regime), but that Paul uses it to refer negatively to Israel's lack of faith in Christ ("Semantic Collisions," 72, 219–27). According to Mohrmann, Paul intentionally changes the meaning of Isa 8:14; 28:16, but uses the texts to add "historical precedent" to his argument (225). But how much historical precedent does a text establish when its historical meaning is changed? By utilizing such a strategy, Paul is jeopardizing his credibility and that of his message by building it on an unsubstantiated foundation. Our exegesis shows that Paul can make a text from the past speak to its present audience without building his case on a meaning that is not really there.

this does not mean that he cannot be the stone itself. The purpose of the statement is to identify the characteristic of a proper object of faith (reliability). Within the larger context, YHWH is the proper object of faith (30:2; 31:1), and the use of the stone imagery echoes 8:14 where Isaiah identifies him as the object of trust.

When Paul cites these two passages, he gives no indication that he means to change the referent of Isaiah's stone from YHWH to anything else. Just as Isaiah admonished Israel to trust God for their deliverance (salvation), so Paul (by citing Isaiah) admonishes Israel to trust God for their righteousness instead of their own attempts to obey the law. Salvation comes by faith in Christ.[136] Although the Isaianic texts may not reflect a messianic referent,[137] in a bold move Paul identifies YHWH with Christ.[138] Confirmation of this interpretation of the stone comes later in the passage when Paul again cites Isa 28:16 (Rom 10:11) and refers unmistakably to Christ.[139] Paul would not likely have changed the referent within this short discussion. Paul therefore identifies Christ with the YHWH of the OT, and admonishes Israel to put their trust in him for their salvation.

CONCLUSION

This chapter argued that although Israel tried to keep the law in order to obtain a right standing with God, they could not. Support for this comes from Paul's statement that Israel pursued the νόμον δικαιοσύνης, "the law whose object is righteousness" (9:31). This means that Israel sought the law in

136. Toews agrees that Israel stumbles over the idea of *sola fide* ("Law," 203). Longenecker infers from Paul's statements about righteous gentiles that Paul's understanding of divine mercy and saving grace was broad enough to include "adherents of other religions and some seemingly secular or 'pagan' Gentiles (who have sometimes been identified as 'those of insider movements' or 'churchlesss believers in Jesus), to whom God has revealed himself in mercy and saving grace (in ways known only to God himself) and who have responded to him by their trust of him and their commitment to Jesus (in ways appropriate to their own cultures or circumstances), and so have been accepted by God as his own people" (*Romans*, 834). If by "ways appropriate to their own culture or circumstances" Longenecker means faith that does have not have Christ as its explicit object, then Longenecker's statement is out of accord with Paul's solution for Israel. As Paul understood the matter, the solution to Israel's plight was conscious faith in Christ, and it was because of that faith in Christ that there existed righteous gentiles.

137. Toews rejects a personal referent for the stone because the Isaianic references are not Messianic, but this is not a problem if Messiah is divine ("Law," 194–98).

138. Huby, *Romains*, 362. Paul will do this again in Rom 10:13, and he has already anticipated it in Rom 9:5.

139. Grieb, *Romans*, 98. For a survey of "stone" passages in connection with Christ, see Jeremias, "λίθος," 271–79.

order to obtain a right standing with God. Such a pursuit was not wrong in and of itself, for law and righteousness are inseparable; a person is supposed to do the law and thus obtain righteousness (Rom 10:5). Israel, however, did not reckon with human inability, and they fell short of their goal of obtaining righteousness ("they did not attain unto law," εἰς νόμον οὐκ ἔφθασεν [9:31]). The reason for their failure was not that they misunderstood what the law was demanding, for the law truly demands works. Nor did they pursue nationalistic works in an effort to maintain their distinct identify (Paul gives no indication in this discussion that he has any more specific works in mind other than the general works that the law demands). Rather, Israel sought to obtain righteousness by works; they pursued the law and its righteousness "not from faith but as from works" (οὐκ ἐκ πίστεως ἀλλ' ὡς ἐξ ἔργων, 9:32a). Blinded by such a pursuit, they stumbled over Christ's offer of salvation by faith alone (9:32b). In this respect, many ethnic Israelites in Paul's day are just like the Israelites of Isaiah's: they trust in human resources to deliver them from judgment instead of trusting God (Isa 8:14; 28:16 in Rom 9:33).

Chapter 3

Romans 10:1–4

INTRODUCTION

Romans 9:30—10:13 presents a step-by-step argument whereby Paul criticizes Israel for pursuing a right standing with God by obeying the Mosaic law when they should have discerned within their own Scriptures both humanity's inability to keep the Mosaic law and the necessity of salvation by faith alone. Rom 9:30–33 lays the foundation for Paul's argument: Israel pursued the νόμον δικαιοσύνης, "the law whose object is righteousness" (9:31a), but fell short of their goal ("they did not attain unto law," εἰς νόμον οὐκ ἔφθασεν [9:31b]) because they pursued the law and its righteousness "not from faith but as from works" (οὐκ ἐκ πίστεως ἀλλ᾽ ὡς ἐξ ἔργων, 9:32a). Like the Israel of Isaiah's day who relied on human alliances to deliver them, and stumbled over the concept of faith, so many Israelites in Paul's day trust in their own efforts to obtain righteousness and to deliver them from eschatological judgment (9:32b–33; Isa 8:14; 28:16).

Paul presents the second step of his argument in Rom 10:1–4. This second paragraph does not begin a new thought, but rather continues the argument by developing and expanding the main ideas of 9:30–33. Paul indicates this in three ways. First, in 10:1, Paul employs μέν without δέ. In such a structure, μέν functions as a marker of continuation.[1] Second,

---

1. BDAG, 630. Blass and Debrunner describes the structure as "good classical usage," and translates it "so far as it depends on my desire" (*Greek Grammar*, 232).

several of Paul's statements in 10:2–3 parallel ideas from 9:30–32: Israel pursuing the law of righteousness (9:31) parallels their zeal for God (10:2) and attempts to establish their own righteousness (10:3); Israel pursuing the law of righteousness not by faith but as if by works (9:32) parallels their zeal that is not based on knowledge (10:2); Israel failing to obtain her goal (9:31) and stumbling over the stumbling stone (9:32) parallels their failure to submit to God's righteousness (10:3).[2] Third, the overall idea of 10:1–4 is the same as 9:30–33: an explanation of why Israel is not presently experiencing salvation.[3]

Paul also continues a similar methodology in 10:1–4. First, he presents his theological argument (10:1–4), and then he supports his argument from the Old Testament (10:5–8).[4] Throughout each of the three major paragraphs in Rom 9:30—10:13, Paul concludes his argument with citations from the OT (Isa 8:14; 28:16 in Rom 9:33; Lev 18:5 and Deut 8:17a; 9:4a; 30:12–14 in Rom 10:5 and 10:6–8, respectively; Isa 28:16 again in Rom 10:11, and Joel 2:32 in 10:13). Due to the large discussion surrounding both Rom 10:1–4 (especially 10:4) and the OT citations in Rom 10:5–8, we will treat these sections in separate chapters. This chapter addresses Paul's theological argument in Rom 10:1–4, and the two chapters which follow address his use of the OT in Rom 10:5 and 10:6–8.

Rom 10:1 establishes the tone for 10:1–4 by expressing Paul's heartfelt anguish for Israel's need of salvation. Each verse that follows further develops and explains the previous statement.[5] If Rom 10:1 expresses Paul's desire for Israel's salvation, then 10:2 explains why non-Christian ethnic Jews need salvation: they are zealous for God but not according to knowledge. Rom 10:3 then explains the nature of Israel's lack of knowledge: in their ignorance of the righteousness of God and quest to establish their own

---

2. Das also highlights the parallels between Rom 10:1–3 and Phil 3:4–11: "The Jews' 'zeal for God' parallels Paul's own 'zeal' as a persecutor of the church. Israel's 'ignorance' of God's righteousness stands in contrast with Paul's own 'knowledge' of Christ Jesus in Phil 3:8. Israel's establishing its 'own righteousness' parallels Paul's 'own righteousness' in Phil 3:9" (*Paul*, 248–49).

3. Moo, *Epistle to the Romans*, 631. On the continuity between 9:30–33 and 10:1–4, Badenas also observes that while the first-person reference of 10:1 interrupts the narrative for a moment, it does not change the focus of the argument, for Paul returns in 10:2 to the third-person plural form used in 9:31–32 to refer to the Jews and their pursuit of the law (*Christ*, 108).

4. Longenecker highlights the frequent occurrence of γάρ throughout 10:1–13 and its absence in the preceding and following material as another indication of the unity of the section and its function to explicate the thesis of 9:30–33 (*Romans*, 840).

5. Each verse in 10:2–4 begins with γάρ. 10:5 also begins with a γάρ, which reinforces the idea that 10:5–8 support the theological argument of 10:1–4.

righteousness, they have not submitted to the righteousness of God. Finally, Rom 10:4 explains why Israel should submit to the righteousness of God: because Christ is the end of the law unto righteousness for all who believe.

While it is easy to state the basic argument of Rom 10:1–4, each of these verses presents an area of debate concerning Israel's plight and Paul's solution. In this chapter, we examine one verse per section in order to understand Paul's critique of Israel, particularly with reference to righteousness and the law. The first section examines Paul's assessment of Israel's plight: does he consider them to need salvation in Christ (10:1)? The second section examines the nature of Israel's zeal: is it a general zeal towards God's law or a specific zeal to maintain their distinct status among the nations (10:3)? The third section examines the nature of the righteousness Israel sought to establish for themselves, and the righteousness of God to which they did not submit (10:3). Finally, the fourth section examines the well-known problem of the meaning and interpretation of τέλος νόμου Χριστὸς (10:4). Throughout this chapter, we argue that Paul again describes Israel as needing salvation in Christ because they zealously but insufficiently try to keep the law in order to obtain a right standing with God (Rom 10:1–3; cf. 9:31–32a). In Rom 10:4, Paul makes explicit what he implied in Rom 9:32b–33: Christ ends using the law to obtain a right standing with God for those who believe.

ISRAEL'S PLIGHT (10:1)

Paul opens Rom 10:1–4 by declaring his desire for Israel's salvation: "Brothers, the desire of my heart and my prayer to God for them is with a view to salvation" (Ἀδελφοί, ἡ μὲν εὐδοκία τῆς ἐμῆς καρδίας καὶ ἡ δέησις πρὸς τὸν θεὸν ὑπὲρ αὐτῶν εἰς σωτηρίαν [10:1]).[6] The personal address ("brothers"),[7] the language of the heart's desire,[8] and the expression of prayer[9] open the

---

6. The Byzantine mss substitute τοῦ Ἰσραήλ for αὐτῶν and include ἐστιν before εἰς. Some mss read αὐτῶν but include ἐστιν (ℵ² P Ψ 33. 1505). The shorter reading is supported by p46 ℵ* A B D F G 6. 365. 1506. 1739. 1881. *l* 249. Metzger suggests that ἐστιν was added to clarify the grammar, and that τοῦ Ἰσραήλ may have been substituted when 10:1 "was made the beginning of a lesson read in church services (cf. the reference to Israel in 9.31)" (*Textual Commentary*, 463).

7. Ἀδελφοί refers to brothers and sisters in the faith (BDAG, 18).

8. In the phrase εὐδοκία καρδίας, καρδίας functions as a subjunctive genitive, and εὐδοκία refers to "good pleasure" or "desire" (BDAG, 404). Jewett favors "good pleasure," arguing that "desire" goes beyond the semantic range of the term (*Romans*, 614–15).

9. Jewett suggests that δέησις implies a specific petition (*Romans*, 615).

new paragraph with a heightened sense of intimacy.[10] Although Israel is presently characterized by unbelief (Rom 9:30-33), Paul prays for their salvation[11] because he knows that their rejection is not final (Rom 11:26).[12]

Interpreters have traditionally understood Paul's statements about unbelieving Israelites in Rom 9-11 in terms of his belief that they were separated from God, in danger of his wrath against sin, and needing salvation in Christ (see esp. 9:1-3, 22; 10:1, 18-21; 11:1, 7, 11, 15, 26-28).[13] Despite Israel's present privileges (9:4-5) and their future hope (11:26), Paul considers the vast majority of Israelites to be presently cut off from Christ and in need of salvation. As Dane Ortlund writes, "Despite all the advantages that are theirs by being born a Jew (Rom 3:1-8; 9:3-5), Paul considers his fellow countrymen to be lost, a point already underscored in 9:3."[14]

Some modern interpreters dispute this approach to Paul. They claim that Paul primarily faulted Israel with failing to recognize that God is now fulfilling his promises towards the gentiles. The problem is not that Israel needs salvation, but that Israel does not accept the fact that salvation is now *also* coming to the gentiles. Israel is saved, yet in rebellion to the concept of God's mercy extending to the gentiles.[15]

Lloyd Gaston represents this position well. With reference to Rom 9, he writes, "Romans 9 is not about the unbelief of Israel nor the rejection of Israel."[16] Concerning Israel's error, he writes,

---

10. Cranfield, *Romans*, 1:81; Dunn, *Romans*, 1:31; Longenecker, *Romans*, 840. Toews notes the linguistic similarities between Rom 10:1 and Esth 4:17d LXX ("Law," 207): ηὐδόκουν φιλεῖν πέλματα ποδῶν αὐτοῦ πρὸς σωτηρίαν Ισραηλ, "For I would have been willing to kiss the soles of his feet, to save Israel!" (Esth 13:13, RSV)

11. εἰς functions as an accusative of reference/respect: "my prayer to God for them is with respect to salvation." Wallace, *Greek Grammar*, 369.

12. Cranfield, *Romans*, 2:513. Paul's prayer for Israel's salvation also anticipates Rom 11:18 and its admonition, "boast not against the branches" (KJV). Paul acknowledges Israel's estrangement from God not so that Gentile believers might boast over them but rather pray for them. Luther writes, "For as he [Paul] had to reject the arrogance of the Jews inasmuch as they gloried in their works, he must now oppose the Gentiles, in order that they might not be overbearing as though God preferred them to the Jews" (*Commentary on Romans*, 145-46).

13. This is the standard view beginning with the church fathers; see Bray, *Romans*, 261-62; Origen, *Romans*, 132-33.

14. Ortlund, "Zeal," 249. See also, *inter alios*, Badenas, *Christ*, 108; Johnson, *Romans*, 168; Kruse, *Romans*, 397; Osborne, *Romans*, 263; Toews, "Law," 206.

15. Representatives of this position include Eisenbaum, *Paul*; Gager, *Origins*, 249-54; Gaston, *Paul*; Räisänen, *Paul*, 108n80; Stendahl, *Paul*, 4.

16. Gaston, *Paul*, 99.

Paul does refer elsewhere to Israel's lack of understanding (10:3, 19), to Israel's disobedience (10:21; 11:11–12, 31) and to Israel's lack of faithfulness (3:3; 11:20), all with respect to the Gentile mission. In Rom 2:17–24 Paul refers bitterly to Israel's task of being a light to the Gentiles, a task in which they have failed in his opinion. But he really does not, in Romans 9–11 or elsewhere, charge Israel with a lack of faith or a concept of works-righteousness.[17]

Gaston also writes, "For Paul, Jesus is neither a new Moses nor the Messiah, he is not the climax of the history of God's dealing with Israel, but he is the fulfilment of God's promises concerning the Gentiles, and this is what he accused the Jews of not recognizing . . . Had all Israel followed Paul's example, it may be that we would have had a Gentile church loyal to the righteousness of God expressed in Jesus Christ and his fulfilment of the promises to Abraham, alongside an Israel loyal to the righteousness of God expressed in the Torah."[18] Instead of this ideal scenario, Gaston argues that the NT as a whole forces its readers to choose between Torah and Christ.[19]

E. Elizabeth Johnson has offered a significant response to Gaston's program.[20] She argues that there is insufficient data to support Gaston's argument that the law has a dual function: covenant for Israel, law for gentiles. Since the law's goal is to lead all, without regard to ethnic and religious heritage, to faith in Christ, then there is no need to assume a different human predicament for Jews and gentiles before God. Rather, Paul's letters, particularly Romans and Galatians, argue that God treats Jew and gentiles impartially in judgment and redemption.[21]

The force of Paul's lament also inclines one to view Paul's sorrow over Israel as sorrow over those who are spiritually lost.[22] At the beginning of Rom 9–11, he experiences "great pain and unceasing distress" in his heart (9:2). He states, "I could almost wish myself to be accursed from Christ for the sake of my brothers and sisters." These are not the expressions of one who is disappointed in Israel's failure to perceive that salvation has now also come to the gentiles.

Furthermore, Paul's very prayer in Rom 10:1 indicates his assessment of their spiritual standing. He prays for Israel's salvation (σωτηρία), a word

---

17. Gaston, *Paul*, 99.
18. Gaston, *Paul*, 33.
19. Gaston, *Paul*, 33.
20. Johnson, *Function*, 176–205.
21. Johnson, *Function*, 203–4.
22. Moo, *Epistle to the Romans*, 548n5.

that occurs four other times in Romans (1:16; 10:10; 11:11; 13:11); each occurrence clearly refers to salvation by faith in Jesus. If one grants our interpretation of the stone in 9:32b–33 as a reference to Christ (and 10:11 is indisputable), then 10:1 also occurs in a context referring to salvation from sin by faith in Jesus Christ. The nature of Israel's plight is that they are separated from God and need salvation by faith in Jesus Christ.

THE NATURE OF ΖΗΛΟΝ ΘΕΟΥ (10:2)

Paul continues his assessment of Israel in 10:2. Here he explains why Israel needs salvation: they have zeal for God, but not according to knowledge.[23] One observes very quickly that Paul does not appear to fault Israel for their zeal; his tone is much more positive. He uses the term μαρτυρῶ, which Dunn suggests carries a legal nuance: "a testimony given in open court."[24] Paul testifies concerning Israel[25] that they have zeal for God,[26] a commendable quality in light of the Old Testament (Num 11:29; 25:11, 13; 1 Kgs 19:10, 14; 2 Kgs 10:15; Ps 119:139) and intertestamental literature (Jdt 9:4; Sir 45:23; 48:2; 51:18; 1 Macc 2:24, 26–27, 50, 54, 58; 2 Macc 4:2; 4 Macc 18:12).

However, Paul does fault Israel for having an insufficient kind of zeal: Israel's zeal is "not according to knowledge" (οὐ κατ' ἐπίγνωσιν). Israel may be zealous for God, but they do not know God. We argue that Paul states here that Israel does not know God based on the moral ramifications of ἐπίγνωσις. BDAG argues that in Christian literature ἐπίγνωσις is "limited to transcendent and moral matters."[27] Ortlund defines the term as "spiritual or moral recognition, due acknowledgement of God, perhaps with a

---

23. As noted earlier, verses 2, 3, and 4 all begin with γάρ. BDAG, 189–90, lists three nuances for γάρ: "1) marker of cause or reason, *for*; 2) marker of clarification, *for, you see*; 3) marker of inference, *certainly, by all means, so, then*." All three are possible here, though the second is the most likely: each subsequent statement further clarifies the previous one.

24. Dunn, *Romans*, 2:586; see also Jewett, *Romans*, 615–16. Käsemann suggests this overstates the meaning: the main idea is "the establishment of a public fact" (*Romans*, 280).

25. The Greek text reads αὐτοῖς, a dative of reference ("concerning them"), but Israel is the referent.

26. ζῆλον θεοῦ, an objective genitive construction.

27. BDAG, 369.

connotation of reverence or submission."[28] Once again, Paul is describing Israel's plight: they do not know God, and they need salvation.[29]

Since Rom 10:3 explains the nature of Israel's ignorance, our chief concern in this section is to describe the nature of Israel's zeal. Paul commends Israel for their zeal, and yet their zeal is insufficient to lead to the knowledge of God. Two interpretations of Israel's zeal dominate the literature: zeal depicted generally (zealous obedience of God's law) and zeal depicted specifically (zeal to maintain Israel's distinct identity and boundary markers). We argue that Paul faults Israel for zealously trying to obey God's law, an obedience that is always insufficient in light of human sinfulness.

The principle root for zeal in the Old Testament is קנא, which refers to both zeal and jealousy, human and divine.[30] In the New Testament and the Apocrypha, the principle words are ζῆλος and ζηλόω, which again can refer to zeal and jealousy, human and divine.[31] While divine zeal and jealousy as well as human jealousy are frequent themes in both testaments,[32] our focus here is on human zeal.

Human zeal has several objects, including God and the law,[33] God's house,[34] Israel and Judah,[35] and good works.[36] In his examination of zeal in the Old Testament, Dane Ortlund observes that Old Testament zeal

---

28. Ortlund, "Zeal," 252–53. Mohrmann also highlights how 10:2 anticipates 10:4, for 10:4 explains what Israel is ignorant of ("Semantic Collisions," 229). In Mohrmann's words, "The reader cannot help be pulled forward to 10:4 by Paul's argument."

29. Jewett compares 10:2 with 1:28 to support this idea: just as gentiles have knowledge of God but do not honor him (1:28), so Israel has zeal for God but does not know him (10:2) (*Romans*, 617).

30. HALOT, 1110.

31. BDAG, 427.

32. For divine zeal and jealousy, see Exod 20:5; 34:14; Deut 4:24; 5:9; 6:15; 29:20; 32:19; John 24:19; 2 Kgs 19:31; Ps 79:5; Isa 9:7; 26:11; 37:32; 42:13; 63:15; Ezek 5:13; 16:38, 42; 23:25; 36:6; 38:19; 39:25; Joel 2:18; Nah 1:2; Zeph 1:18; 3:8; Zech 1:14; 8:2; Wis 5:7; 2 Cor 11:2; Heb 10:27. Ortlund, "Zeal Without Knowledge," 86, highlights two aspects of divine zeal in the OT: (1) God's punishment of his enemies, including Israelites who break the covenant; (2) God's protection of and devotion to his people. For human jealousy, see Gen 26:14; 30:1; 37:11; Num 5:14, 30; Pss 37:1; 72:3; Prov 3:31; 6:34; 23:17; 24:1, 19; 27:4; Eccl 4:4; 9:6; Job 5:2; Song 8:6; Isa 11:13; 1 Macc 8:16; Sir 9:1, 11; 30:24; 37:10; 40:4; 45:18; Acts 5:17; 7:9; 13:45; 17:5; Rom 13:13; 1 Cor 3:3; 13:4; 2 Cor 12:20; Gal 5:20; Jas 3:14, 16; 4:2.

33. Num 11:29; 25:11, 13; 1 Kgs 19:10, 14; 2 Kgs 10:15; 119:139; Jdt 9:4; Sir 45:23; 48:2; 51:18; 1 Macc 2:24, 26–27, 50, 54, 58; 2 Macc 4:2; 4 Macc 18:12; Acts 21:20; 22:3; Rom 10:2; Gal 1:14; Phil 3:6.

34. Ps 69:9 cited in John 2:17.

35. 2 Sam 21:2.

36. 1 Cor 12:31; 14:1, 12, 39; 2 Cor 7:7, 11; 9:2; Titus 2:14; 1 Pet 3:13.

is frequently associated with the covenant, idolatry, and fire.[37] This leads him to define zeal as "relational ardor rooted in the covenant instituted by God with Israel that is invariably aroused by a breach of the covenant and which defends his name and his people against all threats, whether internal of foreign."[38] Such zeal moves in three directions: God's zeal against Israel for their covenant unfaithfulness, God's zeal for Israel because of foreign threats, and human zeal for God, i.e., religious fervor.[39]

James Dunn has done the most to define Israel's zeal in terms of their zeal to maintain Israel's distinct identity among the gentiles. He writes, "The classic examples of such zeal (as attested by the number of references to them) were those who were prepared to use the sword to maintain Israel's set-apartness and purity as God's covenant people—Simeon and Levi (Jud 9:4 and Jub. 30.5–20, referring to Gen 34), Phinehas (Num 25:10–13; Sir 45:23–24; 1 Macc 2:54; 4 Macc 18:12), Elijah (Sir 48:2; 1 Macc 2:58) and Mattathias (1 Macc 2:19–26; Josephus, *Ant.* 12.271)."[40] As Dunn reads Paul, "The trouble with Israel's zeal was that it was too nationalistically centered, too much concerned to defend national prerogative as the people of (the one) God."[41] Moving in the same direction, John Toews writes, "The Jewish people were 'zealous for God' and thus for the law. They 'pursued' it out of the deep conviction that only so could they obey God and keep covenant, and they opposed all compromise with it as apostasy."[42] Furthermore, "A key component of this zeal was the exclusion of all non-Jews and non-Jewish things from the covenant community."[43]

Ortlund's work mounts a capable response to Dunn's interpretation of Israel's zeal. He works through the same texts that Dunn cites, yet presents a fuller picture of Israel's zeal than the particular portrait Dunn paints. With reference to Phinehas, while Dunn is right to observe that foreign incursion was the circumstance that instigated Phinehas's zeal, Ortlund observes that Phinehas acted to prevent God's wrath from consuming all who were

---

37. Ortlund, "Zeal," 99–112. The third association indicates "utter vehemence and consuming intensity" (112). The full scope of Ortlund's work is an examination of zeal in the Old Testament, Second Temple Judaism, and Paul (especially Rom 10:2; Gal 1:14; and Phil 3:6).

38. Ortlund, "Zeal," 113–14. This definition covers both human and divine zeal.

39. Ortlund, "Zeal," 114.

40. Dunn, *Romans*, 2:586. Dunn also connects zeal with righteousness because of the reference to Gen 15:6 in the discussion of Phinehas and his zeal in Ps 106:30–31.

41. Dunn, *Romans*, 2:595.

42. Toews, "Law," 209.

43. Toews, *Romans*, 261.

disobeying his commandments (Num 25:13).[44] Ortlund writes, "The core threat, had Phinehas failed to act, was not incursion of foreigners into Israel's camp resulting in national impurity on account of a breach of (horizontal) ethnic boundaries, but faithless disobedience resulting in the destruction of spiritually adulterous Israel by God on account of a breach of (vertical) covenant allegiance."[45] Intermarriage was wrong not simply because it polluted Israel's distinct identity, but because it constituted disobedience to God's commands and would lead to further disobedience (idolatry).[46] The divine commentary on Phinehas's actions supports Ortlund's assessment: Phinehas's zeal was primarily vertical towards God, and had the effect of averting God's wrath against Israel's disobedience (Num 25:11).

Elijah also expresses zeal for obedience to God's law. In 1 Kings 19:10, 14, Elijah directs his zeal towards YHWH because he is concerned that Baal worship will lead the people to forsake YHWH and his covenant.[47] Elijah is concerned for Israel as it pertains to their obedience to God. Nationalistic interests are a core part of zeal, but only as an expression of Israel's overall zeal to obey God and his law.[48]

The same picture of zeal emerges from Ortlund's analysis of Second Temple Judaism. Zeal is both "ethical and ethnic, moral and social, vertical and horizontal, concerned with upright living as well as Israel's set-apartness from the nations."[49] The question is which aspect is fundamental. Ortlund argues for the primacy of the former.[50] He writes, "Jewish ethics necessarily includes [sic] a significant degree of maintenance of ethnic boundaries, and maintaining ethnic boundaries could only be done via obedience."[51] The discussion of Mattathias's zeal for God in 1 Macc 2 supports Ortlund's conclusions: Matthathias's zeal is based on his loyalty to the covenant and the law (1 Macc 2:20–28 [esp. vv. 20, 26], 50–61 [esp. vv. 50, 55, 58]).

When Ortlund applies his findings to Rom 10:2, he interprets zeal as "Jewish ardency to discharge the injunctions of Torah holistically conceived, with an eye toward God."[52] Israel has a distinct identity, but their

---

44. Ortlund, "Zeal," 118–19.
45. Ortlund, "Zeal," 119.
46. Ortlund, "Zeal," 121.
47. Ortlund, "Zeal," 123.
48. For an analysis similar to that of Ortlund, see Smiles, "Concept," 286–92.
49. Ortlund, "Zeal," 226.
50. Ortlund, "Zeal," 226–27.
51. Ortlund, "Zeal," 226.
52. Ortlund, "Zeal," 267.

distinct identity is the result of their zealous obedience.[53] Furthermore, Israel's zeal to keep the Torah has been separated from the gracious nature of God's righteousness, and has therefore funneled into a misplaced attempt to establish one's own righteousness.[54]

We conclude that Ortlund's analysis gives the most comprehensive explanation of the biblical data. In Phil 3:6, Paul connects his own prior zeal with his supposed blameless adherence to the righteousness of the law. Likewise, Israel's zeal is commendable but insufficient (Rom 10:2). Just as they pursue the law and its righteousness by works instead of by faith (Rom 9:31–32a), so they also zealously obey God (Rom 10:2a), and yet they do not know God (Rom 10:2b). While Dunn helpfully highlights one aspect of Israel's zeal (nationalistic expression), he does so at the expense of the larger picture (Israel's zeal to obey the commands of Torah).

THE NATURE OF ΔΙΚΑΙΟΣΥΝΗ (10:3)

Romans 10:3 explains why Israel's zeal is not according to knowledge. Once again, γὰρ occurs at the beginning of the verse, as well as two causal participles (ἀγνοοῦντες and ζητοῦντες) that modify the main verb ὑπετάγησαν. Because Israel is ignorant of the righteousness of God,[55] and because they seek to establish their own righteousness,[56] they have not therefore submitted[57] to the righteousness of God.[58] The main issue of interpretation here concerns the nature of δικαιοσύνη and Israel's attempt to establish their own. Like the discussion of ζῆλον θεοῦ, so here there are two main interpretations of δικαιοσύνη: right standing before God and covenant status.

Once again, James Dunn stands at the forefront of the effort to define "their own righteousness" (τὴν ἰδίαν δικαιοσύνην) in terms of Israel's

---

53. Schreiner also observes, "as in the previous pericope, no mention of boundary markers and exclusion of Gentiles is made here, suggesting that Israel's own ambition to secure righteousness through obedience to Torah is contemplated rather than the attempt to exclude Gentiles from participation in the covenant" (*Romans*, 544).

54. Ortlund, "Zeal," 271.

55. BDAG, 13, also suggests "disregard" as a possible gloss for ἀγνοοῦντες here.

56. The external evidence is divided evenly on the presence (p46 ℵ F G Ψ 33 *Byz* [b] d* Irlat) or absence (A B D P 81 365 629 630 1506 1739 1881 *pc* ar vg co Cl) of the second δικαιοσύνην. Even if one omits the word, the idea is certainly implied.

57. The Greek verb ὑπετάγησαν is passive. Here the passive has a reflexive idea: subject oneself (BDAG, 1042).

58. Notice here that Paul's thought moves from plight to solution: ignorance of God's righteousness and the attempt to establish one's own righteousness (plight) should give way to submission to God's righteousness (solution).

covenant status. Dunn writes, "The charge is clearly directed against what Paul regarded as a basic misunderstanding of how God deals with his people and what he requires of his people—that is, God's righteousness as God's gracious accepting and sustaining power to faith, therefore open to all and not the special prerogative of Israel to be defended by the sword."[59] More specifically, "ἴδιος has more the sense of 'mine' as belonging to me in contrast to what someone else can claim as belonging to him, 'mine' as 'peculiar to me' (BDG). That is, it expresses Israel's covenant-consciousness, righteousness as the appropriate expression of their covenant status, and so peculiarly theirs—'collective righteousness, to the exclusion of the gentiles.'"[60] Israel does not submit to God's program of covenant establishment (one that includes the gentiles in the people of God, but seeks rather to establish the covenant themselves in their own way.[61]

Dunn appeals to BDAG[62] for his definition of ἴδιος as "belonging to me in contrast to what someone else can claim as belonging to him."[63] BDAG does offer this as a legitimate meaning of ἴδιος, explaining the nuance as "pertaining to a striking connection or an exclusive relationship, own."[64] Interestingly, BDAG does not assign Rom 10:3 to this category. Instead, Rom 10:3 falls under the first definition, "belonging or being related to oneself," with the further nuance of *"belonging to an individual."*[65]

One cannot establish either position merely by appealing to a lexicon. Instead, one must consider the nature of δικαιοσύνη and the immediate context of the entire phrase. We noted in our discussion of Rom 9:30–33 that interpreters continue to debate whether δικαιοσύνη refers to a legal standing or a relational status. Most interpreters agree that the idea of a standard or norm is associated with the צדק and δικ- word groups. The debate concerns the nature of that standard: does Scripture place God's

---

59. Dunn, *Romans*, 2:587.

60. Dunn, *Romans*, 2:587.

61. Dunn, *Romans*, 2:588. Dunn also argues that the verb στῆσαι refers to establishing the covenant, thus the reference is not to Israel attempting to earn their own righteous status before God, but to their attempt to do what God alone can do, that is, establish a covenant relationship with his people. For a similar approach to "their own righteousness," see Sanders, *Paul*, 38; Toews, "Law," 214–18; Wright, *Paul*, 1169; Wright, *Romans*, 655.

62. Technically, BDG in Dunn's work but we refer to the most current edition (BDAG).

63. Dunn, *Romans*, 2:587.

64. BDAG, 466–67.

65. BDAG, 466, emphasis original. BDG, 369, classifies ἴδιος under the broad heading "belonging to an individual," with the additional nuance of "according to his own capability."

covenant or God's moral standards (frequently expressed in God's law) at the center of righteousness language?

Mark Seifrid observes that "Only rarely do ברית and צדק-terms appear in any proximity to one another, despite their considerable frequency in the Hebrew Scriptures."[66] Furthermore, the LXX does not translate צדק- terms with the σωτ- root.[67] Seifrid's analysis of the OT data warrants against limiting δικαιοσύνη to covenantal and relational ideas.

An examination of Paul's use of δικαιοσύνη in Romans further supports the association of δικαιοσύνη with God's standards and law. In Rom 3:21, Paul describes a "righteousness of God" (δικαιοσύνη θεοῦ) that is manifested "apart from the law" (χωρὶς νόμου) and yet witnessed to "by the law and the prophets" (ὑπὸ τοῦ νόμου καὶ τῶν προφητῶν). This righteousness comes "through faith in Jesus Christ to all who believe" (διὰ πίστεως Ἰησοῦ Χριστοῦ εἰς πάντας τοὺς πιστεύοντας [3:22]). Paul indicates the nature of this righteousness in the verses immediately preceding 3:21-22. Rom 3:19 speaks of the work of the law that "stops every mouth" (πᾶν στόμα φραγῇ) and makes the world "accountable to God" (ὑπόδικος τῷ θεῷ, 3:19). Paul's language is judicial in nature, and evokes images of the courtroom.[68] Rom 3:20 states that no flesh can be justified (δικαιωθήσεται) by the works of the law, because the law brings "the knowledge of sin" (ἐπίγνωσις ἁμαρτίας).[69] When Paul comes to Rom 3:21-22, he argues that God has now revealed a way to be declared righteous by faith, not by performing the works of the law.[70] Christ's death on the cross establishes God as righteous and the one who declares sinners to be righteous (Rom 3:25-26).[71]

---

66. Seifrid, "Righteousness Language," 51.

67. Seifrid, "Righteousness Language," 51.

68. Dunn, *Romans*, 1:152; Moo, *Epistle to the Romans*, 205. Wright also utilizes the courtroom imagery but with a different explanation (*Romans*, 459-60).

69. BDAG, 50, defines ἁμαρτία as "a departure from either human or divine standards of uprightness," a definition supported especially by such texts as Rom 5:13; 7:7; Jas 2:9; 1 John 3:4; 5:17. In defining ἐπίγνωσις ἁμαρτίας, Dunn allows for "conviction regarding the sinful act, conviction of guilt" (*Romans*, 1:155).

70. Cranfield, *Romans*, 1:201-2; Moo, *Epistle to the Romans*, 221; Schreiner, *Romans*, 180. Although these commentators attach χωρὶς νόμου to πεφανέρωται instead of δικαιοσύνη θεοῦ as I do, the overall interpretation is still the same: God imputes righteousness to those who believe without consideration of their works.

71. The two occurrences of δικαιοσύνη in Rom 3:25-26 refer to God's righteousness as an attribute, but still communicate the idea of a standard, particularly a moral one. God gave Christ as a propitiation for sin in order to show that God was righteous with reference to sin: in justifying sinners, God does not violate his own righteous nature because Christ has satisfied God's justice (3:25). God can therefore be righteous and justify those who believe (3:26).

Romans 4:1–25 contains eight references to δικαιοσύνη (4:3, 5–6, 9, 11 [2x], 13, 22), most of which occur in connection with Paul's discussion of God "crediting" (λογίζομαι) righteousness to those who believe (Abraham being the exemplar of a person who is justified this way [4:3]). Paul indicates at the very beginning of the chapter how he will use δικαιοσύνη throughout. In 4:4–5, Paul articulates the principle that wages are not reckoned as a gift but as what is due to one who works. He then applies the principle to the discussion of justification: "to the one who does not work but believes in the one who justifies the ungodly, his faith is reckoned unto righteousness" (τῷ δὲ μὴ ἐργαζομένῳ πιστεύοντι δὲ ἐπὶ τὸν δικαιοῦντα τὸν ἀσεβῆ λογίζεται ἡ πίστις αὐτοῦ εἰς δικαιοσύνην).[72] The thought continues in 4:6: "David describes the blessedness of the person to whom God credits righteousness apart from works" (Δαυὶδ λέγει τὸν μακαρισμὸν τοῦ ἀνθρώπου ᾧ ὁ θεὸς λογίζεται δικαιοσύνην χωρὶς ἔργων). For such a man, his lawless deeds (ἀνομίαι) are forgiven, his sins (ἁμαρτίαι) are covered, and sin (ἁμαρτίαν) is not reckoned (λογίσηται) to him (4:7–8). Such language indicates that righteousness in Rom 4 is a status given to those who believe.

The two occurrences of δικαιοσύνη in Rom 5:17 and 21 also associate the language of obedience and disobedience with righteousness and unrighteousness. In Rom 5:17, Paul contrasts Adam's trespass (παραπτώματι) with the free gift of righteousness (τῆς δωρεᾶς τῆς δικαιοσύνης) which comes from Christ. In Rom 5:21, Christ conquers the reign of sin through death (ἐβασίλευσεν ἡ ἁμαρτία ἐν τῷ θανάτῳ) with the reign of grace through righteousness to eternal life (ἡ χάρις βασιλεύσῃ διὰ δικαιοσύνης εἰς ζωὴν αἰώνιον). Just as disobedience brings condemnation and death, obedience brings justification, righteousness, and life (5:12–21).

Paul uses δικαιοσύνη four times in Rom 6:13, 16, 18–19. The entire chapter addresses the concept of righteous living as a necessary response to God's justifying grace.[73] Rom 6:13 commands believers to yield their members to God as instruments of righteousness. Rom 6:16 observes that a person is a slave to whatever they yield themselves: either to sin (ἁμαρτίας)

---

72. In his explanation of Jewish boasting as the assumption of a privileged status before God (as opposed to legalism and works-righteousness), Dunn acknowledges, "The only point at which this line of exegesis really comes into question is Rom. 4.4-5. And here it would appear that my exegesis is most vulnerable" ("Yet Once More," 223). Dunn, however, does not give up the case, but instead offers an explanation of the verses that opposes the idea "that Paul was attacking a doctrine of salvation earned by good works."

73. For an exposition of this chapter as well as all of Rom 5–8 with reference to the connection between justification and sanctification, see Pratt, "Justification and Sanctification." A condensed version of Pratt's dissertation appears in Pratt, "Justification and Spiritual Fruit," 162–78.

which leads to death, or to obedience which leads to righteousness. Rom 6:18 indicates that believers obey the imperative of 6:13: because you've been freed from sin, you've become a slave to righteousness. Rom 6:19 declares that believers now yield their members to righteousness. These occurrences of δικαιοσύνη indicate that Paul conceives of righteousness here as a lifestyle that is in accord with an ethical standard, not a covenantal relationship.

The two other uses of δικαιοσύνη in Romans outside of 9:30—10:13 occur in 8:10 and 14:17. In Rom 8:10, believers have life "because of righteousness." Many verses in Romans associate righteousness with life (Rom 1:17; 6:13; 10:5). The nearest parallels to Rom 8:10 are Rom 5:17, 18, 21, where righteousness leads to life.[74] Our analysis of these verses above found that righteousness there refers to a legal status which is imputed to believers. Rom 14:17 parallels the usage of δικαιοσύνη in Rom 6: the kingdom of God is not primarily concerned with food and drink, but with righteous living, and peace and joy in the Holy Spirit.

We conclude from this examination of the occurrences of δικαιοσύνη in Romans that Paul associates righteousness primarily with God's ethical standards, not the covenant. Those standards are often defined by reference to God's law and set in opposition to the language of sin and disobedience. Righteousness is thus a status that one has when they are rightly related to the law. Sinful humans cannot earn such a status, but rather receive it when they exercise saving faith in Jesus Christ.

With this understanding of δικαιοσύνη in mind, we return to the task of defining ἰδίαν in Rom 10:3. If δικαιοσύνη refers to a legal status, then the explanation of τὴν ἰδίαν δικαιοσύνην as Israel's unique covenant status does not work.[75] Instead, a more individualized and personalized nuance best expresses the concept: because many ethnic Israelites were ignorant of the right standing that God gives to those who believe (τὴν τοῦ θεοῦ δικαιοσύνην), and because many ethnic Israelites sought to establish their own right standing with God (τὴν ἰδίαν δικαιοσύνην), they did not submit to the right standing that God provides (τῇ δικαιοσύνῃ τοῦ θεοῦ).[76] Paul's

---

74. Moo, *Epistle to the Romans*, 492.

75. Jewett surveys the many sects in intertestamental Judaism that vied for superiority with competing versions of "their own righteousness" (*Romans*, 618). While the survey is intended to show that "their own righteousness" does not refer to self-righteousness, we argue that what lay at the root of all these groups was an assumption that what they *did* carried greater weight with God that what others did. Paul contrasts any attempt to do with submitting to God and his righteousness in faith.

76. Moo also notes that "the more immediate contrast to 'their own righteousness' is 'God's righteousness.' This suggests that 'their own,' like the contrasting term, 'God's,' is not simply possessive, but has the nuance of source" (*Epistle to the Romans*, 634). So also Barrett, *Romans*, 196. Byrne notes that the reference to the law in 10:4 indicates

statement contrasts two kinds of righteousness (Israel's and God's) and two ways of obtaining it (self-effort and faith).[77] Such a contrast is consistent with Paul's prior argument: he prays for Israel's salvation because they are separated from God and need salvation by faith in Jesus Christ (10:1), and Israel zealously obeys God and yet they do not know God (10:2).[78] Righteousness in Rom 10:3 refers to right standing before God.

THE MEANING AND INTERPRETATION OF ΤΕΛΟΣ ΝΟΜΟΥ ΧΡΙΣΤΟΣ (10:4)

Romans 10:4 concludes Paul's theological argument in Rom 10:1–4.[79] Uniting all the major ideas of Rom 9:30—10:13, Paul joins Christ, the law, righteousness, and faith together in one sentence: "For Christ is the end of the law unto righteousness for all who believe" (τέλος γὰρ νόμου Χριστὸς εἰς δικαιοσύνην παντὶ τῷ πιστεύοντι [10:4]). Paul has described Israel as needing salvation in Christ (Rom 10:1), as those who zealously obey God but do not know him (10:2), and as those who mistakenly attempt to establish their own right standing with God instead of submitting to the righteousness God provides (Rom 10:3). Now Paul explains why Israel should submit

---

that Israel's attempt to establish their own righteousness was an attempt to do so by means of obedience to the law (*Romans*, 311).

77. Self-effort and faith reflect Paul's use of στῆσαι ("to establish") and ὑπετάγησαν ("submit"): one can attempt to establish their own righteousness by their works, or they can submit in faith to the righteousness God provides. BDAG, 482, even highlights the legal nuance of στῆσαι in Acts 7:60: κύριε, μὴ στήσῃς αὐτοῖς ταύτην τὴν ἁμαρτίαν, "Lord, do not hold this sin against them." Thielman argues that Paul's reference to Israel's attempt to establish their own righteousness probably echoes Deut 9:4—10:10, where Moses reminds Israel that it is not their righteousness which gains them the promised land but the wickedness of its inhabitants. The point of the comparison is that Israel's righteousness is insufficient to merit blessings from God, both then and now. Thielman concludes, "Thus in Rom. 10:3 Paul claims that present-day unbelieving Israel is at fault because her own righteousness is insufficient and she has failed to submit to God's gracious eschatological provision for solving her plight" (*Plight*, 113).

78. Byrne notes the irony that although Israel is zealous for God (10:2), at the same time they refuse to submit to God (10:3) (*Romans*, 312). Schreiner notes how the reference to faith in Christ in 10:4 explains what it means to submit to the righteousness of God in 10:3 ("Paul's View," 122).

79. We use "conclude" in a loose sense because, as we noted in the introduction to this chapter, Rom 10:5 begins with another γὰρ. As we noted above, Paul's strategy in Rom 10:5–8 is to cite OT Scriptures that support his argument in Rom 10:1–4. We can therefore view Rom 10:4 as concluding the theological argument of Rom 10:1–4 before Paul introduces the proof for his argument (Rom 10:5–8).

to the righteousness of God: because Christ is the end of the law unto righteousness for those who believe (10:4).[80]

Four issues of interpretation present themselves in Rom 10:4: (1) the meaning of νόμος; (2) the function of εἰς; (3) the meaning of τέλος; and (4) the interpretation of 10:4 as a whole.[81] Each issue presents several interpretive options which must be carefully evaluated. Throughout this final section, we argue that Christ ends using the Mosaic law to obtain a right standing with God for those who believe.

---

80. Schreiner suggests an implied proposition between 10:3 and 10:4, namely, that those who believe in Christ have submitted themselves to the righteousness of God ("Paul's View," 122). This is indicated by the fact that Paul does not in 10:4 clarify the nature of Israel's failure to submit to God's righteousness (10:3), but rather explains why they *should have* submitted to that righteousness.

81. My approach reflects Moo who approaches the issue along similar lines of inquiry (*Epistle to the Romans*, 636). Two other minor areas of interpretation are worth noting. First, while some commentators interpret Χριστός as the predicate nominative (e.g., Badenas, *Christ*, 112), Wallace argues that proper names take priority as subjects in equative clauses (*Greek Grammar*, 43–44). Paul places the predicate nominative τέλος at the front of the sentence for the sake of emphasis (Lenski, *Romans*, 645; Schreiner, "Paul's View," 123; Seifrid, "Paul's Approach," 8). Linss highlights the significance of Χριστός being the subject: "Paul is not defining the law, or rather the end of the law, but he is talking about the meaning of Christ" ("Exegesis," 6).

Second, τέλος νόμου is an objective genitive relationship: Christ ends/fulfills/culminates the law. Moo writes, "When τέλος is followed by the genitive in the NT (as here), the genitive indicates either (1) the whole, of which the τέλος is a part (partitive genitive; cf. 1 Pet. 4:7; 1 Cor. 10:11); (2) the person bringing the τέλος about (subjective genitive; cf. Jas. 5:11); or (3) the thing or person that is brought to an end (objective genitive; cf. Rom. 6:21; 2 Cor. 3:13; Phil. 3:19; 1 Tim. 1:5; Heb. 7:3; 1 Pet. 1:9; 4:17). Rom. 10:4 must be put in this last category; and in most of these texts (with the probable exception of Heb. 7:3 and possible exception of 2 Cor. 3:13) the 'end' to which the person or thing is brought is the culmination of a process, not simply a termination" (*Epistle to the Romans*, 641n43). Moo's partitive genitives could also be included in the third category: "end of all things" (πάντων τέλος [1 Pet 4:7]) and "the ends of the ages" (τὰ τέλη τῶν αἰώνων [1 Cor 10:11]) could refer to the end that comes to all things, and to the end that comes to the ages, respectively.

The Meaning of Νόμος

Interpreters offer four referents for νόμος in Rom 10:4 (1) law in general;[82] (2) OT revelation;[83] (3) legalism;[84] and (4) the Mosaic law.[85] Beginning with the third option, it is not at all certain that Paul ever uses νόμος in this way.[86] The *idea* of legalism may be expressed by the verse as a whole (Christ ends any attempt to use the law to establish a right standing before God), but the *word* νόμος would still refer to the Mosaic law. The first, second, and fourth options are all legitimate referents for νόμος,[87] and therefore the context must determine which is present in Rom 10:4.

Robert Badenas appeals to the context to justify the second referent. He writes, "Νόμος in the sense of Torah (not as mere legal code, but as the revelation of God's will) has been at the centre of Paul's discussion since 9.6, and particularly since 9.31."[88] However, the phrase νόμον δικαιοσύνης (9:31) actually tends in the opposite direction. The connection between law and righteousness set within a discussion of works and faith (9:31–32) indicates that Paul uses νόμον δικαιοσύνης there to refer to the Mosaic law whose object is righteousness.[89]

---

82. Walvoord writes, "In both instances [Rom 10:4-5], νόμος occurs without the article. In the first instance, in vs. 4, it seems clear that the reference is to any moral law. The argument is that Christ is the end of all law, as far as law resulting in righteousness is concerned. The demands of all moral law reach their destination in Christ" ("Law," 286). See also Denney, "Romans," 669; Gifford, *Romans*, 183; Lenski, *Romans*, 645; Murray, *Romans*, 2:51; Sanday and Headlam, *Romans*, 284.

83. Badenas is representative here: "Νόμος in the sense of Torah (not as mere legal code, but as the revelation of God's will) has been at the centre of Paul's discussion since 9.6, and particularly since 9.31" (*Christ*, 113). See also Bandstra, *Law*, 106; Campbell, "Christ," 75.

84. Moule writes, "If one takes τέλος as 'termination', and construes νόμος with εἰς δικαιοσύνην to mean 'law used as a means to righteousness', Paul is saying that Christ put an end to legalism" ("Obligation," 402).

85. Longenecker explains, "In this statement, the Apostle is not thinking primarily of the general qualitative idea of law or even of the principle of legality; though, of course, such concepts are never unrelated to the main point of his thought. Rather, the context shows that here he is specifically considering the Mosaic Law and declaring that it has been completed and abrogated by Christ on a specific level" (*Paul*, 144). See also Cranfield, *Romans*, 2:516; Dunn, *Romans*, 2:591; Kuss, *Römerbrief*, 751; Lagrange, *Romains*, 253–54; Mohrmann, "Semantic Collisions," 235; Moo, *Epistle to the Romans*, 636; Morris, *Romans*, 380; Viard, *Romains*, 224.

86. Moo, "Law," 76, 85–88.

87. BDAG, 677–78.

88. Badenas, *Christ*, 113.

89. Notice also that when Paul comes to cite the Scriptures in 9:33, he does not introduce the citation with ὁ νόμος λέγει, "the law says" (as he does in 3:19 following

Rom 10:4 contains the first reference to νόμος since 9:31. Between the two occurrences, Paul has continued his discussion of Israel's attempt to obtain a right standing with God by the works of the law instead of by faith in Christ. He does not indicate any shift to a more general use of νόμος (either referring to the OT Scriptures or law as a principle). This indicates that the referent for νόμος has not changed between 9:31 and 10:4. In Rom 10:4, Paul uses νόμος to refer to the Mosaic law.

The Function of Εἰς

The εἰς clause can function in one of two ways: (1) with reference to νόμος particularly, or (2) with reference to the whole verse. Under the first option, Paul is saying that Christ ends/culminates/fulfills the law as it relates to righteousness, and that this is true for those who believe.[90] Under the second option, Paul would be saying that Christ ends/fulfills/culminates the law, with the result that there is righteousness for all who believe.[91] The difference between the two options is that the first has a more narrow focus: Christ is the τέλος of the law *as it relates to righteousness*.

The strength of the second view is grammatical. Moo argues that Rom 10:4 would be the only instance in the NT of "εἰς being dependent on a noun (νόμου) from which it is separated by the subject of the sentence (Χριστός)."[92] Mark Seifrid favors a similar approach, arguing that in most Pauline uses of εἰς where εἶναι is stated or implied, εἰς communicates a telic or ecbatic idea, or an idea like a dative of advantage.[93] Seifrid therefore relates the clauses as follows: "Christ as τέλος of the law secures righteousness for all who believe."

However, other aspects of Seifrid's research could be used to support the first position. He observes that "a survey of NT nouns and/or pronouns

---

the catena of OT citations), but with γέγραπται, "it is written." Perhaps Paul does this in order to avoid confusing the possible referents for νόμος.

90. Dunn, *Romans*, 2:590; Longenecker, *Romans*, 843–44; Longenecker, *Paul*, 144; Moule, "Obligation," 402; Schreiner, "Paul's View," 122–23; Schreiner, *Romans*, 547–48; Walvoord, "Law," 286; Williams, "Righteousness," 284.

91. Bechtler, "Christ," 302n52; Byrne, *Romans*, 315; Cranfield, *Romans*, 2:519; Gifford, *Romans*, 183; Mohrmann, "Semantic Collisions," 234; Moo, *Epistle to the Romans*, 637–38; Sanders, *Paul*, 40; Toews, "Law," 241–42; Wright, *Romans*, 656.

92. Moo, *Epistle to the Romans*, 637n34; also Badenas, *Christ*, 116.

93. Seifrid, "Paul's Approach," 9n29. Seifrid does, however, note the exceptions, and identifies such usages as εἰς functioning like a dative of reference. Schreiner appeals to these exceptions in his defense of the first position, interpreting εἰς as an adverbial preposition of general reference ("Paul's View," 122–23).

linked by ἐστίν (or ἐστίν understood) and followed by a preposition, shows that virtually all have the preposition related to the predicate nominative alone."⁹⁴ This is precisely what advocates of the first position argue: Christ is the τέλος of the law as it relates to righteousness. Therefore, the preposition is governing the predicate nominative alone, and not functioning with reference to the entire clause. Furthermore, interpreting εἰς with a telic or ecbatic idea works with the first position as well, especially the telic idea: Christ ends using the law for the purpose of obtaining a right standing with God.⁹⁵ The idea is similar to the phrase νόμον δικαιοσύνης (9:31), the law whose object is righteousness.

The Meaning of Τέλος

The meaning of τέλος in Rom 10:4 has been the subject of considerable debate. Interpreters argue for such meanings as fulfillment, goal, end (in the sense of termination), or some combination of the above.⁹⁶ Each suggestion warrants consideration.⁹⁷

---

94. Seifrid, "Paul's Approach," 9n30.

95. *Contra* Moo who argues that if εἰς introduces a purpose or result statement, then παντὶ τῷ πιστεύοντι must be taken with εἰς δικαιοσύνην, thus ruling out attempts to read παντὶ τῷ πιστεύοντι as a qualifier of the main idea (*Epistle to the Romans*, 637n35).

96. Lexical evidence supports each of these meanings, though a combination of meanings may be more theological than lexical (though see Moo who insists that he is arguing for a single meaning that combines nuances of end and goal [*Epistle to the Romans*, 641n44]). For the lexical offerings (glosses in italics), see BDAG, 998–99: a point of time marking the end of a duration, *end, termination, cessation*; the last part of a process, *close, conclusion*; the goal toward which a movement is being directed, *end, goal, outcome*; last in a series, *rest, remainder*; revenue obligation, *(indirect) tax, toll-tax, customs*; Henry Liddell, *Greek-English Lexicon*, 1772–74: coming to pass, performance, consummation; degree of completion or attainment; achievement, attainment; Lust et al., *Greek-English Lexicon*, electronic edition: *end, conclusion, completion, totality, tax, tribute, in the end, finally*, often adverbial expression of totality; Muraoka, *Greek-English Lexicon*, 675–76: the full amount; levy; the close of a period or process; Delling, "τέλος," 49–57: in the Greek world: achievement, completion/perfection, obligation, offering for the gods, a detachment, group; in the LXX: execution (of a plan), goal/result/reward, tax/tribute/toll, act in divine worship (Ps headings); in Jewish Apocalyptic: end times (varied); in the NT: goal, result, conclusion, cessation, tribute/tax; in the Post-Apostolic Fathers: not very specific.

97. More bibliography for advocates of each definition will be given in the section analyzing the overall interpretation of Rom 10:4. The reason for this is that many who agree on the definition of the word explain the verse with a different nuance. For example, there are six different interpretations of Rom 10:4 that define τέλος as termination, not including views that combine the meanings of τέλος in some way.

Τέλος as Fulfillment

The idea of fulfillment was popular with the church fathers,[98] and has modern advocates such as Charles Cranfield and Markus Bockmuehl.[99] For example, Bockmuehl writes, "I would like to consider a reading of τέλος in this context as *prophetic fulfillment* or *consummation*. While this is not the primary meaning of τέλος, it is nevertheless one which is well and widely attested."[100]

Two factors warrant against this. First, while Bockmuehl's proposed reading is possible, it would be a minority sense in the NT. Bockmuehl offers many references from intertestamental literature to support his rendering of τέλος as prophetic fulfillment, but he only offers two other NT references where τέλος supposedly communicates this idea (1 Cor 10:11; 1 Pet 1:9). Neither of these references is better served by reading τέλος as "prophetic fulfillment."[101] Second, if Paul wanted to communicate the idea of fulfillment, he had a more suitable word available: τελείωσις.[102]

Τέλος as Goal

The meaning of τέλος as goal has been thoroughly defended by Robert Badenas.[103] Badenas argues that the basic connotations of τέλος "are primarily directive, purposive, and completive, not temporal."[104] Furthermore, "Τέλος with genitive is generally used in expressions indicating result, purpose, outcome, and fate, not termination."[105] In the NT era, "τέλος was especially used for designating the sum, the final cause, the goal, the purpose, the

---

98. Badenas, *Christ*, 34; Origen, *Romans*, 135 ("perfection").

99. Bockmuehl, *Revelation*, 151–52; Cranfield, *Romans*, 2:519.

100. Bockmuehl, *Revelation*, 151. Bockmuehl then offers several references from intertestamental literature and a few from the NT where τέλος supposedly communicates this idea.

101. The better renderings are "end" for 1 Cor 10:11 ("the end of the ages have come") and "result" or "outcome" for 1 Pet 1:9 ("the result/outcome of your faith").

102. BDAG, 997; Morris, *Romans*, 380n15.

103. Among other things, Badenas surveys both the history of the interpretation of Rom 10:4 (7–37) and the use of τέλος in biblical and cognate literature, and gives a detailed exegesis of Rom 9:30–10:21 (*Christ*, 38–79, 101–51). Other advocates of the teleological meaning include Bechtler, "Christ," 298–302; Haacker, *Römer*, 234–35; Jewett, *Romans*, 619–20; Pattee, "Stumbling Stone," 183; Toews, "Law," 238–42.

104. Badenas, *Christ*, 79.

105. Badenas, *Christ*, 79.

decisive factor, or the *summum bonum*."[106] Badenas therefore concludes that "Semantics, grammar, and literature strongly favor a teleological interpretation of this phrase."[107] When Badenas examines the fourteen uses of τέλος in Paul, he identifies five as communicating a teleological idea, including all of the occurrences in Romans (Rom 6:21, 22; 10:4; 2 Cor 3:13; 1 Tim 1:5).[108] He especially notes that 1 Tim 1:5 (an undisputed teleological use of τέλος) contains an almost identical grammatical construction as Rom 10:4.[109] He assigns three to five occurrences of τέλος to the temporal use, and he notes that all of its occurrences are in eschatological contexts (1 Cor 1:8; 10:11; 15:24; 2 Cor 11:15; Phil 3:19). The terminal use is therefore the exception rather than the rule, and one ought to assume a teleological use unless the context demands otherwise.[110]

Badenas has done careful work, but we highlight some weaknesses in his argument. First, he concludes that the terminal use is the exception because it occurs in only three to five contexts, whereas the teleological use is the default sense. But Badenas only notes five occurrences of the teleological sense in Paul. If the terminal sense occurs five times, and the teleological sense occurs five times, then the uses are even and neither can claim to be the exception or the rule. If we reduce the terminal occurrences to three, then the teleological use is in the advantage, but only by a small margin. When one considers that the sample size is fourteen uses, an advantage of five to three is not that significant.

Second, it is not certain that all of Badenas's teleological uses of τέλος are actually teleological.[111] The two occurrences in Rom 6:21, 22 favor the

106. Badenas, *Christ*, 80.
107. Badenas, *Christ*, 80.
108. Badenas, *Christ*, 78–79.

109. Badenas, *Christ*, 79. The two constructions are τὸ δὲ τέλος τῆς παραγγελίας ἐστὶν ἀγάπη ἐκ καθαρᾶς καρδίας καὶ συνειδήσεως ἀγαθῆς καὶ πίστεως ἀνυποκρίτου ("But the goal of the commandment is love from a pure heart and a good conscience and a genuine faith" [1 Tim 1:5]) and τέλος γὰρ νόμου Χριστὸς εἰς δικαιοσύνην παντὶ τῷ πιστεύοντι (Rom 10:4).

110. Badenas, *Christ*, 79. Consequently, when Badenas examines the context of Rom 10:4 (114–15), he finds no compelling reason to translate τέλος in a non-teleological sense.

111. This criticism of Badenas's work has been leveled by scholars such as Dunn, *Romans*, 2:598; Moo, *Epistle to the Romans*, 639n41; Schreiner, "Paul's View," 118. Moo also questions Badenas's survey of the LXX evidence: "τέλος occurs approximately 155 times in the LXX. In 110 of these τέλος occurs as the object of the preposition εἰς. This construction indicates completeness—right up to 'the end'—usually with respect to time (e.g., Hab. 1:4: 'because of this the law is slackened and judgment *never* [εἰς τέλος] goes forth') but occasionally with respect to the quality of the action (e.g., Amos 9:8b: 'However, it is the case that I will not *utterly* [εἰς τέλος] destroy the house of Jacob, says

idea of result, not goal: τὸ γὰρ τέλος ἐκείνων θάνατος, "for the result of those things is death" (6:21); τὸ δὲ τέλος ζωὴν αἰώνιον, "but the result is eternal life" (6:22). While 2 Cor 3:13 is more open to dispute, the sense of termination works well in that context: Moses veiled his face so that the children of Israel could not see the end (termination) of what was fading away (εἰς τὸ τέλος τοῦ καταργουμένου), i.e., the glory on his face.[112] This assessment of the Pauline uses of τέλος turns the tables on Badenas: now there is one undisputed occurrence of the teleological sense of τέλος (1 Tim 1:5), thus giving the terminal nuance the numerical advantage.[113]

Τέλος as End

Many commentators favor the view that τέλος refers to some kind of termination in Rom 10:4.[114] Thomas Schreiner argues as we have above that there is one clear example of a teleological use of τέλος in Paul (1 Tim 1:5), and that the lexical evidence favors the terminal sense.[115] He also argues from the close connection between Rom 10:3 and 10:4 that Paul's point in 10:4 is not to make a theological statement about the relationship between gospel and law (which would favor the nuance of "goal"), but to address the problem of 10:3 and explain why people should not try to establish their own righteousness (because Christ ends using the law for righteousness).[116] In light of the lexical data and the argument from context, the meaning of τέλος as termination appears undeniable. The question is whether τέλος communicates the additional nuance of goal in this one occurrence.

---

the Lord'). It also occurs in the heading of 56 Psalms, with uncertain meaning. Of the approximately 45 other occurrences, τέλος refers to a 'tribute' 10 times, while the others are almost all to be translated 'end': the 'end' of a period of time, or the 'end' of human beings, or the 'end' of matters. Few, if any, occurrences are clearly teleological in meaning" (*Epistle to the Romans*, 639n41). Dunn, *Romans*, 2:589, argues that Badenas "treats the LXX data in particular somewhat tendentiously."

112. Schreiner, *Romans*, 545-46.

113. Toews also argues for the teleological meaning on linguistic and contextual grounds ("Law," 238-41). The linguistic response above applies to Toews's case as well; we examine the contextual arguments when we survey the suggested interpretations of Rom 10:4 as a whole.

114. Bell, *Provoked*, 189-90; Delling, "τέλος," 8:56; Denney, "Romans," 669; Dunn, *Romans*, 2:589, 597; Gifford, *Romans*, 183; Lagrange, *Romains*, 253; Lenski, *Romans*, 645; Linss, "Exegesis," 9-10; Leitzmann, *Römer*, 96; Michel, *Römer*, 326; Moule, "Obligation," 402; Pesch, *Römerbrief*, 82; Ridderbos, *Romeinen*, 233; Sanday and Headlam, *Romans*, 285; Schreiner, "Israel's View," 117-19.

115. Schreiner, *Romans*, 545-46.

116. Schreiner, "Paul's View," 122.

Τέλος as a Combination of Meanings

Several authors argue that τέλος communicates multiple nuances in this one occurrence.[117] In favor of "end," Doug Moo highlights the following: (1) the relationship between 10:3 and 10:4 which emphasizes the discontinuity between seeking to establish one's own righteousness through obedience to the law, and obtaining righteousness by faith in Christ; (2) Paul's use of the salvation-historical disjunction between the old and new ages throughout Romans (6:14, 15; 7:1–6); and (3) the emphasis on the discontinuity between the law and Christ in Rom 9:30—10:13 (particularly 9:30-32a; 10:3, 5–8). In favor of "goal," Moo notes that the context discusses pursuing and attaining the law (9:31–32a), and that throughout Rom 9:30—10:13 Paul uses OT texts to describe Christ and the righteousness he has brought (9:32b–33; 10:6–8, 11, 13).[118] Moo therefore concludes that τέλος communicates both nuances:

> These considerations require that *telos* have a temporal nuance: with the coming of Christ the authority of the law of Moses is, in some basic sense, at an end. At the same time, a teleological nuance is also present. This is suggested not only by the contextual factors mentioned above but also by the fact that similar NT uses of *telos* generally preserve some sense of direction or goal. In other words, the "end" that *telos* usually denotes is an end that is the natural or inevitable result of something else. The analogy of a race course (which many scholars think *telos* is meant to convey) is helpful: the finish line is both the "termination" of the race (the race is over when it is reached) and the "goal" of the race (the race is run for the sake of reaching the finish line).[119]

Moo also clearly states that he is not arguing for a double-meaning for τέλος, but that "the *single* meaning of the Greek word here combines nuances of the English words 'end' and 'goal.'"[120]

Intentional ambiguity is not completely foreign to the NT.[121] However, we do not think that Paul intends a combined meaning for τέλος here. If the

---

117. Campbell, "Christ," 76–77 (primary sense is goal, termination is secondary sense); Boor, *Römer*, 244–45; Jolivet, "Christ," 13–30; Ladd, *Theology*, 546; Mohrmann, "Semantic Collisions," 237; Moo, *Epistle to the Romans*, 639–41 ("both goal and [partial] end"); Wilckens, *Römer*, 3:222–23.

118. Moo, *Epistle to the Romans*, 639–41.

119. Moo, *Epistle to the Romans*, 641.

120. Moo, *Epistle to the Romans*, 641n44, emphasis original.

121. See, for example, from the Gospel of John: 1:5 (ἡ σκοτία αὐτὸ οὐ κατέλαβεν, "the darkness did not *overcome/understand* the light"); 1:29 (ὁ αἴρων τὴν ἁμαρτίαν τοῦ

nuance of goal is present, then Paul is (to some degree) making a theological statement about the relationship between the law and Christ. However, Paul's argument does not appear to be moving in this direction.[122] In Rom 9:30–33, Paul contrasts the way gentiles pursue righteousness with the way Israel does. Paul critiques Israel for pursuing the law and its righteousness by works, a mistake also committed by the Israelites of Isaiah's day who tried to deliver themselves from judgment with their own efforts instead of trusting God in faith. In their preoccupation with works, they do not exercise faith. In Rom 10:1–3, Paul continues the argument: Israel needs to be saved because in their zealous attempt to establish their own righteousness, they have disregarded God's righteousness. They need to see that Christ ends such a pursuit (10:4). Paul's point is not that Christ is the goal of the law, but that Christ ends using the law to establish righteousness.

The Interpretation of Rom 10:4

Building now on the lexical data assembled above, the final task of this chapter is to evaluate the many interpretations of Rom 10:4.[123] While some views are similar to others, they each have a particular nuance that makes

---

κόσμου, "the one *takes upon himself/takes away* the sin of the world"); 3:3 (γεννηθῇ ἄνωθεν, "born *again/from above*" [also 3:7]). On the other hand, we must heed the warning of Käsemann in discussing the possible meanings of τέλος: "the message of the NT would no longer be recognizable if exegesis were allowed to exploit every linguistic possibility, and Paul does not leave the least room for attempts of this kind" (*Romans*, 282).

122. Dunn, *Romans*, 2:597; Schreiner, "Paul's View," 121–22.

123. For a historical overview of the different views, see Badenas, *Christ*, 7–37. According to Badenas, the dominant positions of the major periods are as follows: according to Patristic interpreters, Christ fulfills the prophecies and purposes of the OT; in the Middle Ages, interpreters argued that Christ brings the OT law to its plenitude and completion; during the Reformation, the teleological (Luther) and perfective (Calvin) approaches were favored; in the Post-Reformation and nineteenth-century era, the temporal/terminal/antinomian approach prevailed. In the Modern era, the four main approaches match the four definitions of τέλος noted above: (1) τέλος as temporal—τέλος means "termination," "cessation," or "abrogation," and Rom 10:4 expresses the discontinuity between the law and Christ; (2) τέλος as teleological—τέλος means "goal," "purpose," "aim," or "object," and Rom 10:4 expresses continuity between the law/OT and Christ/Christianity; (3) τέλος as completive/perfective—τέλος means "fulfillment," "climax," "plentitude," and Rom 10:4 may express either/both the continuity and the discontinuity between the OT/law and Christ/Christianity; (4) τέλος as polysemous—the temporal/completive and/or teleological meanings are not mutually exclusive but complementary, and Rom 10:4 may mean any of the above. For a full-length treatment of the historical positions from the early church to the Formula of Concord, see Nestingen, "Christ." My own presentation is patterned after Schreiner, "Paul's View," 113–24, though with some differences.

them unique.[124] Our approach is to describe each view, present its strengths, critique its weaknesses, and then argue for our particular view.

Christ Abolishes the Law

Some interpreters argue that the law and its demands are abolished.[125] The OT law does not exercise any authority over NT Christians. Ernst Käsemann writes, "The Mosaic Torah comes to an end with Christ."[126] Similarly, William Wrede writes, "he [Paul] denies the right of the Law to *demand* their fulfillment; he declares that every 'thou shalt' is done away."[127]

The weakness of this view is that this explanation of τέλος νόμου Χριστὸς implies that righteousness could not come to believers while the law was still in effect. But this contradicts the argument of Rom 4:1–13. There Paul argues that David, a man under the law, received righteousness by faith (4:6–8). Furthermore, Abraham, who came before the law, is identified as the father of all those who believe whether circumcised or not (4:11–12). In other words, righteousness has always come to those who believe, both before the law and under the law.[128] If Christ has abolished the law, that does not mean that righteousness is now suddenly available for believers for the first time.

The Messianic Age Ends the Age of the Law

Others argue that Paul is echoing the Jewish belief that the law would play no role in the messianic age. Hans-Joachim Schoeps articulates this view:

---

124. We could organize these views around the different definitions of τέλος, or even under the broad headings of Christology, salvation history, and experience: is Paul making a statement about the relationship between the law and Christ (Christology), the relationship between the eras of law and Christ (salvation history), or about the relationship of individual people to the law and Christ (existential)? However, these broad headings would miss the many nuances interpreters offer to defend their particular view. We also cannot characterize these views according to particular theological systems (dispensationalism, covenant theology, etc.) or approaches to Paul (New Perspective versus Old Perspective). Many who agree on a theological system or approach to Paul still differ in their exegesis of Rom 10:4. We must evaluate each view on its own merits.

125. Käsemann, *Romans*, 283; Linss, "Exegesis," 10–11; Lowery, "Christ," 245–46; Wrede, *Paul*, 125–26.

126. Käsemann, *Romans*, 283

127. Wrede, *Paul*, 125–26.

128. Notice also that the righteousness that comes apart from the law in Rom 3:21 does not come by abolishing the law but independently of the law.

The 2,000-year era of the Mosaic law which followed on the 2,000 years of *Tohuwabohu* (Sanh. 97a, Ab. Zara 9a: Jer. Meg. 70d) has now ended and the era of the Messiah has begun. The law had validity until 'all things were fulfilled'. Now the fulfillment has been effected. According to this midrash of the aeons, Judaism and the law have no further meaning than that of marking the end of an epoch.[129]

Schreiner argues that this view does not enjoy the support of the alleged Jewish evidence.[130] Furthermore, even if Jewish literature did support this view, there is no indication that Paul accepted it.[131] In addition, we argue that this explanation of τέλος νόμου Χριστὸς is too abstracted from the rest of Rom 10:4 and the immediate context. When Paul discusses Christian freedom from the law, he has more than just ages in mind. Rather, something has happened to Christians and their standing before God that affects their relationship to the law (Rom 6:14–15; 7:4–6).

The Law Has Ended as a Way to Righteousness

The third position argues that the law is now an invalid way to seek righteousness.[132] With the coming of Christ, the law as a way of salvation by works has ended. Johannes Munck writes, "It is by Christ's death on the cross, and the atonement thus gained, that an end is made once and for all to the law as the way to salvation."[133]

This view implies that one could achieve salvation by the law before Christ came. But Paul does not conceive of salvation or the law this way. As noted above, Rom 4:1–25 insists that salvation has always been by faith, whether before, during, or after the law (see also Gal 3:1–29). In addition, Paul describes the law as a force that convicts of sin (Rom 3:19–20; 5:13), and aggravates one to sin (Rom 7:7–25). In attempting to keep the law, one discovers their natural rebellion to the law (Rom 7:7–8). Furthermore, if

---

129. Schoeps, *Paul*, 171. See also Schweitzer, *Paul*, 188.
130. Schreiner, "Paul's View," 115.
131. Schreiner, "Paul's View," 115.
132. Dodd, *Romans*, 165; Dülmen, *Theologie*, 126 (van Dülmen takes the passage in several senses, but her summary comments best fit here); Heil, "Christ," 485–86; Heil, *Romans*, 71; Hodge, *Romans*, 303–4 (Hodge sets this view within the context of covenant theology: Christ ends the law as a rule of justification, that is, a covenant of works); Lagrange, *Romains*, 254; Munck, *Christ*, 83–84; Reumann, *Righteousness*, 88; Witherington, *Romans*, 261.
133. Munck, *Christ*, 83–84.

one could keep the law and earn righteousness, then Christ's death would be unnecessary (Gal 2:21).

Christ Ends the Ceremonial Law

Some argue that Christ ends part of the law. Pelagius's theology tends in this direction. While his commentary on Rom 10:4 does not directly address the issue,[134] those who have assessed Pelagius's larger body of work place him in this category. In his examination of the history of the interpretation Rom 10:4, James Nestingen writes, "Thus something of the law does terminate in Christ for Pelagius. At least the ceremonial law loses its significance."[135] Robert Evans, in his survey of Pelagius's theology, also writes, "It is clear that Pelagius attributes chief significance to the 'moral' aspects of the law of Moses and that he gives only a temporary and secondary value to its ceremonial requirements."[136] For Pelagius, there is no antithesis between the gospel and the law. Rather, the NT itself is law, and the difference between the law of Moses and the gospel is merely a difference of kinds of laws.[137]

While most interpreters agree that the ceremonial law has ended with Christ, few (if any) appeal to this text to justify that deduction. There is no indication from lexis or context that a portion of the law has been abrogated.[138] We cannot impose on individual texts even legitimate systematic deductions which the author did not intend to communicate.

Christ Prophetically Fulfills the Law

The fifth view argues that Christ fulfilled the types, shadows, and prophecies of the law. As noted above, Markus Bockmuehl glosses τέλος as "prophetic fulfillment" and "consummation."[139] Christ is the true Torah, the meaning and fulfillment of the law itself.[140]

---

134. Pelagius, *Romans*, 122. Pelagius simply gives a one-sentence summary of the meaning of the verse: "On the day one believes in Christ, it is as if one has fulfilled the whole law (cf. Gal. 5:3)."

135. Nestingen, "Romans 10:4," 88.

136. Evans, *Pelagius*, 99.

137. Evans, *Pelagius*, 106–7.

138. Moo argues, "As Mosaic law, *nomos* is basically for Paul a single indivisible whole" ("Law," 84).

139. Bockmuehl, *Revelation*, 151.

140. Bockmuehl, *Revelation*, 152.

But was we noted in our discussion of τέλος above, the NT uses of τέλος do not support such a specific nuance as prophetic fulfillment.[141] Furthermore, Badenas notes that the Greek-speaking church explained τέλος in Rom 10:4 with the words σκοπός, πλήρωμα, and τελείωσις, which communicated such ideas as purpose, object, plentitude, and fulfillment.[142] One wonders why Paul did not use those terms if that is what he meant.

Christ Obeyed the Law

Many older commentators interpret Rom 10:4 as a reference to the active obedience of Christ.[143] John Owen, the editor of Calvin's commentaries,[144] writes, "we may also regard the law in its moral character, as the rule and condition of life; then the end of the law is its fulfilment, the performance of what it requires in order to attain life: and Christ in this respect is its end, having rendered to it perfect obedience. This last meaning is most consistent with the words which follow, and with the Apostle's argument."[145]

Once again we encounter an idea that is doctrinally true but not intended here.[146] First, the word τέλος does not communicate the idea of obedience. Second, this view requires reading νόμος as a reference to the moral law, a restriction which does not work in this context. The previous reference to νόμος is Rom 9:31, where Paul refers to Israel's pursuit of the law of righteousness (νόμον δικαιοσύνης). The law of righteousness is Israel's covenant, a covenant that the gentiles do not possess (hence the reason they do not pursue righteousness [Rom 9:30]). Paul's statement in Rom 10:4 continues the focus on Israel's pursuit of a right standing by means of obeying their law/covenant.

141. BDAG, 998–99, does not offer this as a potential gloss either.

142. Badenas, *Christ*, 34.

143. Chalmers, *Romans*, 396–97; Gill, *Exposition*, 518; editorial note in Calvin, *Romans*, 383n1; Owen, *Faith*, 343. This view has modern advocates as well: Barth argues that Rom 10:4 refers to Christ fulfilling the law in terms of fulfilling the worship and mission to which Israel was called (*People of God*, 39–40); Dumbrell speaks of Christ demonstrating the perfect covenant obedience that Moses required of Israel ("Paul," 309); Royster, a modern commentator writing from the Orthodox tradition, writes of Christ doing all that was prescribed by the law (*Romans*, 260–61).

144. The John Owen who edited Calvin's Commentaries lived from 1788–1867 and served as the Vicar of Thrussington. He is to be distinguished from the earlier and better-known John Owen of 1616–83. On the latter, see Trueman, *John Owen*.

145. Editorial note in Calvin, *Romans*, 383n1.

146. For a defense of the doctrine, see McCormick, "Active Obedience." As we will see in the next chapter, there are also those who argue that Rom 10:5 refers to Christ's active obedience.

Christ Ends the Exclusivity of the Law

A view associated with the New Perspective on Paul is the idea that Christ ends Israel's confinement of the law to themselves. Israel mistakenly thinks that the law establishes their privileged position as the people of God, when in truth Christ has ended the old epoch of the Mosaic covenant and Israel's special privileges associated with it.[147] James Dunn writes,

> Paul then is probably thinking here of the law of Moses understood not as a definition of righteousness (9:31), but the law misunderstood in terms of "works" (9:32), the law misunderstood as a means of establishing and fixing firmly righteousness as Israel's special prerogative (10:3). All that is now finished! Christ is the end of any such function of the law; since the coming and work of Christ that misunderstanding of the law has no more scope.[148]

Dunn's last statement reflects a key part of his position: Christ ends not the law itself, but Israel's *misunderstanding* of the law. In other words, Dunn implies that νόμος does not refer to the Mosaic law, but to Israel's misunderstanding and abuse of the Mosaic law. In response, Paul's argument in Romans 9:30—10:13 is not concerned with Israel's perspective on the law, but on Israel's relationship to the law. They sought the law and its righteousness but did not attain to it, not because they misunderstood it, but because they sought it in the wrong way (by works instead of by faith [9:31–32a]). Like the Israel of Isaiah's day, they refused to heed the call to trust God by faith (Rom 9:32b–33). Paul does speak of Israel lacking knowledge (Rom 10:2), and being ignorant (Rom 10:3a), but he does so in connection with their refusal to submit to God's righteousness (Rom 10:3b). Israel has not committed a mistake; they have refused to submit to God's gospel (cf. Rom 10:16–21).[149]

Stephen Pattee advances a position similar to Dunn's by arguing that Habakkuk's emphasis on universalism and faith (see the presence of πᾶς in Hab 2:5–6, 8, 17, 19–20 and πίστις in Hab 2:4) influenced Paul's thinking in

---

147. Bechtler, "Christ," 296–302, 308 (Bechtler argues for the same idea as Dunn but does so by arguing that τέλος means "goal" and not "end"; Dunn, *Romans*, 2:589–90, 596–97; Gaston, *Paul*, 141–42; Getty, "Apocalyptic Perspective," 101–2; Howard, "Christ," 336; Jewett, *Romans*, 620; Pattee, "Stumbling Stone," 155–211; Refoulé, "Romains, x, 4," 339; Sanders, *Paul*, 40–41; Stowers, *Romans*, 304–8.

148. Dunn, *Romans*, 2:596.

149. Dunn's argument is also based on his assessment of intertestamental Judaism, the nature of righteousness, and the nature of Israel's works. We have addressed these latter two issues in the previous chapter and the previous sections of this chapter.

Rom 10:1–4.[150] Pattee argues that Paul understood Hab 1:4 and 3:13 to teach that the goal of the law was to save the Anointed (notice the verbal parallels: νόμος, τέλος, and δίκαιος in 1:4; σωτηρία, εἰς, and χριστός in 3:13). The resurrection of Christ, which saves Christ from death and all who believe from sin, is the climactic revelation of the τέλος νόμου.[151] Pattee therefore concludes that the Jews by their lack of faith in Christ demonstrate that they do not understand what God was doing in the law and in Christ: saving *all* nations.[152] God cannot be charged with unfaithfulness for he is doing what he always purposed to do: save all people, not just Israelites.[153] In response, we argue that Pattee is allowing the supposed implications of Habakkuk to overturn the plain sense of Paul. Pattee builds his argument on a string of verbal similarities between Romans and Habakkuk, but verbal similarity does not prove conceptual influence. Pattee's proposed interpretation should be able to stand on the words of Rom 10:1–4 alone, and apart from the alleged influence of Habakkuk.

Christ Is the True Meaning of the Law

Many recent interpreters argue that Christ is the goal of the law in the sense that the real message of the law is that people should trust Christ for their righteousness.[154] The law commands, but what the law really (ultimately) commands is faith. For those with faith to see it, the law ultimately points to Christ and his righteousness. Cranfield writes, "Christ is the goal, the aim, the intention, the real meaning and substance of the law—apart from Him it cannot be properly understood at all."[155]

John Toews supports this view by arguing that linguistic evidence favors the teleological meaning of τέλος, and that the teleological meaning best accounts for the purpose of the εἰς clause. Furthermore, Toews argues that the context favors this interpretation because Paul's contrast in Rom

150. Pattee, "Stumbling Stone," 166.
151. Pattee, "Stumbling Stone," 175, 188.
152. Pattee, "Stumbling Stone," 190, 194.
153. Pattee, "Stumbling Stone," 194.
154. Badenas, *Christ*, 112–18; Barth, *Dogmatics*, 244–45; Barth, *Shorter Commentary on Romans*, 126; Campbell, "Christ," 77; Cranfield, *Romans*, 2:519–20; Davies, *Faith*, 188; Fitzmyer, *Romans*, 584; Fuller, *Gospel*, 84–85; Johnson, *Romans*, 169; Keener, *Romans*, 124–25; Meyer, "Romans 10:4," 68; Rhyne, "*Nomos Dikaiosynēs*," 492–93; Toews, "Law," 238–45.
155. Cranfield, *Romans*, 2:519. Cranfield also writes, "the righteousness to which the law was summoning them was all the time nothing other than that righteousness which God offers to men in Christ" (*Romans*, 2:520).

9:30—10:13 is not between law and Christ but between faith and works as two different approaches to the law.[156]

This view has the great difficulty of proving that the essence of the law is faith and not works. The question is not whether the OT Scriptures bear witness to salvation by faith, but whether the law can really be read as ultimately demanding faith and not obedience to its commands. When proponents of this position appeal to Rom 9:32a to prove this (Israel sought the law by works instead of by faith), they overstate the case. Paul's point in Rom 9:31–32a is that the law and its righteousness cannot be obtained by works, but only by faith. The close connection between law and righteousness (νόμον δικαιοσύνης) indicates that Paul is not merely discussing pursuing the law, but pursuing the law with the intent of obtaining its righteousness. Paul's point is that this righteousness can be obtained only by faith. He does not say that the essence of the law is faith, or that the law itself is properly pursued by faith, but that the law with its object of righteousness can be obtained only by faith.

Paul's logic in Rom 9:30–33 does imply that there is a larger *purpose* to the law than that of commanding.[157] But this is different from arguing that the law's ultimate *meaning* is faith in Christ.[158] For Paul, the era of the law is something of a parenthesis, but it is a parenthesis with a purpose (Gal 3:1–29).[159] The law promises life in exchange for obedience (Lev 18:5; Rom 10:5), and it commands in order to reveal human unrighteousness (Exod 20:19; Rom 3:19–20). Within the context of the OT as a whole, the law highlights human sin (Rom 7:7–25) while looking back to Abraham who was justified by faith (Gen 15:6; cf. Rom 4:1–25), and ahead to a time when God himself will circumcise the hearts of his people so that they will obey him (Deut 30:1–14; Rom 10:6–8). The law, rightly used, does ultimately lead to faith in Christ. But it does so, not by commanding faith, but by commanding

---

156. Toews, "Law," 238–45. Interestingly, the comments given in Toews, *Romans*, 262, sound more like the view articulated by Dunn, but the more detailed treatment in "Law" places him here.

157. Indeed, if τέλος meant "goal" in Rom 10:4, we would favor the interpretation of the verse that argues that God's ultimate purpose in giving the law was to lead people to faith in Christ.

158. Westerholm: "*it is not legitimate to apply what Paul says of the Scriptures in general to the Sinaitic laws without further ado*. It does not follow, for example, that because Paul thought *the Scriptures* witness to faith, or contain the divine promise, he could not have contrasted *the Sinaitic legislation* with faith and God's promise" (*Perspectives*, 300, emphasis original).

159. Carson, "Mystery," 412; Bruce, *Paul*, 190.

an obedience which no sinful person can perform, and then presenting faith as the means to obtain that righteousness.[160]

Christ Ends and Culminates the Law

Those who favor a complex of ideas for τέλος argue that Christ brings the law to its climax and also ends its reign.[161] Moo articulates this view well:

> As Christ consummates one era of salvation history, so he inaugurates a new one. In this new era, God's eschatological righteousness is available to those who *believe;* and it is available to *everyone* who believes. Both emphases are important and reflect one of the most basic themes of the letter (cf. 1:16; 3:22, 28–30; 4:16–17). Because the Jews have not understood that Christ has brought the law to its culmination, they have not responded in faith to Christ; and they have therefore missed the righteousness of God, available only in Christ on the basis of faith. At the same time, Christ, by ending the era of the law, during which God was dealing mainly with Israel, has made righteousness more readily available for Gentiles.[162]

This view highlights the salvation-historical aspect of Paul's reasoning while also allowing for the multiple nuances τέλος can communicate.[163]

This view is tempting in that it allows one to capture the many nuances of Paul's argument and express them in one central theological statement.[164] However, it risks infusing the verse with more significance than

---

160. Westerholm writes, "God's design for the law must have been, in part, to go on record as demanding what is 'holy and righteous and good,' but also (indeed, even more) to demonstrate the rebellious character of humanity in Adam through the shortcomings of the most privileged segment of Adamic humanity (3:19–20). Paradoxically, then, the righteousness demanded *by* the law can only be attained *apart from* the law, by faith in Christ" ("Paul," 234, emphasis original).

161. Achtemeier, *Romans*, 168; Barrett, *Romans*, 146–47; Bruce, *Paul*, 190; Bruce, *Romans*, 190; Das, *Paul*, 250–51 (Das combines the two views that Christ is the true meaning of the law and that Christ ends the law as a way of salvation); Edwards, *Romans*, 250; Kruse, *Romans*, 405; Mohrmann, "Semantic Collisions," 236–37; Moo, *Epistle to the Romans*, 641–43; Seifrid, "Paul's Approach," 6–10; Southall, *Rediscovering Righteousness*, 236; Wright, *Romans*, 658.

162. Moo, *Epistle to the Romans*, 641–42, emphasis original.

163. *Contra* Dunn who argues that this interpretation "turns what is primarily a soteriological, or better, salvation-history, point into a primarily christological one" (*Romans*, 2:590). Moo *is* arguing that salvation history is the primary category, but that the meaning of the word also has a teleological nuance (*Epistle to the Romans*, 640–41).

164. Moo notes, "Verse 4 is, then, the hinge on which the entire section 9:30–10:13

Paul intended. As Schreiner notes, "The close connection between vv. 3–4 demonstrates that Paul is not making some global theological statement on the relationship between gospel and law in v. 4. He is responding to the specific problem raised in v. 3 of people wrongly using the law to establish their own righteousness."[165] The argument of Rom 9:30—10:13 focuses on Israel's failure to obtain a right standing with God, a failure which is due to their preoccupation with the works of the law, not a failure to perceive the salvation-historical shift in God's administration of the covenants. The tight construction of Rom 10:2–4, and the particular focus of the passage as a whole decrease the likelihood that Paul would use τέλος in an intentionally pregnant manner.

Christ Is the Purpose of the Law

Many theologians argue that the overall purpose of the law is to lead men to faith in Christ.[166] The law exposes humanity's unrighteousness and inability to obey the law in order to lead them to faith in Christ for righteousness. John Calvin articulates this theological idea in his comment on Rom 10:4:

> the law had been given for this end,—to lead us as by the hand to another righteousness: nay, whatever the law teaches, whatever it commands, whatever it promises, has always a reference to Christ as its main object; and hence all its parts ought to be applied to him. But this cannot be done, except we, being stripped of all righteousness, and confounded with the knowledge of our sin, seek gratuitous righteousness from him alone.[167]

The theology of this view is sound. The question, once again, is whether this is what Paul intends to communicate in Rom 10:4. As noted above, the close connection between 10:3 and 10:4 indicates that Paul is focusing on the specific problem of 10:3, and not making a theological statement

---

turns. It justifies Paul's claim that the Jews, by their preoccupation with the law, have missed God's righteousness (9:30–10:3): for righteousness is now found only in Christ and only through faith in Christ, the one who has brought the law to its climax and thereby ended its reign. It also announces the theme that Paul will expound in 10:5–13: righteousness by faith in Christ for all who believe" (*Epistle to the Romans*, 642).

165. Schreiner, "Israel's View of the Law," 122.

166. Aquinas, *Romans*, 279; Byrne, *Romans*, 312; Calvin, *Romans*, 384–85; Calvin, *Inst.* 2.7.2–3; Chrysostom, *Homilies*, 472; Mounce, *Romans*, 207; Nygren, *Romans*, 379–80; Osborne, *Romans*, 265–66; Westerholm, "Paul," 234; see also Westerholm, *Perspectives*, 329–30, though Westerholm speaks there more of the end of the law's validity as a way to righteousness rather than its place in the overall purpose of God.

167. Calvin, *Romans*, 384.

about the purpose of the law.¹⁶⁸ This view also adds some ideas to Rom 10:4 that are not explicit from the text. While Rom 10:4 states that Christ is the τέλος of the law, this view alleges that *God's* purpose (τέλος) in giving the law was to lead people to faith in Christ. This rearranges and amplifies the meaning of the text beyond what the words themselves justify.

Christ Ends Using the Law to Establish One's Righteousness

We argue that Christ ends the individual's use of the law for the purpose of obtaining righteousness.¹⁶⁹ The phrase εἰς δικαιοσύνην directly modifies τέλος νόμου, and the final clause (παντὶ τῷ πιστεύοντι) identifies those who benefit from Christ ending the law: believers.¹⁷⁰ Believers see that righteousness comes through faith in Christ, and not obedience to the law.¹⁷¹

Three factors incline us to this view. First, the lexical data and the context support the meaning of τέλος as "end" in the sense of termination. Christ is putting something to an end.¹⁷² Second, the phrase εἰς δικαιοσύνην directly modifies τέλος νόμου, not the entire equative clause.¹⁷³ Christ ends the law *with reference to righteousness* (and the pursuit of righteousness). Third, the flow of thought in Rom 10:1–3 leads naturally to a statement in Rom 10:4 about Christ ending the pursuit of righteousness by works for those who believe. Paul prays for Israel's salvation because they zealously obey God, but not according to knowledge. They lack knowledge about the right way to obtain a right standing with God, and they try to establish their own right standing before God. Because of this, they have not submitted to

---

168. Schreiner, "Israel's View," 122.

169. Bultmann, "Christ," 54; Denney, "Romans," 669; Gifford, *Romans*, 183; Hultgren, *Romans*, 383–84; Kaiser, "Law," 186; Ladd, *Theology*, 546; Lohse, *Römer*, 292–93; Longenecker, *Paul*, 145–53; Martin, "Paul," 278–79; Morris, *Romans*, 381; Moule, "Obligation," 402; Murray, *Romans*, 2:50; Origen, *Romans*, 135–36; Porter, *Romans*, 196; Räisänen, *Paul*, 54–56; Sanday and Headlam, *Romans*, 285; Schreiner, "Paul's View," 121–24; Schreiner, *Romans*, 546–47; Schlatter, *Romans*, 213.

170. In other words, Christ does not end the law in any universal sense. He ends the individual pursuit of the law in order to obtain right standing with God. When a sinful human trusts Christ for salvation, then Christ ends the law unto righteousness for them.

171. Longenecker observes how Paul contrasts the gospel with pagan religions in that pagan religions set out a path to be followed while the Christian gospel proclaims a person to whom one is committed, "the crucified, risen, exalted, and 'coming again' Messiah and Lord" (*Romans*, 842).

172. Christ ending the law is the implied verbal idea behind the verbless construction τέλος νόμου Χριστὸς.

173. Seifrid, "Paul's Approach to the Old Testament," 9n30.

God's way of providing righteousness. Christ ends this zealous pursuit and refusal to submit for those who believe in him.

Opponents of this view argue that it implies that prior to Christ one could use the law to establish one's righteousness.[174] Kruse writes, "Paul would deny that the law was ever intended to provide the way to obtain righteousness, and therefore such a view trivializes the relationship between Christ and the law."[175] In response, Paul identifies Christ as the end of the law because Christ is the ultimate manifestation of the message that humans must trust God alone for their salvation.[176] This logic reflects the flow of Rom 3:21–22: the OT Scriptures have always borne witness to the righteousness of God, and yet that righteousness is *now* (νυνὶ) manifested apart from the law (3:21), a righteousness that comes through faith in Christ (3:22).[177]

CONCLUSION

This chapter argued that Paul continues his critique of Israel's pursuit of a right standing with God by obeying the Mosaic law instead of by faith. Israel needs salvation in Christ (Rom 10:1) because they zealously try to keep the law but not in an informed manner (Rom 10:2). More specifically, Israel is ignorant of God's way of providing righteousness, and tries instead to establish (earn) their own right standing with God (Rom 10:3a). Because of this, they do not submit to the righteousness God provides to those who have faith (Rom 10:3b). Israel should submit to God in faith because Christ ends using the law to obtain a right standing with God for those who believe (Rom 10:4). The same critique that Paul developed in Rom 9:30–33 appears again with further detail in Rom 10:1–4. We must now examine Paul's scriptural proof for that second stage of his argument.

---

174. Badenas, *Christ*, 116; Campbell, "Christ," 75; Kruse, *Romans*, 403.

175. Kruse, *Romans*, 403.

176. Schreiner, "Israel's View," 123.

177. Dunn opposes this view on the grounds that first-century Judaism didn't try to earn or merit righteousness by obeying the law (*Romans*, 2:597). Our exegesis of Rom 9:30—10:13 thus far shows that at least *some* Jews did, particularly the Jews that Paul is writing about here.

Chapter 4

Romans 10:5

INTRODUCTION

The Old Testament plays a major role in Paul's argumentation throughout Rom 9:30—10:13. The first paragraph (9:30-33) concludes with citations from Isa 8:14; 28:16. The final paragraph (10:9-13) includes a second citation of Isa 28:16 (10:11) and concludes with a citation of Joel 2:32 (10:13). Between these two paragraphs lies Rom 10:1-8. We have already examined Paul's theological argument in 10:1-4 where Paul argues that Israel should end their insufficient attempts to gain a right standing with God by obeying the law and instead submit to the righteousness God provides through faith in Christ. That argument develops Paul's thesis in Rom 9:30-33 that Israel was trying to keep the law in order to obtain a right standing with God, but on account of human inability fell short of their goal. Just as Paul concluded that argument with citations of the OT, so he also supports his argument in 10:1-4 with citations from the OT in 10:5-8.[1] Rom 10:5 cites Lev 18:5, and Rom 10:6-8 cites Deut 8:17a; 9:4a; and 30:12-14.

This chapter examines Paul's use of Lev 18:5 in Rom 10:5. Paul uses Lev 18:5 as his first proof that Christ ends using the law to establish one's

---

1. Rom 10:5 begins with γὰρ, indicating that 10:5 explains why Christ ends using the law to establish one's righteousness. Rom 10:6 begins with δὲ, thus linking the citation of 10:6-8 to 10:5. As a whole, Rom 10:5-8 gives the final clarification (and proof) to the theological argument of 10:1-4.

righteousness: "For Moses writes about the righteousness that comes from the law, 'A person who does these things will live in them'" (Μωϋσῆς γὰρ γράφει τὴν δικαιοσύνην τὴν ἐκ [τοῦ] νόμου ὅτι ὁ ποιήσας αὐτὰ ἄνθρωπος ζήσεται ἐν αὐτοῖς).[2] We argue that Paul cites Lev 18:5 to represent the theological principle embedded in the law that eternal life comes to those who keep the law's demands. In order to prove this, we first examine the meaning of Lev 18:5 within its original context. Second, we examine the use of Lev 18:5 within the OT itself and within Jewish literature. Third, we critically examine the different approaches to Paul's use of Lev 18:5 before articulating our interpretation of Paul's hermeneutical and theological reasons for citing Lev 18:5 in Rom 10:5.

LEV 18:5 WITHIN ITS ORIGINAL CONTEXT

We begin with an examination of Lev 18:5 within its original context. Leviticus primarily contains detailed regulations relating to Israel's worship and ethics set within a narrative framework.[3] The author attributes these instructions directly to God (YHWH) himself, who speaks his word to Moses and Aaron.[4] The purpose of these regulations is to ensure that Israel will be a holy people for the Lord (Lev 11:44; 19:2; 20:26).[5]

Leviticus divides into two main sections. The first major section regulates Israel's official worship (Lev 1–16). The Lord instructs Israel regarding

---

2. We examine the text-critical and grammatical issues of this verse in the final section of this chapter.

3. Harrison, *Leviticus*, 13–14, identifies Leviticus as "a manual of priestly regulations and procedures," "containing technical regulations which the priests were to apply to the conduct of worship and the regulating of the community's life in Israel." See also Wenham, *Leviticus*, 15.

4. Moses alone is the most frequent direct recipient of the divine instructions (Lev 1:1; 4:1; 5:14; 6:1, 8, 19, 24; 7:22, 28; 8:1; 12:1; 14:1; 16:1; 17:1; 18:1; 19:1; 20:1; 21:16; 22:1, 17, 26; 23:1, 9, 23, 26, 33; 24:1, 13; 25:1; 27:1). However, one time Aaron is the direct recipient (Lev 10:8), and four times Moses and Aaron are both named (Lev 11:1; 13:1; 14:33; 15:1). Moses is to communicate these instructions to Aaron (e.g., 6:9, 25; 16:2) and to the children of Israel (e.g., 1:2; 4:2; 7:23, 29).

5. Harrison identifies the theme of the book as "the insistent emphasis upon God's holiness, coupled with the demand that the Israelites shall exemplify this spiritual attribute in their own lives" (*Leviticus*, 14). Hamilton identifies 150 occurrences of the Hebrew root קדשׁ ("holy") in Leviticus, about 20 percent of all occurrences in the Old Testament. He argues that maintaining ceremonial and moral holiness was an essential requirement in the covenant relationship that Israel enjoyed with YHWH (Exod 22:31; Lev 11:44; 20:7, 26; Deut 14:2 [*Handbook on the Pentateuch*, 233]). Rooker identifies holiness as the central theme of the book (*Leviticus*, 46–47). For more discussion of the theology of holiness in Leviticus, see Wenham, *Leviticus*, 18–25.

sacrifices (Lev 1–7), the priesthood (Lev 8–10), cleanness and uncleanness (Lev 11–15), and the Day of Atonement (Lev 16). The second major section (Lev 17–27) is demarcated by a concentrated emphasis upon holiness.[6] The section addresses sacrifice and food (Lev 17), private religion and morality (Lev 18–20), and then gives further instructions regarding Israel's worship (Lev 21–27).

Lev 18:1–30 emphasizes the necessity of sexual purity. The chapter begins and ends with an exhortation to avoid the practices of gentile nations (vv. 1–5, 24–30).[7] As God's special people, Israel must observe God's laws and not imitate the sinful practices of the Egyptians in their former home or the Canaanites in the land where they are going. If they defile themselves as the Canaanites did, then the land will vomit Israel out as it did the Canaanites. The particular laws governing sexual relations are given between the two framing exhortations (vv. 6–23). Israel must avoid incestuous unions (vv. 6–18), intercourse with a woman during her menstrual cycle (v. 19), adultery (v. 20), offering children to Molek (v. 21), homosexuality (v. 22), and bestiality (v. 23).

Leviticus 18:5 concludes the first framing exhortation: "Keep my statutes and my judgments, which if a person does them, he will live in them, I am YHWH" (ושמרתם את־חקתי ואת־משפטי אשר יעשה אתם האדם וחי בהם אני יהוה). Paul cites the second half of this verse in his description of the righteousness of the law: "the person who does these things will live in them" (ὁ ποιήσας αὐτὰ ἄνθρωπος ζήσεται ἐν αὐτοῖς). While the connection between performance of the law and life lends itself very naturally to Paul's discussion of righteousness and the law in Rom 9:30—10:13, we must first establish the significance of the connection in Leviticus.

Interpreters offer three explanations of this verse within its OT context. First, some argue that Lev 18:5 offers eschatological (eternal) life to those who keep the law.[8] John Calvin writes, "The passage [cited in Rom 10:5] is taken from Lev. 18:5, where the Lord promises eternal life to those who would keep his law; for in this sense, as you see, Paul has taken the passage,

---

6. As noted above, holiness is the central theme of the book. However, Lev 17–26 contains the majority of the occurrences (85 out of 150) of the root קדש (Hamilton, *Pentateuch*, 282). Lev 17 has therefore been traditionally recognized as beginning a new section of the book (Rooker, *Leviticus*, 228). Many critics designate Lev 17–26 the "holiness code" and classify it as material that was written after the opening chapters of Leviticus. However, Wenham wisely observes that even if one could discern separate sources in Leviticus, this does not necessarily indicate that they ever circulated independently of one another (*Leviticus*, 7).

7. Mohrmann, "Making Sense," 59.

8. Bonar, *Leviticus*, 329–30; Calvin, *Romans*, 387.

and not only of temporal life, as some think."⁹ Like Calvin, Andrew Bonar notes that some take the passage as referring to temporal life, but argues that the use of the text in Rom 10:5 and Gal 3:12 makes it clear that Lev 18:5 is referring to the eternal life promised to those who perfectly keep the law.¹⁰

Second, many argue that Lev 18:5 requires Israel to faithfully obey God's commandments as a response to the saving grace manifested in the Exodus event and Sinai covenant.¹¹ Mark Rooker concludes his analysis of the verse with these words: "The phrase 'the man who obeys them will live by them' should thus be viewed as promising a meaningful, secure life for those who are faithful to God and who exhibit their faithfulness by obedience to the Law. Hence, the verse pertains more to sanctification than justification, as the repeated phrase 'I am the Lord your God' makes plain (18:2, 20)."¹²

Third, many argue that, on one level, Lev 18:5 requires Israel's faithful obedience as a response to his saving grace, and, on another level, the commandment bears witness to the larger idea that perfect obedience secures eternal life.¹³ Micah McCormick writes, "In light of redemptive-historical themes and typological connections, Israel had a right to infer 'eternal life' lessons from Leviticus 18:5. Temporal land-life is the most obvious referent. Still, eternal life, while not on the surface, is latent in the text."¹⁴ This interpretation suggests a single meaning with multiple referents for Lev 18:5.

We can answer this overall question of interpretation by answering four subordinate questions related to the details of the text.¹⁵ First, which statutes and judgments are in view? Do חקה and משפט refer to the specific

---

9. Calvin, *Romans*, 387.

10. Bonar, *Leviticus*, 329–30.

11. Buswell, *Systematic Theology*, 313; Childs, *Introduction*, 187; Dunn, *Theology*, 152–53; Harris, "Leviticus," 597–98; Harrison, *Leviticus*, 184–85; House, *Old Testament Theology*, 149–50; Kaiser, "Leviticus 18:5," 21–25; Kaiser, "Law," 184–85; Lagrange, *Romains*, 254; Mohrmann, "Semantic Collisions," 101–2; Rooker, *Leviticus*, 40–41; Strickland, "Inauguration," 233–34; VanGemeren, "Law," 33; Venema, "Law," 223; Rad, *Old Testament Theology*, 194.

12. Rooker, *Leviticus*, 241.

13. Estelle, "Leviticus 18:5," 118; Gathercole, "Torah," 126–45; McCormick, "Active Obedience," 142–43; Meyer, *End*, 218; Schreiner, *40 Questions*, 63; Wenham, *Leviticus*, 253; White and Beisner, "Covenant," 159–60. Levine states that both views are possible, and does not argue for one view over another (*Leviticus*, 119).

14. McCormick, "Active Obedience," 143.

15. Patterned after the analysis of McCormick, "Active Obedience," 139–46.

sexual laws of 18:6–23,[16] or to all of God's laws?[17] In favor of the former view, the framing exhortations (vv. 1–5, 24–30) could function to isolate the intervening sexual laws as the locus of Israel's obedience.[18] However, nearly identical exhortations to keep God's commands occur throughout Leviticus without specifying particular commands (19:37; 20:22; 22:31; 25:18; 26:3). "Keep my statutes and my judgments" (and similar exhortations) is a common way in Leviticus to admonish Israel to keep the terms of the covenant.[19] Also, the threat to vomit Israel from the land (18:28) is later reiterated as a punishment for breaking the covenant (26:33), indicating that the principles of obedience and punishment expressed in the framing exhortations have reference to more laws than the specific sexual laws of 18:6–23.[20]

Second, what is the relationship between "doing" and "living"? Is doing synonymous with living (do the statutes and commands, that is, live in accordance with them),[21] or is life the conditional result of doing (if a person does these things, then he will live)?[22] Both options are grammatically possible,[23] but the first suffers from an obvious redundancy.[24] It goes without saying that the one who obeys the commands will live in the sphere of the commands. Furthermore, Lev 26:3 contains almost identical language to Lev 18:5 (אִם־בְּחֻקֹּתַי תֵּלֵכוּ וְאֶת־מִצְוֹתַי תִּשְׁמְרוּ וַעֲשִׂיתֶם אֹתָם), yet makes the conditional element explicit: *if* (אִם) Israel walks in God's statutes, and keeps his judgments and does them, *then* he will give them peace and prosperity in their land (see 26:4–13 for a description of these blessings). Likewise, if

16. Balentine, *Leviticus*, 150–55; Hartley, *Leviticus*, 293; Estelle, "Leviticus 18:5," 114; Milgrom, *Leviticus 17–22*, 1522; Mohrmann, "Making Sense," 76; Mohrmann, "Semantic Collisions," 101–2; Rooker, *Leviticus*, 239.

17. Bonar, *Leviticus*, 329–30; Harris, *Leviticus*, 598; McCormick, "Active Obedience," 140. Sprinkle concludes that "While the 'statutes and judgments' are a general description of all (i.e., non-specific) the laws of H, the narrative unit of 18–20 suggests a mild focus on the purity laws related to the land in 18–20" (*Law*, 34).

18. Mohrman, "Making Sense," 76.

19. For similar language outside of Leviticus, see Exod 15:26; 19:5–6; Deut 6:3; Ps 78:10; Jer 7:23.

20. McCormick, "Active Obedience," 140.

21. Kaiser, "Law," 184–85.

22. Estelle, "Leviticus 18:5," 117–18; McCormick, "Active Obedience," 141; Moo, *Epistle to the Romans*, 647n13; Rooker, *Leviticus*, 240; Sprinkle, *Law*, 31–34 (cf. 18:29); Wagner, *Heralds*, 160–61; Wenham, *Leviticus*, 253.

23. Williams, *Hebrew Syntax*, 97, 99. Levine says that the "simple sense" of the clause favors the first view, but that syntax does allow for the second option (*Leviticus*, 119). The ESV, KJV, NKJV, NASB, HCSB translate the clause with a conditional element ("if"). The RSV, NRSV render the clause modally ("by doing"). The NAB and NIV mildly reflect the conditional element by introducing the subordinate clause with "for."

24. Gathercole, "Torah," 127–28; McCormick, "Active Obedience," 141n12.

Israel does not listen and do all these commands (26:14), and if Israel breaks the covenant (26:15), then impoverishment and destruction will come upon them (26:16–39). The if-then structure of 26:3, 14 indicates that Lev 18:5 expresses a similar idea.

Third, what is the nature of the life offered? Does חיה refer to earthly, temporal benefits,[25] or to eternal life?[26] Most commentators argue for a temporal reference: the life promised refers to an individual remaining a member of the nation, and to the nation remaining in the promised land.[27] This does appear to be the immediate referent, especially when considered in the light of 18:24–28 and 26:3–13.[28] If Israel keeps the terms of the covenant, then they will enjoy peace and prosperity in the promised land.

However, many commentators also see a typological use of earthly life to bear witness to the concept of eternal life.[29] The temporal blessings of the covenant and the life in the land point Israel to greater realities.[30] Heb 11:16 opens a window into the comprehension of the OT saints when it reports that "they were looking for a better country, that is, a heavenly one." Life in the promised land anticipated the final restoration of all things to an Edenic state, where life in the land was accompanied by the absence of death.[31] Even the sacrificial system had a "built-in obsolescence" (Heb 8:6–12), indicating that the Mosaic economy as a whole looked forward to something greater to come.[32] The promise of life in the land anticipates eschatological life.

25. Bellinger, *Leviticus and Numbers*, 110; Gathercole, "Torah," 140; Harrison, *Leviticus*, 185; Hartley, *Leviticus*, 293; Milgrom, *Leviticus 17–22*, 1522; Moo, *Epistle to the Romans*, 647–48; Moo, *Romans*, 331; Rooker, *Leviticus*, 140–41; Seifrid, "Paul's Approach," 12; Sprinkle, *Law and Life*, 33–34; Wenham, *Leviticus*, 253.

26. Bonar, *Leviticus*, 329–30; Calvin, *Romans*, 387.

27. Moo, *Epistle to the Romans*, 647–48. Moo also writes, "'Living' in the Old Testament context refers to the enjoyment of covenant privilege and not necessarily to eternal life" (*Romans*, 331). So also Wenham: "What is envisaged is a happy life in which a man enjoys God's bounty of health, children, friends, and prosperity. Keeping the law is the path to divine blessing, to a happy and fulfilled life in the present" (*Leviticus*, 253).

28. Although it is not the last chapter, Lev 26 functions like a conclusion to the book. It sets before Israel the terms of the covenant, promises blessing as a reward for obedience, and threatens judgment for disobedience. It also holds out the promise of restoration if Israel repents of her unfaithfulness to the covenant. For occurrences of חיה in connection with Israel's covenant-life, see Deut 4:1; 5:33; 6:24; 8:1, 3; 16:20; 30:16, 18.

29. Estelle, "Leviticus 18:5," 118; Gathercole, "Torah," 126–45; McCormick, "Active Obedience," 142–43; Meyer, *End*, 218; Schreiner, *40 Questions*, 59; Seifrid, "Romans," 656; Wenham, *Leviticus*, 253; White and Beisner, "Covenant, Inheritance, and Typology," 160.

30. McCormick, "Active Obedience," 142.

31. McCormick, "Active Obedience," 143. See also Robertson, *Understanding*, 7–13.

32. Some authors attribute such typological ideas to later Jewish interpretation. Gathercole argues that in the second to first centuries B.C., there was an

This leads to the final subordinate question: what kind of obedience is God demanding? Is he requiring perfect obedience to his law,[33] or faithful obedience (i.e., obedience that is less than perfect but an expression of loyalty to God and his covenant)?[34] Once again, most agree that the immediate referent is faithfulness rather than perfection. The OT Scriptures refer to certain persons as blameless and obedient, a description grounded not in their perfection or their experience of salvation (though they certainly were saved), but in their obedience to the Mosaic covenant (Gen 6:9; Job 1:21; Ezek 14:14, 20; 2 Chron 31:20; see also Gen 17:1; Deut 6:25).[35] Furthermore, the Mosaic economy provided forgiveness for transgressions of the covenant by means of the sacrificial system.[36] Finally, when the Scriptures describe Israel's covenant unfaithfulness, they do not speak in terms of failing to perfectly obey, but of forsaking God and his covenant (Lev 26:15; Judg 10:6, 13; 1 Kgs 9:9; 18:18; 19:10; Jer 2:13; 5:19; 19:4). The Mosaic commandments show God's people how to faithfully obey him in response to his grace (Exod 20:1-2).

However, just as the reference to life bears witness to the concept of eternal life, so the commands to covenant faithfulness also bear witness to the necessity of perfect obedience.[37] The Mosaic covenant contains many admonitions to perform *all* of the law's demands (Deut 5:29, 33; 6:2, 24; 8:1; 10:12). In addition, the very existence of the sacrificial system testifies to the necessity of perfect obedience.[38] While it is true that offering the prescribed sacrifices in faith is part of covenant faithfulness, sacrifices for sin are necessary because God requires perfect obedience, and no one perfectly obeys God. While Israelites can be considered "righteous" in the sense that they do the right thing and are faithful to God when they obey the law (Deut 6:25), so the OT also speaks to the necessity of receiving a right standing

---

"eschatologizing" exegetical tendency that deferred the promises of life in this age to the age to come ("Torah," 129–32). Meyer writes, "The 'life' of Lev 18:5 is equivalent to the Deuteronomic lengthening of days, and it refers to an abundant life in the promised land. Paul's appropriation of the OT text relies on an eschatological extension, which takes realities from the old age and transposes them into their eschatological counterpart in the new age" (*End*, 218). See also Estelle, "Leviticus 18:5," 118n45; Rosner, *Paul*, 63; Sprinkle, *Law*, 68, 76, 100. The verses cited in our argument above indicate that these realities were intended by the original author. While they may have become more apparent to later readers, they were still present in the original text.

33. Bonar, *Leviticus*, 329–30.
34. Howard, "Christ," 334–35; Kaiser, "Leviticus 18:5," 24; Rooker, *Leviticus*, 240–41.
35. McCormick, "Active Obedience," 144.
36. Kaiser, "Leviticus 18," 25.
37. McCormick, "Active Obedience," 145–46; Wenham, *Leviticus*, 253.
38. McCormick, "Active Obedience," 145.

with God by faith (Gen 15:6; Ps 32:1–2; cf. Rom 4:1–8). Sinful humans must receive a right standing (perfection) before God by faith because God demands perfection, which no sinful person can provide.[39] The Mosaic commandments reveal the necessity of this perfect obedience to God.[40]

Based on the analysis above, we conclude that Lev 18:5 describes the faithful obedience that Israel must render to YHWH as a response to his salvation, while pointing to the larger truth that perfect obedience leads to eternal life. Lev 18:5 commands Israel to obey God's statutes and commandments in order that they may enjoy life. Israel must faithfully obey the statutes and judgments of the Mosaic covenant in order to enjoy peace and prosperity in the promised land. At the same time, the constant reminder of the necessity of obedience, and the necessity of sacrifice to atone for disobedience, pointed Israel to the larger truth that their enjoyment of eschatological life would be dependent upon their ability to stand perfect before God.

LEVITICUS 18:5 WITHIN THE OT AND JEWISH LITERATURE

We now survey the use of Lev 18:5 within the Old Testament and other Jewish writings. The phrase appears multiple times within later OT books, and frequently in intertestamental literature. The interpretation of this text within the OT and later Judaism suggests we are on the right path in articulating multiple referents for the main ideas of Lev 18:5.

Lev 18:5 within the OT

Leviticus 18:5 occurs in two later OT books, Ezekiel and Nehemiah.[41] Both passages give sustained attention to Israel's violation of the Mosaic covenant.

---

39. Estelle, McCormick, and Seifrid also note the individualistic thrust of Lev 18:5b ("Leviticus 18:5," 114–15; "Active Obedience," 143n19; and "Romans," 656, respectively). While the first clause in Lev 18:5 employs a third-person plural verb (ושמרתם), the second clause (which Paul cites) employs two second-person singular verbs (וחי יעשה). Estelle calls this "a kind of democratization of the law" ("Leviticus 18:5 and Deuteronomy 30:1–14," 115). Paul's citation preserves the individualistic language (ἄνθρωπος ὁ ποιήσας).

40. The Mosaic commandments do not, however, command one to exercise faith in order to be righteous. The sacrificial system points one to the availability of forgiveness, and the example of Abraham demonstrates that righteousness comes by faith. The law commands in order to convict; faith leads the convicted sinner to God for salvation.

41. Schreiner also refers to Prov 4:4 and 7:2, since they reflect the principle that if one obeys the commandments they will live (*40 Questions*, 60). Mohrmann adds

The conditional element remains, but the contexts emphasize the failure to meet those conditions.

Ezekiel 20:11, 13, 21

Three citations of Lev 18:5 appear in Ezek 20:11, 13, 21.[42] In many ways, Ezekiel 20 reads like a commentary on Lev 26.[43] Like Ezek 16 and 23, it rehearses the history of Israel, highlighting their persistent disobedience to God's commands (see esp. 20:4, 8, 13, 16, 21, 24, 30).[44] Although God is slow to punish Israel (20:9, 14, 17, 22), their persistent disobedience leaves him with little choice but to pour out his wrath upon them (20:23–26).

Throughout this rehearsal of Israel's disobedience, Ezekiel cites Lev 18:5: God gave Israel his statutes (חקה) and his judgments (משפט), "which, if a person does them, he will live in them" (אשר יעשה אותם האדם וחי בהם, 20:11). However, Israel has not kept God's statutes (חקה) and judgments (משפט), "which, if a person does them, he will live in them" (אשר יעשה אותם האדם וחי בהם, 20:13). They did not walk in the statutes (חקה) or observe the judgments (משפט), "which, if a person does them, he will live in them" (אשר יעשה אותם האדם וחי בהם, 20:21).[45] This threefold recitation of Lev 18:5 perhaps indicates that Ezekiel views this verse as an appropriate summary of the entire Mosaic Covenant.[46] While Ezekiel does not view the

---

Deut 4:1 and 30:16 based on verbal and conceptual overlap ("Semantic Collisions," 102–5). One would expect the OT to reflect the ideas and even the wording of such an important verse as Lev 18:5 in its later writings, especially those that address Israel's responsibility under the covenant. We therefore limit ourselves in our examination of the OT data to those passages which directly cite Lev 18:5, not just the same principle or wording.

42. Sprinkle also argues that Ezek 18 and 33 allude to Lev 18:5 ("Law," 276). Again, we concentrate our analysis on the direct citations, though we will incorporate the larger context of Ezekiel into our overall interpretation.

43. Compare Ezek 20:5–10 with Lev 26:1–13. Both chapters rehearse God's deliverance of Israel from Egypt and her concomitant responsibility to obey God and to keep his covenant.

44. Sprinkle, "Law," 285.

45. The language is nearly identical to Lev 18:5 (אותם in Ezek 20:11, 13, 21 is spelled with the ו), thus retaining the potential for the conditional translation. Avemarie notes that the phrase לא יחיו בהם ("by which they could not have life" [RSV]) in Ezek 20:25 all but guarantees a conditional idea in Lev 18:5 and Ezek 20:11, 13, 21. In Avemarie's words, "the phrase לא יחיו בהם can hardly be understood as 'they are not to live *in accordance with* them'" ("Paul," 127n4, emphasis original).

46. Watson observes that Paul's citations of Lev 18:5 in Romans and Galatians "are said to encapsulate the very essence of the law, summing up the law's entire rationale and content in a single lapidary utterance" (*Hermeneutics*, 314).

law and the covenant negatively, he does view Israel's response negatively.[47] Despite God's repeated displays of mercy, they have failed to respond to the covenant appropriately. This fits the immediate referent of Lev 18:5: God enters into a covenant relationship with Israel, and demands obedience as the appropriate response to his grace.

However, this does not preclude the second referent suggested for Lev 18:5, that the commandment bears witness to the necessity of perfect obedience, and to God's initiative to provide that obedience. Before Ezek 20 concludes, the prophet describes a time when God will restore Israel to her land, purge out rebels from her midst, and manifest his holiness among them (20:37–44). This theme of future restoration receives further treatment in Ezekiel 36:27; 37:14, 24. Ezek 36:27 describes a time when God will put his Spirit within his people, and cause them to walk in his statutes (חקה) and judgments (משפט). Ezek 37:14 concludes the valley of dry bones vision with God's promise to put his Spirit within his people with the result that they live (חיה). Ezek 37:24 describes the Davidic king who will enable Israel to do all God's statutes (חקה) and judgments (משפט). Preston Sprinkle has helpfully analyzed the shift that occurs in Ezekiel from chapters 18, 20, 33 (if a person does, then he will live) to 36:27; 37:14, 24 (the Spirit will give life and enable you to do).[48] From Ezekiel's perspective, Israel could not keep the demands of Lev 18:5, thus highlighting the need for divine agency to provide life and obedience.[49] While Ezek 20:11, 13, 21 bear witness to the fact of Israel's failure, the commentary on that situation in Ezek 36:27; 37:14, 24 bears witness to man's inability to obey God and the necessity of divine intervention. Lev 18:5 thus refers to Israel's present responsibilities under the Mosaic covenant, and humanity's inability to please God by any obedience.

Nehemiah 9:29

Nehemiah 9:29 uses Lev 18:5 in a similar manner. Nehemiah rehearses God's gracious dealings with Israel (9:7–15), including his gift of the law (9:13–15). However, Israel has failed to keep the covenant (9:16–29). She did not obey God's commandments (מצוה) or judgments (משפט), "which, if a person does them, he will live in them" (אשר יעשה האדם וחי בהם, 9:29).

---

47. Block observes that the prophet takes a positive view of God's law: obedience to God's laws is the key to life (cf. Ezek 18:9, 19, 21–23; Deut 4:6–8; 30:15–19 [*Ezekiel, Chapters 1–24*, 632]). So also Badenas, *Christ*, 120.

48. Sprinkle, "Law," 292.

49. Sprinkle, *Law*, 40.

They persisted in their disobedience, and suffered the consequence of exile (9:30-31). This reflects the immediate referent of Lev 18:5: God's grace forms the relationship with Israel (9:5b-15, 31-35), and Israel has the responsibility to obey God's laws as a response to such mercy (9:16-17a, 26, 28-29).[50]

However, the context also emphasizes God's mercy and Israel's need of salvation. When God gave Israel into the hand of their enemies, he also sent saviors to deliver them from those enemies (9:27). God's great mercy and grace precluded him from making a complete end to Israel during their exile (9:31). Nehemiah therefore bases his appeals on God's covenant and love, not Israel's obedience (9:32). These appeals recognize that there is nothing Israel can do to rescue themselves from divine wrath. Israel needs a savior, and the Mosaic covenant, summarized in the words of Lev 18:5, bears witness to this need.

Lev 18:5 within Intertestamental Jewish Literature

Research into the use of Lev 18:5 within Jewish writings has yielded fruitful results.[51] Throughout its many occurrences, the verse is used to iden-

---

50. Sprinkle writes, "the Leviticus formulation is used to describe what Israel should have done but failed to do, thus forfeiting the covenant blessing of life" (*Law*, 44).

51. Three helpful studies are Avemarie, "Paul," 127-29; Gathercole, "Torah," 128-39; Sprinkle, *Law*, 45-130. One of the difficulties of assessing the use of Scripture in other documents is assessing what constitutes a quotation, allusion, etc. We follow the uses identified by Avemarie, Gathercole, and Sprinkle. Gathercole identifies his criteria in that texts must refer to two elements of Lev 18:5b in order to constitute part of the interpretive history ("Torah," 129). This criteria leads him to omit discussion of two texts (Bar 4:1 and *Let. Aris.* 127) that Dunn refers to in his discussion (*Theology*, 153n26). While these two texts do communicate principles that are similar to that of Lev 18:5 (Bar 4:1: keeping the commandments leads to life; *Let. Aris.*127: observing the commandments is the good life), we agree with Gathercole that the language is too dissimilar to include these texts in a discussion of the interpretation of Lev 18:5. Strangely, Gathercole does choose to interact with Dunn's reference to 1QS 4.6-8 (*Rule of the Community* or *Manual of Discipline*), which contains one of the elements of Lev 18:5, the reference in 4.6 to "all those who walk in it" (Gathercole himself admits that "the allusion to Lev 18:5 is extremely vague" ["Torah," 133-34]). If 1QS 4.6 is alluding to Lev 18:5, then it reflects the double-referent interpretation we have advocated. Wise et al., *Dead Sea Scrolls*, 121, translate 4.6b-7a as, "Through a gracious visitation all who walk in this spirit will know healing, bountiful peace, long life, and multiple progeny, followed by eternal blessings and perpetual joy through life everlasting." The divine blessing is founded on grace, but still dependent on obedience. The reference to the life given on the basis of obedience easily moves from a reference to a blessed life now to eternal life in the future. Avemarie and Gathercole also discuss some rabbinic references to Lev 18:5, but we will omit discussion of those due to our interest in the use of this text by

tify what one must do in order to enjoy (usually eternal) life.⁵² Within intertestamental Judaism, the elements that contribute to the secondary referent are more clearly identified: there is more focus on the individual, life is interpreted as eternal life, and the conditional nuance becomes explicit.

*The Septuagint*⁵³

The Septuagint (LXX) translates Lev 18:5b as a conditional statement: ἃ ποιήσας ἄνθρωπος ζήσεται ἐν αὐτοῖς, "if a person does these things, he will live in them." While the Hebrew imperfect verb יַעֲשֶׂה does not demand a conditional translation,⁵⁴ the subordination of ποιήσας to ζήσεται makes it difficult to read the LXX in any other way.⁵⁵ The same translation occurs in Neh 9:29 (2 Esdras 19:29), ἃ ποιήσας αὐτὰ ἄνθρωπος ζήσεται ἐν αὐτοῖς. LXX Ezek 20:11, 13, 21 uses the future verb ποιήσει instead of the participle ποιήσας. While this downgrades the conditional element from an explicit element to a possible nuance, the possibility is still there. In summary, none of these translations deny the conditional element, and two of them make it explicit.

Philo

The works of Philo contain one reference to Lev 18:5.⁵⁶ In the allegorical work, *On Mating with the Preliminary Studies* (*De Congressu Quaderendae Eruditionis Studies*), Philo cites Lev 18:1–5 and then comments, "So then the true life is the life of him who walks in the judgements and ordinances of God, so that the practices of the godless must be death."⁵⁷ Gathercole and Sprinkle interpret these comments as a reference to the regulatory function

---

Paul and not later Judaism ("Paul," 128–29 and "Torah," 138–39, respectively).

52. The verse's frequent occurrence has led Sprinkle to identify Lev 18:5 as the "John 3:16 of Early Judaism" (*Law*, vii).

53. We include the LXX translation in Jewish literature instead of the OT proper since translations are one step removed from the original writing and can reflect assumed interpretations.

54. Williams identifies ten uses of the imperfect, of which the conditional is one (*Hebrew Syntax*, 69–73). However, we have argued above that the conditional element avoids the redundancy of the incomplete-action translation ("the person who does these things will live in them").

55. Avemarie, "Paul," 127; Sprinkle, *Law*, 50.

56. According to Sprinkle, *Law*, 114.

57. Philo, *Congr.* 87; Colson and Whitaker, *Philo*, 4:501.

of the law: the good life consists of keeping God's commandments.[58] However, Avemarie notes, "The fact that he [Philo] opposes true life not to wrong life but to death clearly evinces his soteriological perspective."[59]

Pseudepigrapha

Three references to Lev 18:5 occur in the OT Pseudepigrapha. First, Pseudo-Philo's *Liber Antiquitatum Biblicarum* refers to Lev 18:5 when it retells the Exodus story. *L.A.B.* 23:10 reads, "And I did not let my people be scattered, but I gave them my Law and enlightened them in order that by doing these things they would live and have many years and not die."[60] This citation closely resembles the immediate referent of Lev 18:5: the gift of the law is based on God's grace, and the people obey it in order to continue to enjoy the blessings of the covenant. Sprinkle's analysis of *L.A.B.* as a whole highlights the theme of God's mercy upon Israel despite their disobedience.[61] However, the verse still bears witness to the idea that Israel's future enjoyment of God's blessings will be based on their obedience to God's laws.

The *Psalms of Solomon* bear witness to the connection between obedience to the law and obtaining life. *Pss. Sol.* 14:2–3a reads, "[The Lord is faithful] To those who live in the righteousness of his commandments, in the Law, which he has commanded for our life. The Lord's devout shall live by it forever."[62] God shows his faithfulness (14:1) to those who live in the righteousness of his commandments. The purpose of the law is to give life, and one obtains life by obeying it. While the Psalm lacks any notion of self-righteousness (*Pss. Sol.* 14 resembles the canonical Ps 1), it does insist that obedience to Torah is necessary to obtain eternal life.[63]

Finally, 4 Ezra 7:21 contains a possible reference to Lev 18:5. The text reads, "For God strictly commanded those who came into the world, when they came, what they should do to live, and what they should observe to

---

58. Gathercole, "Torah," 128; Sprinkle, *Law*, 114.

59. Avemarie, "Paul," 128. Not only is Lev 18:5 itself subject to multiple interpretations, but so is its use in later writers.

60. Charlesworth, *Old Testament Pseudepigrapha*, 2:333.

61. Sprinkle, *Law*, 129–30.

62. Charlesworth, *Old Testament Pseudepigrapha*, 2:663.

63. Sprinkle, *Law*, 100. Gathercole cites this passage as an example of the frequent tension in Jewish literature that bases salvation both on obedience and gracious divine election ("Torah," 133).

avoid punishment."⁶⁴ The verse does communicate the "do and live" idea, though it is unclear whether eternal life is in view or not.⁶⁵

Dead Sea Scrolls

The Dead Sea Scrolls contain three references to Lev 18:5. First, CD III, 12b–17a (the *Damascus Document*), reads as follows:

> But when those of them who were left held firm to the commandments of God He instituted His covenant with Israel forever, revealing to them things hidden, in which all Israel had gone wrong: His holy Sabbaths, His glorious festivals, His righteous laws, His reliable ways. The desires of His will, which Man should carry out and so have life in them, He opened up to them. So they "dug a well," yielding much water. Those who reject this water He will not allow to live.⁶⁶

Several elements deserve attention. First, as the opening line indicates, this citation occurs in the midst of a discussion of Israel's disobedience. The discussion resembles Ezekiel's use of Lev 18:5: this is what Israel ought to have done and did not.⁶⁷ Second, the language of obligation ("which Man should carry out") reflects the idea that obedience is the proper response to the covenant.⁶⁸ Third, the reference to "life" in 3:20 ("those who hold firm to it shall receive everlasting life") indicates that the life in view here is eternal life.⁶⁹ According to CD III, 15, obedience to the rules of the Qumran community is a precondition for attaining eternal life.⁷⁰

The *Damascus Document* was discovered in the genizah of the Ben-Ezra synagogue in Cairo in 1896 or 1897.⁷¹ It is a medieval copy of some of

---

64. Charlesworth, *Old Testament Pseudepigrapha*, 1:537.

65. Gathercole, "Torah," 138. Avemarie claims that the context favors relating this reference to life and punishment in the future world ("Paul," 128).

66. Wise et al., *Dead Sea Scrolls*, 54.

67. Sprinkle, *Law*, 68.

68. Gathercole and Sprinkle identify the halakic rulings of the community as the immediate referent for the commands which ought to be obeyed ("Torah," 135, and *Law*, 68, respectively).

69. Wise et al., *Dead Sea Scrolls*, 54.

70. Gathercole, "Torah, Life, and Salvation," 136; Sprinkle, *Law and Life*, 68. Mohrmann also interprets the reference to life as eternal life, and observes, "This section CD emphasizes 'living,' and gives the impression that only a few in Israel, past or present, have actually deserved it" ("Semantic Collisions," 110).

71. Evans, *Ancient Texts*, 141.

the documents discovered at Qumran.⁷² One of those documents discovered at Qumran (4Q266) contains material that occurs at the end of the *Damascus Document* and discusses the procedure for punishing offenders.⁷³ The relevant section contains the second reference to Lev 18:5, and reads, "Thou hast chosen our fathers, Thou hast given to their descendants the statutes of Thy truth, and the judgments of Thy holiness, which, if humankind shall do, they shall have life" (4Q266 11, 11–12).⁷⁴ If CD III, 15 reflected Ezekiel's use of Lev 18:5, then 4Q266 11, 11–12 reflects Nehemiah's.⁷⁵ As the author of the fragment rehearses God's gracious dealings with his people, he pauses to observe that if Israel will keep the terms of the covenant, then they will have life. Here the emphasis is upon the conditional element: if Israel will obey, then they will live.⁷⁶

The third reference to Lev 18:5 occurs in the highly fragmentary *Words of the Luminaries* (4Q504 6 II, 17). The preceding and following words have not survived, and it is therefore impossible to analyze the reference in its most immediate context. The passage reads, "For you . . . and you do not acknowledge innocent . . . as one punishes a son . . . the holy ones and the pure ones . . . the man and lives in them . . . the oath which you [swore]."⁷⁷ Much of the fragment in which the reference occurs exists in this state. Sprinkle assesses the allusion in the light of the *Words* as a whole, and highlights the conditional element: "Lev 18:5 was understood as an offer of life forfeited through the rebellion of Israel, but still capable of being met through renewed obedience to the law."⁷⁸

The Targumim

Targum Onqelos and *Targum Jonathan* interpret life in Lev 18:5 as eternal life. The person who performs the commandments will live "in the life of eternity" (בחיי עלמא).⁷⁹ While the Targumim postdate the NT, they may bear witness to a Jewish understanding of the text in existence during the time of Jesus and Paul.⁸⁰ *Targum Ezekiel* also reads "in the life of eternity" (בחיי

---

72. Evans, *Ancient Texts*, 141.
73. Wise et al., *Dead Sea Scrolls*, 77–78.
74. Wise et al., *Dead Sea Scrolls*, 78.
75. Sprinkle, *Law*, 75.
76. Gathercole, "Torah," 136; Sprinkle, *Law*, 75–76.
77. Martínez, *Dead Sea Scrolls*, 417.
78. Sprinkle, *Law*, 85.
79. *Targum Neofiti* does not modify the phrase.
80. Evans, *Ancient Texts*, 185–86.

עלמא), and many scholars identify this Targum as pre-Rabbinic.[81] Whoever produced these Targumim interpreted the life of Lev 18:5 and Ezek 20:11, 13, 21 as eternal life.

Conclusion

The many uses of Lev 18:5 in the intertestamental writings consistently reinforce the idea that one must do the law in order to live. Obedience to the law is a precondition for life. Often the life in view is eternal life: one must do the law (or its halakic interpretation) in order to enjoy life in the world to come. The secondary referent that was latent in the original has become apparent to its later interpreters.

PAUL'S USE OF LEV 18:5 IN ROM 10:5

We now examine Paul's use of Lev 18:5 in Rom 10:5. The standard critical editions (NA²⁸, UBS⁴) read, Μωϋσῆς γὰρ γράφει τὴν δικαιοσύνην τὴν ἐκ [τοῦ] νόμου ὅτι ὁ ποιήσας αὐτὰ ἄνθρωπος ζήσεται ἐν αὐτοῖς. Some variation exists in the manuscript tradition, particularly regarding the presence or location of ὅτι. Some manuscripts omit the ὅτι entirely,[82] while others place it immediately after γράφει.[83] The latter placement extends the quotation and makes τὴν δικαιοσύνην τὴν ἐκ τοῦ νόμου the object of ποιήσας.[84] The longer quotation is not represented in any OT manuscripts, but could be an expanded quotation if genuine. However, Metzger offers three arguments in favor of placing the ὅτι after νόμου: (1) early and diversified external support; (2) a later move to γράφει is more likely than a move to νόμου; (3) the expression ποιεῖν τὴν ἐκ νόμον δικαιοσύνην is non-Pauline.[85] These reasons give sufficient cause to follow the text of the major editions.[86] The present reading therefore presents δικαιοσύνην as an accusative of reference:

---

81. Gathercole, "Torah," 137.
82. א² B Ψ 945 *l* 249 *al.*
83. א* A D* 33* 81 630 1506 1739 1881 *pc* co.
84. Metzger, *Textual Commentary*, 524.
85. Metzger, *Textual Commentary*, 524–25.
86. The comments by Metzger come from the first edition of the *Textual Commentary*, which is used in company with UBS³. UBS⁴ and the second edition of the *Textual Commentary* do not note the variant. Other variants of a more minor nature involve whether to include αὐτὰ following ποιήσας, and whether the sentence should conclude with αὐτῇ or αὐτοῖς.

"Moses writes *concerning* the righteousness that comes from the law."[87] Seifrid observes that this is the only place where Paul first describes the content of the citation before giving the citation itself.[88]

Paul's citation does differ slightly from the MT and LXX. A formal Greek translation of the MT would likely yield ἃ ποιήσει ἄνθρωπος αὐτὰ καὶ ζήσεται ἐν αὐτοῖς.[89] As noted above, the LXX reads ἃ ποιήσας ἄνθρωπος ζήσεται ἐν αὐτοῖς. Paul's citation does not correspond perfectly to either of these. The biggest difference is that Paul has added the definite article to the participle, thus removing the explicit conditional element in favor of a general statement: "a man who does these things will live in them."[90] Paul has also added αὐτὰ, albeit without a specific antecedent. The differences are not drastic enough to suppose an alternative source; Paul has given a somewhat free rendering of the verse.[91]

Five major interpretations of Paul's use of Lev 18:5 emerge from the relevant literature. The correspondences between these views and the three major critiques of Israel's error which this dissertation addresses will become apparent throughout the examination. We analyze each view in turn, and argue for the validity of the fifth.

Obeying the Law because of Grace

The first view asserts that Paul uses Lev 18:5 in accord with its immediate referent in its original context: obedience to the law flows from a prior experience of grace.[92] Moses' description of the righteousness of the law is a description of the sanctified life of obedience to the law pursued by those

---

87. Wallace, *Greek Grammar*, 203–4.

88. Seifrid, "Romans," 654. Seifrid also observes that although Paul throughout this section of Romans frequently introduces OT citations by identifying the biblical figure who is the source of the utterance (cf. 9:27, 29; 10:19, 20; 11:9), Rom 10:5 is the only place where Paul uses the present tense of γράφω in reference to a human author of Scripture. Dunn suggests that the present tense "denotes the continuing force of this word of Moses for Paul's own people" (*Romans*, 2:600). Porter identifies γράφει as the narrative present (*Romans*, 196).

89. This is very similar to the reading of LXX Ezek 20:11, 13, 21.

90. The future tense verb "will live" still implies a conditional element: one will live *if* he does these things.

91. Hultgren, *Romans*, 385.

92. Davies, *Faith*, 30, 192–94, 198; Dunn, *Romans*, 2:600–601; Dunn, *Theology*, 153; Harris, "Leviticus," 598; House, *Old Testament Theology*, 150; Kaiser, "Leviticus 18:5," 24–25, 27–28; Kaiser, "Law," 184–85; Strickland, "Inauguration," 249–51; Toews, "Law," 283–84.

who are justified by faith. Both OT citations in Rom 10:5–8 bear witness to the priority of faith.[93]

The strength of this view is that it does not raise any hermeneutical concerns about Paul's use of the Old Testament. According to Kaiser, Paul simply cites this verse in accordance with its original meaning in order to show that it is a description of true righteousness, and the same thing as the word of faith which Paul preaches.[94] Just as works followed faith in the old economy, so faith has the priority in the new economy.

James Dunn suggests a different strategy in Paul's citation, but still articulates a similar meaning of Lev 18:5. According to Dunn, Paul and the Israelites know that God first establishes the covenant relationship by grace, and that Israel's proper response is faith. The role of the law is secondary: it regulates the life of those whom God has chosen. Paul's complaint in Rom 10:5 is that his fellow Jews have emphasized that secondary role of the law at the expense of faith and grace.[95] The Jewish way of living, as expressed by Lev 18:5, no longer defines those who belong to the covenant; it has been "rendered out of date by Christ."[96]

One other variant of this view deserves attention before we give our analysis. Stephen Pattee argues that the fulfillment of the law commanded by Lev 18:5 is exemplified in the command of Lev 19:18 to love one's neighbor as one's self.[97] The Jews acted hypocritically because they claimed to fulfill the law but actually violated one of the law's most fundamental requirements (Lev 19:18) when they failed to give gentiles coequal status in the soteriological purpose of God.[98] To demonstrate the link between Lev 18:5 and Lev 19:18, Pattee cites Jewish writings that combine statements on

---

93. Kaiser argues that the γάρ . . . δὲ construction spanning 10:5–6 should be translated, "for . . . and" (cf. Rom 7:8; 11:15 ["Leviticus 18:5," 27]). However, see the discussion under the fifth view.

94. Kaiser, "Leviticus 18:5," 27.

95. Dunn, *Theology*, 153.

96. Dunn, "Righteousness," 221–23; Dunn, *Romans*, 2:612. See also Dumbrell, *Romans*, 104–5; Mohrmann takes a similar approach, arguing that Paul uses Lev 18:5 to define the old limits of the people of God which had now been redefined in Christ ("Semantic Collisions," 243–44). Southall embraces Dunn's view but also believes the active obedience view is a second, subsidiary point of Paul's that maintains the dual meaning of τέλος as Israel's error which has come to an end and Christ as the goal of the law (*Rediscovering Righteousness*, 248–53).

97. Pattee, "Stumbling Stone," 212–23.

98. Pattee, "Stumbling Stone," 240–44.

fulfilling the law with citations of Lev 19:18.⁹⁹ He also cites NT evidence such as Luke 10:25–28 and Matt 19:16–22.¹⁰⁰

These approaches to Lev 18:5 suffer from four weaknesses. First, we have raised questions against interpreting Lev 18:5 solely in terms of a statement about Israel's responsibility under the Mosaic covenant. While the immediate referent is to Israel's obedience in response to the covenant, the verse also has a secondary referent to the necessity of perfect obedience in order to secure eternal life, a secondary referent brought out by the use of this verse within the OT itself and later Jewish literature. This secondary referent also argues against Dunn's limited understanding of the role of Lev 18:5: while the Mosaic Covenant had gracious elements, it still bore witness to Israel's obligation and inability to obey God satisfactorily, and to their need for the final sacrifice, Christ.

Second, even if Lev 18:5 referred exclusively to Israel's responsibility to keep the terms of the covenant, in light of the interpretation(s) of this verse within intertestamental Judaism, it is not certain that Paul's audience would have read Lev 18:5 in accordance with that original meaning. This does not prohibit Paul from using Lev 18:5 in accordance with its original meaning, but as noted in our survey of the Jewish literature, many Jews interpreted Lev 18:5 as requiring them to obey the law in order to obtain eternal life. For Paul to cite this text and assume a different meaning without explanation runs the risk of his point being lost on his readers.¹⁰¹

That observation leads to the third criticism: Paul seems to imply a very different meaning for his text by citing it as a description of the righteousness of the law. The phrase τὴν δικαιοσύνην τὴν ἐκ [τοῦ] νόμου does not seem to be a very appropriate phrase to describe the righteous living that is appropriate to the covenant. That idea is foreign to Rom 9:30—10:13,¹⁰²

---

99. Pattee, "Stumbling Stone," 223–26.

100. Pattee, "Stumbling Stone," 235–39.

101. Dunn argues that intertestamental Judaism read Lev 18:5 as he does, as a description of the regulatory function of the law for an already-saved people (*Theology*, 152–53). This understanding of Lev 18:5 has been challenged by Gathercole ("Torah," 126–45). House argues that Paul cites Lev 18:5 "to correct the misconception that salvation and righteousness come by works" (*Old Testament Theology*, 150). But how does Paul correct a misconception regarding the role of works in salvation by citing a verse that emphasizes the necessity of works in obtaining eternal life? Unless Paul knew exactly how his readers would understand his text, we doubt that he would have cited it without further explanation. Within the present context, one expects a reference to obedience and life to be referring to the pursuit of life by means of obedience to the law.

102. Schreiner writes, "Nowhere in this context is the doing of the law rooted in faith" (*Romans*, 553).

and does not accord with Paul's use of the same phrase in Phil 3:6.[103] If Paul is trying to disprove the efficacy of works in salvation by citing a text that teaches that works follow justification while describing that citation as a description of the righteousness of the law, then he has chosen a very indirect way to make his point.

Finally, regarding Pattee's approach to the meaning of Lev 18:5, the interpretive connection he makes between Lev 18:5 and Lev 19:18 does not exist outside of his hypothesis. The interpretation of Lev 19:18 as a summary statement of the law is not the same thing as saying that Lev 18:5 equals Lev 19:18. Lev 18:5 does not summarize the law: it states the necessity of obeying the law. Even those texts in the NT which cite Lev 18:5 in conjunction with Lev 19:18 do not limit the range of commandments one must do to the commandment to love one's neighbor as oneself. Luke 10:25–28 reads that one must love the Lord with all of one's heart, soul, strength, and mind (Deut 6:5), and love one's neighbor as one's self (Lev 19:18). The one who do these things (both commandments) will live (a possible allusion to Lev 18:5).[104] The same logic applies to Matt 19:16–22: Christ cites many commandments that one must do in order to have eternal life, including the prohibitions against murder, adultery, theft, bearing false witness, and dishonoring one's parents. Christ does cite Lev 19:18 last, perhaps indicating that this summarizes the previous commandments, but then Christ's admonition to the rich young ruler to sell all that he has and follow Christ shows that there is still more he must "do" in order to gain eternal life. Christ's citation of these commandments functions as a representative sample of the whole law which one must do in order to inherit eternal life.[105]

The Active Obedience of Christ

The second view argues that Lev 18:5 refers to the active obedience of Christ.[106] Christ is the one who performs the righteousness of the law (10:5)

---

103. Again, Schreiner writes, "Given that Phil. 3:9 speaks negatively of 'righteousness from law,' it is extremely unlikely that the same phrase in Rom. 10:5 is being used positively" (*Romans*, 553).

104. Sprinkle argues that Luke 10:28 does not refer to Lev 18:5 ("Genesis 42:18," 193–205).

105. Also, the words in Matt 19:16–17 do not necessarily cite or allude to Lev 18:5. They connect doing the commandments with having eternal life (which may function as a clue to the current understanding in that time of the connection between the law and eternal life), but they do not utilize the wording of Lev 18:5.

106. Bandstra, *Law*, 103–4; Barth, *Dogmatics*, 245–46; Barth, *Shorter Commentary*, 127; Barth, *People of God*, 39; Cranfield, *Romans*, 2:521–22; Hendriksen, *Romans*, 343;

and provides righteousness for all who believe in him (10:6–8). This view posits a soft contrast between the righteous status Christ has by his perfect life of obedience (10:5) and the righteous status people have through faith in him (10:6–8).[107]

This view does appeal to a legitimate doctrine. Nevertheless, there does not appear to be a good reason to introduce Christ's active obedience at this point in the argument.[108] Paul's citation does not focus on a person but on the nature of legal righteousness (Μωϋσῆς γὰρ γράφει τὴν δικαιοσύνην τὴν ἐκ τοῦ νόμου). Within the citation, Paul retains the general terms ὁ ποιήσας and ἄνθρωπος, thus making a specific reference to Jesus unlikely.[109] A. J. Bandstra attempts to introduce Christ's obedience into the context here by noting the similarities between the descent and ascent motifs of Rom 10:6–8 and Christ's descent and ascent in Phil 2:7–10.[110] However, the context and language of the two passages are too dissimilar for this to succeed.[111]

Stowers, *Romans*, 308.

107. Cranfield, *Romans*, 2:521–22.

108. Moo, *Epistle to the Romans*, 647. Moo also notes that reading Lev 18:5 as a reference to active obedience would conflict with Paul's use of Lev 18:5 in Gal 3:12. While this is not impossible, it is highly unlikely in light of the common material between the two passages. Interpreters often discuss Gal 3:1–29 in connection with Rom 9:30—10:13. Some criticize this on the grounds that it supposedly mutes Rom 9:30—10:13 in favor of Gal 3:1–29. However, Moo's comment regarding the similar content between the two passages reminds interpreters that they ought to interpret them in the light of one another. One would not expect two passages written by the same author and addressing similar ideas to come to radically different conclusions. Toews claims that the wording of Lev 18:5 in Rom 10:5 is fundamentally altered from that of Lev 18:5 in Gal 3:12, and that such altered wording indicates that exegetes should assume a different meaning in Rom 10:5 ("Law," 253–54). However, the fundamentally altered wording is based on Toews decision to place the ὅτι after γράφει in the original wording of Rom 10:5. Even if we grant Toews decision on the text, it does not lead to the conclusion that exegetes should assume a different meaning. Both texts are discussing the nature of the law, and its relationship to works, righteousness, and faith.

109. Schreiner, *Romans*, 551.

110. Bandstra, *Law*, 103–4.

111. Schreiner, "Paul's View," 126; Seifrid, "Paul's Approach," 14. Schreiner also notes that Phil 3:9 is much more parallel to Rom 10:5 than Phil 2:7–10, and that interpreting Rom 10:5 in the light of Phil 3:9 would yield a much different interpretation than Bandstra suggests.

Jewish Legalism

The third view claims that Paul uses Lev 18:5 to represent the position of his legalistic opponents.[112] Willem VanGemeren writes, "Paul's citation from Moses (Lev. 18:5) is an illustration of how the Jews had mistakenly argued that justification came by keeping the law (v. 5)."[113] Paul does not think that Lev 18:5 actually encourages legalism, but he cites the verse because it has become something of a slogan among his Jewish opponents. Paul then uses another text (Deut 30:12–14 in Rom 10:6–8) to show that legalism cannot be true and is therefore an impossible interpretation of Lev 18:5.

This position avoids the charge that Paul is pitting Moses against Moses, or that he is arguing that the Old Testament teaches salvation by works. We have also seen that many intertestamental Jewish writings cited this text to promote the idea that obedience was a necessary precondition to obtaining eternal life. However, in this context, Paul gives no indication that he is citing a view contrary to his own.[114] He does not cite an idea based on Lev 18:5, but Lev 18:5 itself. In fact, Paul highlights *Moses* as the one speaking in Rom 10:5, not his legalistic opponents.[115]

Commanding Faith

The fourth view maintains that Paul reads Leviticus 18:5 as commanding faith.[116] The righteousness now given in Christ is the righteousness that

---

112. Keener, *Romans*, 125; VanGemeren, "Response," 281–84. This view was formerly held by Schreiner (see "Paul's View," 133–34 and *Romans*, 555–56). Schreiner now argues for the fifth view (see *40 Questions*, 62–63). Silva makes this argument with reference to the use of Lev 18:5 in Gal 3:12 ("New Testament Use," 159).

113. VanGemeren, "Response," 283–84.

114. Moo and Naselli, "Problem," 710.

115. Kaiser, "Leviticus 18:5," 27.

116. Avemarie, "Paul," 142–44; Badenas, *End*, 120–25; Bekken, *Word*, 169–70 (Bekken allows for a polyvalent reading of Lev 18:5 which would also affirm the legitimacy of the next view when the law is read in the sense of bare commandments [*Word*, 181–82]); Bring, "Paul," 49; Bultmann sees Rom 10:5 as describing a life that can be obtained if one can keep the law, but then describes that very pursuit as sinful (*Theology*, 259–69); Davies, *Faith*, 198; Fuller could also go under the first view for he views the obedience of faith both as the obedience which is faith and the obedience which produces faith (he argues throughout his book that the two concepts should not be separated, and that the consistent message of both testaments is that the law and the gospel command this obedience of faith [*Gospel*, 66–88]); we place him here due to the primacy of the obedience which is faith which most interpreters acknowledge; Flückiger, "Christus," 155; Hays, *Echoes*, 76–77; Humphrey, "Rhetoric," 142–43; Jewett, *Romans*, 625; Wagner, *Heralds*, 160–61; Wright, *Climax*, 244–45; Wright, *Romans*, 658–63.

Moses described in the law.[117] N. T. Wright writes, "Paul's point is that those who share Christian faith are in fact 'doing the law.'"[118] The citations from Deuteronomy 8:17a; 9:4a; 30:12–14 in Rom 10:6–8 further define the nature of the performance referred to in Rom 10:5: to believe in Christ is to do the law.[119]

This view challenges a traditional law-gospel framework for Rom 9:30—10:13.[120] Advocates of this view note that Paul does not condemn Israel for pursuing the law (9:31), but for pursuing it by works and not by faith (9:32). Paul does not think that the law commands perfect obedience in order to inherit eternal life. Such views are supposedly foreign to Paul and Israel who would have viewed eternal life as the gracious gift of God, and the law as a guide for one's life (and one that made provision for sin). This is not to say that advocates of this view argue that sinful people can perfectly obey God's law. Rather, they argue that God does not set perfect obedience before people as something they should attempt, even as a means to the end of their realizing their sinfulness and abandoning such a pursuit. They argue that the terms of God's covenant are always faith alone, and that these are the terms which the law commands. In fact, some argue that Paul could not criticize the Jews for seeking righteousness via obedience if that is what Lev 18:5 supposedly commands.[121] Instead, he critiques Israel for failing to see that Christ is the culmination of the law (9:33; 10:4), and that the law has always commanded faith (9:31–32a).

Despite the growing popularity of this view in recent years, it suffers from several weaknesses. First, it ignores Paul's frequent contrasts between righteousness by faith in Christ and righteousness by the works of the law (Rom 4:13–15; 9:30—10:13; Gal 3:10–12; Phil 3:6–9).[122] God's covenant with Israel was not established by the law but rather preceded the law (Rom 4:13; Gal 3:1–17). Therefore, the promise of salvation does not come through the law but rather through faith (Rom 4:14; Gal 4:18). The law brings wrath, for it highlights the reality of one's personal transgressions (Rom 4:15). Righteousness must come apart from the law (Gal 2:21; 3:21).

---

117. Bring, "Paul," 49.

118. Wright, *Romans*, 660.

119. Badenas, *Christ*, 123–25; Davies, *Faith*, 190; Wright, *Romans*, 658–64.

120. Moo, who opposes this fourth position, writes, "This theological 'law'/'gospel' antithesis is at the heart of this paragraph, as Paul contrasts the righteousness that is based on 'doing' the law (v. 5) with the righteousness that is based on faith (vv. 6–13)" (*Epistle to the Romans*, 644).

121. Badenas, *End*, 121; Davies, *Faith*, 194.

122. McCormick, "Active Obedience," 170–71; Meyer, *End*, 222–23; Moo, *Encountering*; Moo, *Epistle to the Romans*, 646; Sprinkle, *Law*, 171.

Second, the context of Rom 10:5 does not support the idea that the law commands faith. We freely admit that Paul does not fault Israel for pursuing the law (Rom 9:31). However, we challenge the idea that Paul thought of Israel's pursuit of the law as if it were disconnected from the pursuit of a right standing with God. As we have already argued, the point of the phrase νόμον δικαιοσύνης is to highlight the tight connection between the law and righteousness: to pursue the law is to pursue righteousness, and Paul criticizes Israel for doing this by works instead of by faith (9:32).

The critique continues in Rom 10:1–4. Israel needs salvation because, although they are zealous for God, they do not know God. They seek to establish their own righteousness by works instead of submitting to the righteousness of God by faith.[123] They ought to submit to the righteousness of God by faith because Christ ends every attempt to keep the law for a right standing with God. What follows in Rom 10:5 is Paul's attempt to prove part of the assertion of Rom 10:4, that is, that righteousness cannot come from the law.[124] It would not contribute to his case to cite a text that supposedly teaches that the law has demanded faith all along.[125]

Third, throughout this letter, Paul often highlights the commanding nature of the law, not in terms of ultimately commanding faith, but in terms of obedience to its precepts (Rom 2:13; 7:7; 13:9). Righteousness is promised for those who do the law (Rom 2:13), but no person can perfectly obey the law's commands (Rom 7:1–25; see also Gal 3:10–12, which also cites Lev 18:5). The law therefore highlights human transgression, and ultimately points to another righteousness, namely, the righteousness of faith (Rom 3:28; 5:12–21).[126] The law does ultimately bear witness to righteousness by faith, not because it commands faith, but because its commandments highlight the necessity of faith (Rom 3:19–22; see also Gal 3:1–29).

We can say that Israel on one level misunderstood the law: they misunderstood the law's ultimate purpose. This, however, is different from saying that Israel misunderstood what the law actually commanded. Israel

---

123. Schreiner argues that doing the commandments in Rom 10:5 is equivalent to attempting to establish one's own righteousness (10:3). Israel did not submit to the righteousness which comes from God (Rom 10:3), and instead attempted to establish a righteousness which comes from the law (Rom 10:5 ["Paul's View," 128]).

124. The citations from Deuteronomy in Rom 10:6–8 prove the other half of the assertion, namely, that Christ provides the righteousness people need.

125. Moo writes, "Faith and believing on the one hand and works and doing on the other are one of the most pervasive contrasts in the Pauline letters. For him to place them in a complementary relationship here would be for him to discard one of the most important building blocks in his theology" (*Epistle to the Romans*, 646).

126. Schreiner notes that Paul does speak positively of the law at times, but he never identifies righteousness as coming from the law ("Paul's View," 130).

understood that perfectly clearly: the law commands obedience. They did not, however, realize that those commandments are not an end in themselves, but a means to a further end, namely, that of faith in Christ.[127]

Therefore, Paul's critique of righteousness by the law is not simply a critique of a misunderstanding and misuse of the law.[128] God manifests his righteousness apart from the law (Rom 3:21). Life in the Spirit releases one from the bondage of the law (Rom 7:6). The law is a temporary guardian that operates until faith comes (Gal 3:22-25). The purpose of the law is to bring people to faith by commanding an obedience they cannot provide. For this reason, Paul says the law is not characterized by faith, but rather by works (Gal 3:10-12).[129]

Pursuing a Right Standing with God by Obeying the Law

The final view argues that Lev 18:5 represents the essence of the law, namely, that obedience leads to blessing.[130] Whether the focus is on Israel's proper

---

127. Paul's argument in Rom 9:30—10:13 is similar to the train of thought in Phil 3:1-14. Paul considered himself at one time to have adequately kept the law ("blameless," according to Phil 3:6), and so now does Israel (Rom 9:30-33). This consideration did not lead Paul to faith in Christ, as it is not now leading Israel to faith (Rom 10:1-4). Eventually, Paul had to discard his righteousness from the law in favor of the righteousness which comes by faith in Christ (Phil 3:7-9), and he encourages Israel to do the same (Rom 10:5-13).

128. Davies, *Faith*, 196-97; Fuller, "Paul," 35-37; Fuller, *Gospel*, 86-87. Schreiner helpfully notes that even if Paul were criticizing Israel for misunderstanding the law, he would still be faulting them for trying to establish their own righteousness by obeying the law, and that the wording of Rom 10:5 would very naturally lend itself to this concept ("Paul's View," 129).

129. "The law is not characterized by faith" is our gloss for ὁ δὲ νόμος οὐκ ἔστιν ἐκ πίστεως (Gal 3:12). According to BDAG, 297, one of the nuances of the preposition ἐκ is, "of the underlying rule or principle, *according to, in accordance with*."

130. Aageson, "Typology," 62-63; Achtemeier, *Romans*, 168-69; Barrett, *Romans*, 198; Bechtler, "Christ," 303-6; Bell, *Provoked*, 190; Bruce, *Romans*, 190-91; Byrne, *Romans*, 317; Calvin, *Romans*, 383-87; Dodd, *Romans*, 165; Estelle, "Leviticus 18:5," 139-42; Fitzmyer, *Romans*, 587; Gathercole, "Torah," 143; Getty, "Paul," 467-68; Gundry, "Inferiority," 208-9; Heil, *Paul's Letter to the Romans*, 112; Hodge, *Romans*, 304-5; Huby, *Romains*, 355-56; Hultgren, *Romans*, 386; Käsemann, *Romans*, 285; Keck, *Romans*, 251; Lagrange, *Romains*, 254; Kuss, *Römerbrief*, 755; Longenecker, *Eschatology*, 223-24; Luther, *Lectures on Romans*, 89; McCormick, "Active Obedience," 173-75; Meyer, *End of the Law*, 210-27; Michel, *Römer*, 327-28; Moo, *Epistle to the Romans*, 647-50; Murray, *Romans*, 2:150, 249-51; Nygren, *Romans*, 380; Rhyne, *Faith*, 105; Rosner, *Paul*, 71-72; Sanday and Headlam, *Romans*, 285-86; Schlatter, *Romans*, 213-14; Schreiner, *40 Questions*, 62-63; Seifrid, *Christ*, 120-22; Seifrid, "Paul's Approach," 15; Seifrid, "Romans," 655-56; Sprinkle, *Law*, 176; Stuhlmacher, *Romans*, 156; Thielman, *Plight*, 113-15; Venema, "Law," 224; Viard, *Romains*, 225; Vos, "Hermeneutische

response to the covenant, or to the necessity of perfect obedience for eternal life, Lev 18:5 emphasizes doing, and makes life contingent on performance.[131] For Paul, this emphasis on works is what characterizes the law (Rom 9:31; Gal 3:10–12).[132] Paul therefore cites this text as an example of the use of the law for righteousness which Christ ends.[133]

Paul contrasts this pursuit of righteousness via obedience (Rom 10:5) with the availability of righteousness by faith (Rom 10:6–8).[134] Since the law

---

Antinomie," 259; Waters, "Romans 10:5," 211–12, 237–38; Watson, *Hermeneutics*, 332; Wells and Zaspel, *New Covenant Theology*, 145–46; Westerholm, *Justification*, 21; Westerholm, *Perspectives*, 326–28; White and Beisner, "Covenant, Inheritance, and Typology," 162.

131. Not every interpreter in this section would argue that Lev 18:5 bears witness to the necessity of perfect obedience for eternal life, but would affirm that Paul uses Lev 18:5 to represent the nature of the law as commanding works. For example, Moo writes, "Paul does think that the law embodies, in its very nature, the principle that perfect obedience to it would confer eternal life (see 2:13 and 7:10). It may be this principle that Paul intends to enunciate here via the words of Lev. 18:5. However, we think that Paul's point is a more nuanced one. His purpose in quoting Lev. 18:5 is succinctly to summarize what for him is the essence of the law: blessing is contingent on obedience" (*Epistle to the Romans*, 648). So also Sprinkle: "We also find inadequate some of the more traditional views that understand Lev 18:5 as a legalistic formula or as demanding perfection. What is wrong with Leviticus is that it makes blessing contingent upon human behaviour" (*Law*, 189). We combine both positions under this one because both agree on the main idea behind Lev 18:5 and Paul's use of it: Lev 18:5 represents the unobtainable goal of salvation by works. We favor the view that Lev 18:5 bears witness to the necessity of perfect obedience for eternal life.

132. Seifrid notes Paul's alteration of the text from ποιήσας to ὁ ποιήσας, and suggests, "This generalizing of the text reflects Paul's interpretation of the passage as a summary of the entire law" ("Romans," 655). Paul can summarize the entire law with these words: do and you will live.

133. *Contra* Toews who claims that this view does not do justice to the γάρ at the beginning of Rom 10:5 ("Law," 252).

134. Cranfield argues that a contrast between 10:5 and 10:6–8 best explains the use of δέ in verse 6 (*Romans*, 2:520). Moo evaluates the evidence and notes the following: "First, γάρ . . . δέ is not a correlative pair in Greek, and it is artificial therefore to isolate places where they occur together as if they have a standard meaning. Second, however, even if the words are examined in this artificial combination, the results are just the reverse of what Howard and the others [such as Kaiser] claim. In Rom. 1–8, e.g., this sequence occurs 22 times: in three δέ is continuative (4:15; 7:8–9; 8:24); in four explanatory ("that is," "now"; 1:11–12; 2:1b–2; 6:7–8; 5:13); and in 15 contrastive (2:25; 5:7–8, 10–11, 16; 6:10, 23; 7:2, 14, 18b, 22–23; 8:5, 6, 13, 22–23, 24–25)" (*Epistle to the Romans*, 650n23). Moo's grammatical observations demonstrate that there is more driving the argument for contrast than the "law-gospel bias of modern interpreters," as Toews claims ("Law," 253). Dunn does not embrace a law-gospel framework, but still argues for an antithesis on grammatical grounds ("Righteousness," 218). Thielman also notes, "given the chronological proximity of Galatians to Romans, it is difficult to see why Paul's contrast of Lev. 18:5 with Hab. 2:4 in Gal. 3:10–12 should not be considered

focuses on doing, and since no man can do all that the law requires, such a pursuit must be discarded in favor of righteousness by faith.[135] This has been true throughout salvation history, and it constitutes Paul's main critique of contemporary Israelites: they seek to be justified by obedience to the law when they should seek righteousness through faith in Christ.[136] This contrast between believing and doing occurs repeatedly throughout Rom 9:30—10:13 (9:30-32; 10:3-4; 10:5-8; see also the emphasis on faith in 10:9-13).[137]

Critics of this view charge that if Moses taught blessing via obedience (or salvation by perfect obedience), then he could have not condemned Israel for pursuing it.[138] In response, we argue that although the law embodied the principle that obedience leads to blessing, Israel had a responsibility to understand the law in light of redemptive history as a whole. In other words, if Abraham was justified by faith prior to the giving of the law, then Israel ought to have been able to discern that the law was not advocating a new pathway to justification. Rather, the law was serving a limited purpose: highlighting human sin in order to emphasize the necessity of salvation by faith (Rom 5:13-14; Gal 3:23-25). This, in fact, is exactly how Paul interprets redemptive history in Rom 4:1-25 and Gal 3:1-29.[139]

---

analogous to what Paul says here" (*Plight*, 113n94).

135. Schreiner notes that Paul does not refer directly to human inability in this section because he has already established its reality in 1:18—3:20 (and we would argue in 7:1-25 as well). Israel does not err when they seek to obey God (God commands obedience); they err when they base their right standing before God on their obedience to God's commandments ("Paul's View," 131).

136. Moo writes, "Throughout salvation history, faith and doing, 'gospel' and 'law' have run along side-by-side. Each is important in our relationship with God. But, as it is fatal to ignore one or the other, it is equally fatal to mix them or to use them for the wrong ends. The OT Israelite who sought to base his or her relationship with God on the law rather than on God's gracious election in and through the Abrahamic promise arrangement made this mistake. Similarly, Paul suggests, many Jews in his day are making the same mistake: concentrating on the law to the exclusion of God's gracious provision in Christ" (*Epistle to the Romans*, 649-50).

137. Schreiner, "Paul's View," 129.

138. E.g., Badenas, *End*, 121; Davies, *Faith*, 194. Fuller, *Gospel*, 77, charges the law-gospel paradigm with giving the law two meanings.

139. Carson, "Mystery," 411-12. This also answers the charge that a contrast between Rom 10:5 and 10:6-8 means that Paul is citing Moses against Moses. Rather, Paul is discerning two principles within the OT Scriptures. The first principle is that of faith, exemplified by the patriarch Abraham. The second principle is that of works, embodied in the Mosaic covenant. These two principles do not result in a contradictory message, because the second principle is supposed to be subordinated to the first. The principle of works functions to highlight the necessity of faith. The second leads to the first. As we will see in our exposition of Rom 10:6-8, the gospel message exemplifies the principle of faith. The law has one meaning, and communicates that meaning with a particular

CONCLUSION

In his ongoing critique of Israel's pursuit of righteousness by faith, Paul cites Lev 18:5 as his first proof that Christ ends using the law to establish one's righteousness. On one level, Lev 18:5 teaches that Israel will continue to enjoy God's blessings if they obey the law's commands. On another level, that principle that obedience leads to blessing bears witness to the timeless theological truth that perfect obedience leads to eternal life. The use of Lev 18:5 within the OT itself and intertestamental Judaism bears witness to the legitimacy of these multiple referents for Lev 18:5. The verse therefore becomes a powerful proof text for Paul to utilize in his argument that contemporary Israelites should cease trying to keep the law in order to earn a right standing with God and instead place their trust in Christ. Christ ends using the law to establish one's righteousness because the law only gives righteousness to those who perfectly obey it.

---

soteriological purpose.

Chapter 5

Romans 10:6–8

INTRODUCTION

Romans 10:4 declares that Christ ends using the law to obtain a right standing with God for all who believe. Paul's statement there contains both a positive and a negative element. Negatively, Christ ends using the law to obtain a right standing with God. Positively, the person who would attempt to keep the law for a right standing with God should instead exercise faith in Jesus Christ. Faith alone brings one into a state of salvation and obtains the righteousness of God (Rom 10:1–3).

Paul uses the OT in Rom 10:5–8 to prove both elements in the theological assertion of Rom 10:4.[1] Paul cites Lev 18:5 in Rom 10:5 to demonstrate the negative assertion. Lev 18:5 describes the righteousness of the law: the person who *does* the commandments will live. However, as Lev 18:5 also indicates, and as its use throughout the OT demonstrates, no one can do what the law demands. Therefore, all attempts to use the law to establish a right standing before God are futile and must come to an end.

Since salvation cannot come by the law, salvation must come through faith in Christ. Paul therefore cites Deut 8:17a; 9:4a; and 30:12–14 in Rom 10:6–8 to develop the positive side of Rom 10:4, namely, that Christ brings righteousness to those who believe.[2] While Lev 18:5 describes the righ-

---

1. Käsemann, *Romans*, 275; Moo, *Epistle to the Romans*, 647.
2. Moo, "Paul's Reading," 401; Rhyne, *Faith*, 110–11; Seifrid, "Paul's Approach," 16.

teousness of the law, Deut 8:17a; 9:4a; and 30:12–14 describe the righteousness of faith.[3]

However, while Paul's purpose in citing the OT in Rom 10:6–8 may be clear, his understanding and interpretation of the verses are not, particularly with reference to the use of Deut 30:12–14.[4] Paul's use of Deut 8:17a; 9:4a is not subject to much dispute: the short phrase[5] introduces what one must not say in order to be righteous by faith.[6] Paul's use of Deut 30:12–14 is much more complex. In its original context, Deut 30:12–14 appears to make a statement regarding Israel's ability to obey the law: God has brought the commandment near to them, even put it within them, and they can obey it. Paul, however, removes all references to the law and doing from his citation, and interprets them as a reference to Christ and the gospel. Furthermore, Paul employs the citation not as a reference to obeying the law, but as a description of the righteousness that comes by faith. Paul's hermeneutic demands explanation, as well as his rationale for contrasting two OT citations.

This chapter therefore examines Paul's use of Deut 8:17a; 9:4a; 30:12–14 in Rom 10:6–8. We argue that Paul cites these passages as a description (and proof) of righteousness by faith because they articulate the same principle as the gospel: just as the Israelites in the OT did not need to do any works to find God's commandment (he had brought it near to them so that they could do it), so there is no need for Paul's contemporary Israelites to do any works to find Christ: they ought to seek a right standing with God by faith in Christ. To prove this thesis, we first examine the meaning of the Deuteronomic passages within their original contexts. Second, we trace the use of Deut 30:12–14 within intertestamental literature. Third, we compare Paul's citations with the MT and LXX, and note any significant alterations or textual variants. Finally, we evaluate the many theories of how Paul interprets Deut 8:17a, 9:4a, and 30:12–14, and the theological point he is making.

---

3. The previous chapter noted the grammatical evidence for an adversative reading of δὲ in Rom 10:6. In addition, the interpretation of Lev 18:5 in Rom 10:5 posited there essentially demands it. The interpretation of Rom 10:6–8 presented in this chapter confirms the contrast.

4. Moo refers to "the tempest that rages over his [Paul's] use of language from Deut 30:11–14 in Rom 10:6–8" ("Paul's Reading," 400). Bock calls it "an exegetical minefield" ("Single Meaning," 132).

5. The phrase μὴ εἴπῃς ἐν τῇ καρδίᾳ σου is identical in Deut 8:17a; 9:4a and cited once in Rom 10:6a.

6. We still examine these verses in their original context in order to justify this assertion.

DEUTERONOMY 8:17A, 9:4A, AND 30:12-14 WITHIN THEIR ORIGINAL CONTEXTS

We first examine the meaning of Deut 8:18a; 9:4a; and 30:12-14 within their original contexts. Deuteronomy is the book of the covenant (Deut 29:21; 31:26),[7] and recounts the second giving of the law to the children of Israel.[8] Moses' speeches structure the book: his first speech, the historical prologue, recounts Israel's history between Sinai and the present day (Deut 1-4); his second speech gives the general (Deut 5-11) and specific stipulations of the covenant (Deut 12-26); his third speech outlines the blessings and curses of the covenant, and exhorts Israel to keep the covenant (Deut 27-30); the final chapters highlight the succession of leadership from Moses to Joshua (Deut 31-34).[9] Throughout the book, Moses aims to move the people to obedience and commitment to the Lord and his covenant.[10]

Deuteronomy 8:17a; 9:4a

Deut 8:17a and 9:4a occur in the second speech of Deuteronomy. Both verses warn the people of Israel against presuming that they have done or can do anything to secure God's blessing. Deut 8:17 reads, "and you say in your heart, my power and the strength of my hand have gotten me this wealth." The statement comes in a series of warnings to Israel to beware lest they forget the Lord when they enter the promised land and begin to enjoy its blessings (Deut 8:11-18). Many translations therefore translate the first phrase of Deut 8:17 (ואמרת בלבבך) with the "beware lest" language

---

7. On the relationship between Deuteronomy and the Near Eastern vassal treaty, see Craigie, *Deuteronomy*, 22-24.

8. The title Deuteronomy literally means "second law." It is based on the Greek translation of משנה התורה in Deut 17:18 as δευτερονόμιον, which passed into the Latin Vulgate as Deuteronomium. However, Tigay suggests that the title Deuteronomy stems from a misunderstanding of the phrase in Deuteronomy 17:18. The Hebrew phrase actually means "a copy of the Teaching." Nevertheless, Tigay grants that Deuteronomy is an apt designation for the book (*Deuteronomy*, xi). Merrill concurs with this judgment, and notes that Deuteronomy is not merely a second giving of the law, but a development of the covenant message first given to Moses at Sinai forty years earlier (*Deuteronomy*, 22). Craigie notes that the Hebrew title אלה הדברים more accurately describes the content of the book, which focuses on Moses' final words addressed to Israel before his death and their entrance into the promised land (Deut 34:1-12 [*Deuteronomy*, 17]).

9. See the outlines in Craigie, *Deuteronomy*, 67-69, and Dennis, *ESV Study Bible*, 328-29.

10. Craigie, *Deuteronomy*, 17.

of 8:11–12 (or some form thereof).[11] Israel must not presume that their own power has procured for them the divine blessing of houses, flocks, and wealth that Israel will enjoy in Canaan.

The warning continues in Deut 9:1–6. Here the focus is on YHWH driving out the Canaanites, and Israel is commanded, "Do not say in your heart, when the LORD your God has driven them out before you, 'My righteousness caused the LORD to bring me in to possess this land'; it is the wickedness of these nations that causes the Lord to drive them out before you." Two reasons are given for Israel's success: divine favor and Canaanite wickedness.[12] Israel must not think that their righteousness has secured the Lord's blessing.[13] On the contrary, God describes Israel as a "stiff-necked people" (9:6), a description that reminds them of their own wickedness that forfeits God's blessings.[14] These two references constitute a strong warning against presuming that one's obedience has merited God's blessing.

Deuteronomy 30:12–14

Deut 30:12–14 occurs within Moses' third speech, which outlines the blessings and curses of the covenant (Deut 27–30). Deut 29:1 highlights the fact that the content of these chapters is part of the renewal of the Mosaic covenant with Israel in Moab. Towards the end of Deut 29, Moses warns Israel, "Beware, lest there be any man or woman, or tribe or clan whose heart turns away this day from YHWH your God" (29:18 [29:17 MT]). Such a person will suffer the curse of the covenant (29:19–21). In addition, should Israel as a whole turn away from the Lord, then they will suffer exile and the desolation of their land (29:22–28). Despite the fact that God has revealed to Israel everything they need to know in order to obey God (Deut 29:29, perhaps anticipating 30:11–14), the harbinger of future disobedience permeates the entire chapter.

Deut 30, however, opens with a note of hope. When the curses of the covenant come upon Israel, and they find themselves in a foreign land, then they will return to YHWH and obey him with all their heart and soul (Deut 30:1–2). When that happens, God will have compassion on Israel

---

11. ESV, RSV read "Beware lest." NASB reads "Otherwise." NIV reads "You may say."

12. Craigie, *Deuteronomy*, 189, 193–94; Kalland, "Deuteronomy," 76, 78; Moo, *Epistle to the Romans*, 651.

13. Tigay suggests that הצדקה in 9:4 may refer specifically to loyalty or devotion, especially in light of the fact that the rest of the chapter is a demonstration of Israel's lack of loyalty (see vv. 7, 24 [*Deuteronomy*, 97]).

14. Craigie, *Deuteronomy*, 193–94.

and restore them to their homeland (Deut 30:3-5). He will circumcise Israel's heart, and they will love him (Deut 30:6). He will curse Israel's enemies and prosper Israel when they obey him with all their heart and soul (Deut 30:7-10).

Moses begins his final admonition by highlighting the nearness of God's word and Israel's ability to obey it (Deut 30:11-14). The first sentence expresses the main thought of the paragraph: "For this commandment which I command you today is not too difficult for you nor is it distant" (30:11).[15] The next two verses explain why the commandment is not too difficult or distant: "It is not in the heavens so that you have to say, 'Who will go up into the heavens for us and get the commandment for us so that we can hear and do it?' And it is not across the sea so that you have to say, 'Who will cross the sea for us and take it for us so that we can hear and do it?'" (30:12-13) The final sentence reiterates the main idea and gives another reason why the two previous questions are unnecessary: "Because the word is near you, in your mouth and in your heart so that you can do it" (30:14). As a whole, the paragraph tells Israel that that the covenant is not too difficult for them to obey. There is no need for any additional revelation obtained by superhuman quests into heaven or across the sea.[16] Rather, God has brought his word near to Israel: it is in their mouth and in their heart so that they can obey it. The chapter concludes by calling Israel to a decision: they must choose life or death, the blessing or the curse (30:15-20).[17]

The main interpretive question of Deut 30:11-14 concerns whether this paragraph highlights conditions that were true as Israel prepared to enter the promised land (Deut 29:29), or whether it referred to a future time after Israel returned from exile (Deut 30:1-10). Some argue that the future orientation of Deut 30:1-10 continues into 30:11-14.[18] In favor of a

---

15. Several scholars note that the commandment here refers to the covenant which God is (re)making with Israel (cf. 6:1 [Craigie, *Deuteronomy*, 364; Hall, *Deuteronomy*, 447; Kalland, "Deuteronomy," 189; Keil and Delitzsch, *Commentary*, 1:977; Rad, *Deuteronomy*, 184]).

16. Although crossing the sea may not seem so extraordinary to modern-day readers, Hall observes, "In Mesopotamian literature crossing the sea was seen as an especially difficult task and only the gods or heroes could do it. In the Gilgamesh Epic, Gilgamesh had to go far beyond the sea in search for life" (*Deuteronomy*, 447n14). So also Craigie, *Deuteronomy*, 365.

17. Craigie, *Deuteronomy*, 361.

18. Barker, "Deuteronomy," 86-87; Barker, *Triumph*, 182-93; Estelle, "Leviticus 18:5," 127; McConville, *Deuteronomy*, 429; McConville, *Grace*, 138; Millar, *Deuteronomy*, 176; Ridderbos, *Deuteronomy*, 271; Sailhamer, *Pentateuch*, 473-74; Strickland, "Inauguration," 250; Thielman, *Plight*, 113-14; Wright, *Romans*, 659-60. Brueggemann suggests the context is post-exilic as well, but not for prophetic reasons (*Deuteronomy*, 267-68).

future reference, in Deut 30:6, Moses identifies heart circumcision as one of the blessings that will accompany Israel's return from exile. The circumcision of the heart results in Israel obeying the voice of YHWH and keeping his commandments (Deut 30:8). When Moses states in Deut 30:14 that the word is in their heart, this position argues that he must be referring to that future generation which has experienced the promise of Deut 30:6.[19] Furthermore, Deut 30:11–14 is verbless, and the context must supply the tense of the clauses. The כי at the beginning of Deut 30:11 indicates that 30:11–14 is predicated on 30:1–10 and therefore has a future orientation.[20]

Others argue that while Deut 30:1–10 does look ahead to a future day, the focus of Deut 30:11–14 shifts back to Israel's present circumstances.[21] In favor of this present reference, Moses uses the word "today" to describe the time frame of the word's accessibility: "this commandment which I command you *today*" (Deut 30:11); "I have set before you *today* life and good, death and evil" (Deut 30:15, emphasis supplied). Deut 30:15 initiates the final admonition of the chapter, and is addressing Israel on the plains of Moab.[22] The use of "today" in Deut 30:11 therefore indicates that the same audience is in view.[23] One also notes the similarity between the nearness of the word and the ability to obey it in Deut 30:11–14, and the emphasis on present revelation and ability in Deut 29:29: "the hidden things belong to YHWH our God, but the revealed things belong to us and our descendants

---

19. Coxhead, "Dueteronomy 30:11–14," 308–9; McConville, *Deuteronomy*, 429. Wright states that Deut 30 "presumes that Israel has been sent into exile and is now going to turn to YHWH from the heart, and proceeds to explain what it really means to 'do' the law and so to 'live'" (*Romans*, 659).

20. Barker, *Triumph*, 185–86; Coxhead, "Deuteronomy 30:11–14," 306–8. Philo cites Deut 30:10–13 in *Praem*. 79–80 as a single unit.

21. Bock, "Single Meaning," 133–34; Craigie, *Deuteronomy*, 364; Kalland, "Deuteronomy," 189; Merrill, *Deuteronomy*, 390; Moo, *Epistle to the Romans*, 652; Thompson, *Deuteronomy*, 286; Tigay, *Deuteronomy*, 285. Driver opposes the idea that 30:11–14 is based on the future contingency on 30:10, but also finds it highlight unlikely that 30:11–14 was originally the sequel of 30:1–10 (*Deuteronomy*, 330–31).

22. Moses is putting the choice to obey or disobey before the children of Israel in the concluding verses 30:15–20. Furthermore, "today" occurs again in 30:16, and "this day" occurs twice in 30:18–19.

23. Strickland argues that Deut 30:11 refers to a commandment given in the present but fulfilled in the future. He bases this conclusion on a comparison with Deut 30:8, where a contrast is made between a present commandment and future obedience ("Inauguration," 251). However, the strength of the comparison is its weakness: Deut 30:8 clearly distinguishes between the commandment being given in the present and fulfilled in the future ("you shall again obey the voice of the LORD and keep all his commandments that I command you today" [ESV]; see also 30:2). Deut 30:11 makes no such distinction.

after us, so that we can do all the words of this law."²⁴ Deut 30:11–14 appears to continue the theme of Deut 29:29 (not 30:1–10) and speaks to Israel as they stand ready to enter the promised land. God's revelation of his word leaves them without excuse. He has made the terms of the covenant clear, and now Israel must fulfill them.

Moses' use of the metaphor of heart circumcision throughout Deuteronomy also favors the second position. While Deut 30:6 does anticipate a future time when God will circumcise the hearts of his people, the present necessity of such an inward work is emphasized in Deut 10:16. There Moses commands the people, "Circumcise the foreskin of your heart, and do not stiffen your necks any longer." The metaphor highlights the necessity of an inward change which must take place within God's covenant people.²⁵ When this heart circumcision takes place, then a person is no longer stiff-necked.²⁶ In light of Deut 30:8, circumcising the heart also leads to obeying YHWH's commandments, highlighting the connection between heart circumcision and the inward presence of the word. This connection is later emphasized by the prophets in their description of the New Covenant, where they use the language of God putting and writing his law in the hearts of his people (Jer 4:4; 31:31–34; Ezek 36:26–27).²⁷ When one experiences heart circumcision, then the word is present there too.²⁸

---

24. Coxhead attempts to defer the nearness of the Torah to a future time by arguing that Moses hints at a modification of Torah. In other words, since Deuteronomy favors the idea that the law is presently near, the only way to explain Deut 30:12–13 is to suppose that another Torah is coming that will be near in the future ("Deuteronomy 3:11–14," 310). This logic assumes a future orientation rather than proving one (this argument is presented as the third proof for the future orientation of Deut 30:11–14). Also, Coxhead's explanation of the future Torah as Christ is not consistent with Christ's own teaching. In Matt 5:17–20, Christ speaks of fulfilling the Law and the Prophets, not being the law. The NT speaks of the law of Christ (1 Cor 9:21; Gal 6:2), but does not equate the law with Christ.

25. Craigie, *Deuteronomy*, 205. Miller notes, "History by this time has indicated that such obedience cannot come without God's gift of a heart to know and obey" (*Deuteronomy*, 213).

26. Ridderbos describes heart circumcision as "the removal of the wrong disposition that turned away from God" (*Deuteronomy*, 270). See also Craigie, *Deuteronomy*, 205.

27. Ps 119:11 indicates that having the word in one's heart is the same as having the law in one's heart.

28. Heart circumcision is the biblical metaphor for regeneration (see McCune, *Systematic*, 51). John 3:3 uses the metaphor of being "born again" or "born from above" (γεννηθῇ ἄνωθεν). John 3:5 refers to being born "from water and spirit" (ἐξ ὕδατος καὶ πνεύματος), which likely refers to God's promise in Ezek 36:25–27 to wash Israel with pure water and put a new spirit within them (so Carson, *John*, 195). While Deut 10:16 does command Israel to circumcise their hearts, we do not press this language to mean that Israel was able to regenerate themselves. Rather, they should seek the inward

When Moses states that the word is in Israel's heart (Deut 30:14), this does not mean that Deut 30:11-14 anticipates the future, but rather that the present generation of Israelites has obeyed the commandment of Deut 10:16.[29] Each Israelite and each generation of Israelites must submit to the covenant and receive heart circumcision.[30] Those who do not receive it disobey God and receive his judgment.[31] The promise of the future is that God will circumcise their hearts again when they return to him with all their hearts (Deut 30:1-10).[32] The focus of Deut 30:11-14 is on the present generation which is submitting to the covenant and preparing to enter the promised land.

---

change that God accomplishes by his Word and Spirit. Like the commands to believe in the NT, the ability to do so presumes the inward work of God that makes one willing and able to believe. Bock and Barker argue that Deut 10:16 and 30:6 refer to different things because in Deut 10:16 God calls for a circumcised heart whereas in Deut 30:6 he promises to provide one ("Single Meaning," 133n27 and *Triumph*, 163-64, respectively). However, this ignores the larger theological picture articulated above. That God commands something does not preclude the idea that God must also still provide the ability to perform it.

29. Harrison, commenting on Deut 30:11-14, notes, "the passage presupposed an attitude of loving obedience (Deut 30:6-10) rather than a legalistic attempt to attain righteousness" ("Romans," 111). Fuller argues that Deut 30:11-14 refers to the present generation, but that the audience is unregenerate (*Gospel*, 67-68). We would argue that the language of the word being in the heart indicates that they must be regenerate. The language of Deut 29:4 ("to this day the LORD has not given you a heart to understand or eyes to see or ears to hear" [ESV]) does not refer to unregenerate hearts, but hearts that have not fully realized just how gracious God has been to Israel (so Kalland, "Deuteronomy," 179).

30. Notice how Deut 29:18-28 moves seamlessly between language addressing individuals (29:18-21) and language addressing the people as a whole (29:22-28).

31. Keil and Delitzsch note, "however near the law had thus been brought to man, sin had so estranged the human heart from the word of God, that doing and keeping the law had become invariably difficult, and in fact impossible; so that the declaration, 'the word is in thy heart,' only attains its full realization through the preaching of the gospel of the grace of God, and the righteousness that is by faith" (*Commentary*, 1:977).

32. Again we note that the promise that God will circumcise the hearts of his people in the future does not imply that they are capable of circumcising their own hearts in the present. The command to circumcise one's heart means that one should seek YHWH for an internal transformation, and is functionally a command to exercise repentance and faith. Like the command to love YHWH (Deut 6:5), it is rooted in the prior love of YHWH for his people (Deut 7:7-8). Keener notes that Paul's expectation regarding the New Covenant is not that regeneration will suddenly be available in the future, but that it will occur on a widespread scale (Jer 31:33 [*Romans*, 126]). Christensen notes similarity between the Mosaic and New Covenants when he writes, "In one sense, then, the 'new covenant' Jeremiah envisioned (Jer 31:31-34) was a return to the original intention of the covenant relationship between God and his people as expressed in Deuteronomy" (*Deuteronomy 21:10-34:12*, 744).

Conclusion

Deut 8:17a; 9:4a; 30:12–14 address the present generation of Israelites under Moses who are preparing to enter the promised land. Moses warns this generation that they must not presume that their power and virtue have merited them the blessings of a second attempt to enter the promised land (Deut 8:17a; 9:4a). They are naturally a stiff-necked people and need an inward change (heart circumcision) in order to obey God (Deut 9:6; 10:16). However, the current generation shows evidence that they have received this inward work of God and are prepared to obey his law (Deut 30:11–14). Divine grace has brought the commandment to God's people and enabled them to obey it.

This language of Israel's ability to obey the law does not contradict Paul's earlier statements about Israel's inability to earn righteousness by the law. As noted in the examination of Lev 18:5, the law performs multiple functions. On one level, the law of God bears witness to the necessity of perfect obedience which no human can perform; it functions to make people aware of their sin and need of righteousness by faith. However, the law also functions as a guide for God's covenant people to observe in response to his saving grace. Moses highlights this second element here: for those Israelites who are prepared to enter the promised land and have received heart circumcision, the law is something which they can and must obey in response to God's mercy.[33] God has brought the commandment to them, he has written it in their heart, and now they must do it.

THE USE OF DEUTERONOMY 30:12–14 IN INTERTESTAMENTAL LITERATURE

In his study of Paul's use of Deuteronomy 30:12–14 in Rom 10:6–8, N. T. Wright points out the importance of thinking one's way into a world of thought that Paul took for granted.[34] Such effort guards against assuming that ancient writers meant one thing with their words when they in fact meant something completely different. Studies on the use of the OT in the NT examine the intertestamental use of the texts in question in order to accomplish that very task. With reference to Paul's citations from Deuteronomy, the first two references (8:17a; 9:4a) do not appear to have attracted much use in intertestamental Judaism.[35] On the other hand, Deut 30:12–14

---

33. Hall, *Deuteronomy*, 448.
34. Wright, *Romans*, 659.
35. Strack and Billerbeck cite no references (*Kommentar*, 3:278–82), nor does

has a rich history of interpretation. Bock claims that within Judaism the images of Deut 30:12-14 "became almost proverbial in force."³⁶ Understanding how the Jews of Paul's day read Deut 30:12-14 helps illuminate how Paul himself utilized it.³⁷

Seifrid ("Romans," 657). The language of Deut 9:4a does appear in *T. Mos.* 12:8 where Moses tells Joshua, "it is not on account of the piety of this people that you will drive out the nations" (see Charlesworth, *Old Testament Pseudepigrapha*, 1:934). The ideas are parallel in that Deut 9:4a forbids Israel from supposing that their own piety has earned them the promised land, and *T. Mos.* 12:8 directly state's that Israel's piety has not earned them the promised land. The occurrence in *T. Mos.* 12:8 indicates the appropriateness of our reading of Deut 9:4a in context.

36. Bock, "Single Meaning," 134.

37. Some echoes of the language of Deut 30:12-14 exist within the OT, but enough differences exist to conclude that they are not citations. For example, Job 28:12-14 reads, "But where can wisdom be found? Where does understanding dwell? No mortal comprehends its worth; it cannot be found in the land of the living. The deep says, "It is not in me"; the sea says, "It is not with me" (NIV). However, Job refers to wisdom, not Torah, and highlights human inability to obtain wisdom rather than divine revelation of the commandment. Likewise, Prov 30:3-4 refers to going up to heaven and coming down in order to obtain wisdom, but again the difference is between Torah and Wisdom, and Prov 30:4 does not refer to crossing the sea, or make direct reference to divine revelation (though Prov 30:5-6 possibly does). Suggs cites these Proverbs texts as evidence for Paul's Christ=Wisdom=Torah paradigm, which he uses to explain Paul's use of Deut 30:12-14 in Rom 10:6-8 ("Word," 305-6). Regardless of the accuracy of Sugg's paradigm, and even if conceptual overlap between Wisdom and Torah existed when these Proverbs texts were written, they still do not constitute a direct citation of Deut 30:12-14.

Furthermore, some references in intertestamental literature contain an ascent and descent theme, but this is not enough to warrant a citation of Deut 30:12-14. For example, Wis 16:13 reads, "For thou hast power over life and death; thou dost lead men down to the gates of Hades and back again" (RSV). Jub 24:31 refers to going up to heaven and down to Sheol, but that imagery resembles Ps 139:8 more than Deut 30:12-14. Therefore, we limit our focus to those passages that contain the actual wording of Deut 30:12-14.

The Rabbinical material contains many references to Deut 30:12-14 (see Str-B, 3:279-82). Seifrid surveys the Rabbinical literature and highlights a number of uses of the passage: proof that Torah's revelation is complete; exhortations to study Torah; Torah is available and comprehensible; description of an impossible task ("Paul's Approach," 19-20). However, these references date to the post-Pauline period and cannot inform us of how Paul used the text. The same can be said of the possible allusion to Deut 30:12-14 in *Gos. Thom.* 3: "Jesus said, 'If those who lead you say to you, 'See, the kingdom is in the sky,' then the birds of the sky will precede you. If they say to you, 'It is in the sea,' then the fish will precede you. Rather, the kingdom is inside of you, and it is outside of you. When you come to know yourselves, then you will become known" (Robinson, *Nag Hammadi*, 126). Later material does not likely reveal what informed prior exegesis. See Mohrmann for parallels in Ancient Near Eastern literature ("Semantic Collisions," 143-44).

Apocrypha and Pseudepigrapha

Several books in the Apocrypha and Pseudepigrapha use the language of Deut 30:12-14. Baruch 3:9-4:4 exalts the importance of wisdom, and contains two admonitions to Israel to seek wisdom (3:9, 14). The passage describes the giants of old who "perished because they had no wisdom" (3:28 [RSV]). The next verses then employ Deut 30:12-13 to describe human inability to obtain divine wisdom: "Who has gone up into heaven, and taken her, and brought her down from the clouds? Who has gone over the sea, and found her, and will buy her for pure gold?" (3:29-30 [RSV]) However, while humans have no ability or interest to obtain this wisdom on their own (3:31), God does (3:32-35), and has revealed it to Israel: "He found the whole way to knowledge, and gave her to Jacob his servant and to Israel whom he loved. Afterward she appeared upon earth and lived among men" (3:36-37 [RSV]). Baruch 4:1 then indicates that God has revealed his wisdom by means of his law: "She [wisdom] is the book of the commandments of God, and the law that endures forever. All who hold her fast will live, and those who forsake her will die" (4:1 [RSV]).[38]

Sirach 1:3; 24:5-6 contain allusions to Deut 30:12-13 that are almost so weak as not to warrant inclusion in our examination. We highlight them because of the connection the author makes between the sea and the abyss, a connection that seems to have informed Paul's use of Deut 30:13. Sir 1:3 reads, "The height of heaven, the breadth of the earth, the abyss, and wisdom—who can search them out?" (RSV). Likewise, Sir 24:5-6 reads, "Alone I have made the circuit of the vault of heaven and have walked in the depths of the abyss. In the waves of the sea, in the whole earth, and in every people and nation I have gotten a possession." When Paul cites Deut 30:13, he replaces the reference to the sea with a reference to the abyss. These texts indicate that there was a conceptual overlap between the abyss and the sea, and thus Paul makes a legitimate substitution.[39]

The language of Deut 30:12-13 makes a stronger appearance in 4 Ezra 4:7-8. The larger discussion in 4 Ezra 4:1-12 resembles the conclusion of Job where Job is forced to confess that humans cannot entirely comprehend

---

38. Notice the similarity of Bar 4:1 with Lev 18:5: those who hold fast to the law will live. According to Suggs, Baruch makes the crucial link in defining Wisdom in terms of Law ("Word," 307-9). However, Deut 30:12-14 is reflected in many intertestamental texts, and Paul's citation differs enough from Baruch to doubt whether it lies behind Rom 10:6-8 (see Seifrid, "Paul's Approach," 22-23; Toews, "Law," 293). Badenas "The key phrase both in Romans and in Deuteronomy, namely, 'the Word is near', is lacking in Baruch" (*Christ*, 127). Furthermore, Rom 10:8 does not equate the Word/Commandment with Christ, but with the Gospel (Moo, *Epistle to the Romans*, 653n35).

39. For more on this substitution, see the analysis below of *Targum Neofiti*.

God's ways (Job 38–40). When Ezra cannot tell the angel Uriel the weight of fire, measure wind, or bring back the past, Uriel responds, "If I had asked you, 'How many dwellings are in the heart of the sea, or how many streams are at the source of the deep, or how many streams are above the firmament, or which are the exits of hell, or which are the entrances of Paradise?' perhaps you would have said to me, 'I never went down into the deep, nor as yet into hell, neither did I ever ascend into heaven.'"[40] Uriel employs the language of Deut 30:12–13 as a point of comparison: if you cannot explore the extremities of God's creation, then you cannot comprehend God. The language highlights human inability to understand God's ways.

The use of Deut 30:12–13 in the Apocrypha and Pseudepigrapha consistently highlights human inability to discern God's ways. Deut 30:12–14 may itself imply this: God has brought his law near to man because man could never obtain it (cf. Deut 29:29). However, the key verse that highlights God bringing his law to man (Deut 30:14) is absent from the references. While Baruch 3:36–4:1 does emphasize divine revelation of wisdom, it interestingly does not employ the language of Deut 30:14. Therefore, the main contribution of the Apocrypha and Pseudepigrapha is their emphasis on human inability to reach God.[41]

Philo

Philo cites Deut 30:12–14 in four of his works: *On the Virtues* (*De Virtutibus*), *On Rewards and Punishments* (*De Praemiis et Poenis*), *On the Posterity of Cain* (*De Posteritati Caini*), and *On the Change of Names* (*De Mutatione Nomium*).[42] *Virt.* 183 reads, "Admirable indeed too the admonitions to repentance, in which we are taught to refit our life from its present misfit into a better and changed condition. He tells us that the thing is not overgreat nor very distant, neither in the ether far above nor at the ends of the earth, nor beyond the great sea, that we should be unable to receive it, but

---

40. Charlesworth, *Old Testament Pseudepigrapha*, 1:529–30.

41. *Contra* Wright who claims that Jews of the Second Temple period read Deut 30 in terms of "the new obedience which brings new life" (*Romans*, 659n377). That characterization does not fit the literature surveyed here (although Wright cites some of the same texts). This theme will emerge somewhat in Philo, and perhaps 4QMMT, but it was not the only approach to the text. Wright has painted with too broad of a brush.

42. For a monograph devoted exclusively to the study of the use of Deut 30:11–14 within the first two of these passages, see Bekken, *Word*. The third and fourth passages (*Post.* 84–85 and *Mut.* 236–37) use the passage in a more general manner, or illustratively of the threefold nature of good. We focus on the first two passages here.

very near, residing in three parts of our being, mouth, heart and hands."[43] The reference to Deut 30:12–14 is clear, and emphasizes the necessity and even ease of conversion. Bekken notes that Philo applies this text to Jews and gentiles, and that the citation of Deut 26:17 in *Virt.* 184 clarifies that the conversion in view is conversion to the true people of God.[44] Paul may utilize similar elements in his use of this text: he employs Deut 30:12–14 as a contrast to Lev 18:5 emphasizing the ease with which one obtains the righteousness of faith. He also employs the passage in his explanation of why many Israelites are not currently part of the Israel within Israel (cf. Rom 9:6).

Praem. 79–84 emphasizes the necessity of hearing and obeying the law. *Praem.* 79–80 cites Deut 30:10–13 to introduce the discussion, and utilizes the text to encourage people to obey the law because one must do it and not merely hear it in order to be blessed (see esp. *Virt.* 82). Bekken argues that Philo interprets the blessings one receives as eschatological victory over one's enemies. A similar thought may appear when Paul utilizes Deut 30:12–14 to emphasize the availability of eschatological salvation in Christ (cf. Rom 9:22–29; 10:14–21).

Qumran

A reference to Deut 30:1–2 occurs in the Qumran document 4QMMT (*A Sectarian Manifesto*). While the reconstructed document as we possess it does not cite Deut 30:11–14, N. T. Wright highlights this document as important for understanding Paul's use of Deut 30:12–14 in Rom 10:6–8, and therefore we examine its contribution here. Like many documents from Qumran, 4QMMT is highly fragmented, but does contain a clear citation of Deuteronomy 30:1–2 in Section C, lines 12b–16: "And it is writ[ten,] 'that when [al]l these thing[s happ]en to you in the Last Days, the blessing [and] the curse, [that you call them] to m[ind] and return to Him with all your heart and with [al]l [your] soul,' . . . at the end of [the age,] then [you shall] l[ive]."[45] The author then discusses the blessings which came during the time of Solomon (ll. 17–18) and the curses which began during Jeroboam son of Nebat's reign and continued until the Babylonian exile (ll. 19–21). Now is the time when Israel will return to the law (l. 22), and therefore the author

---

43. Colson, *Philo*, 8:275–77.
44. Bekken, *Word*, 112.
45. Wise et al., *Dead Sea Scrolls*, 461.

of the text has written "some of the works of the Law" (l. 27)⁴⁶ which will be reckoned to Israel as righteousness if they do what is right and good.⁴⁷

Martin Abegg notes that Galatians, Romans, and 4QMTT are the only documents in antiquity which discuss the relationship between works and righteousness.⁴⁸ Wright reads 4QMMT as an example of the sectarian mindset that characterized intertestamental Judaism.⁴⁹ The author has discerned that Israel is living in the age of eschatological blessing, and he believes that keeping the halakic regulations of his community will secure the divine blessing.⁵⁰ Paul situates himself within the same story, but argues that faith, not sectarian regulations, characterizes the people of God and leads to eschatological blessing.⁵¹

Wright's assessment has certain weaknesses. First, the citation of Deut 30:1–2 in 4QMMT makes sense if the author views himself as living in the days of eschatological blessing; the original context of Deut 30:1–2 looks ahead to the days after Israel's exile when they experience divine visitation. However, this does not solve the problem of Paul utilizing Deut 30:12–14 in his description of righteousness by faith because it is not certain that Deut 30:12–14 looks ahead to the eschatological period, and 4QMMT does not provide an example of someone in intertestamental Judaism reading Deut 30:12–14 as a reference to the eschatological period.⁵²

Second, Wright's assessment of those who insist on doing the works of the law as sectarian is not accurate. Sectarianism is certainly a result of emphasizing certain works in opposition to faith. However, the real underlying problem in such an emphasis is that it makes a person relate to God

---

46. "Some of the works of the Law" translates מקצת מעשי התורה. Transliterating the first letter of each Hebrew word (not including the definite article) yields MMT, from which the document title is derived.

47. Wise et al., *Dead Sea Scrolls*, 462.

48. Wise et al., *Dead Sea Scrolls*, 454.

49. Wright, *Romans*, 661. Dunn also notes, "the motivation behind Peter's withdrawal from table-fellowship with Gentile Christians in Antioch (Gal 2.12) was of a similar character and rationale as the withdrawal of the MMT group from their larger community" ("4QMMT," 340).

50. Wright, *Romans*, 661.

51. Wright, *Romans*, 661. Dunn makes a similar point: "מעקי התורה and ἔργα νόμου both seem to refer to 'works of the law' understood as defining a boundary which marks out these of faith/faithfulness from others" ("4QMTT," 343).

52. Even if 4QMMT did provide such an example, that would not justify the author's use of Deut 30:12–14 in that way, nor Paul's (assuming that we have rightly interpreted Deut 30:12–14 as a reference to Israel's experience before entering the promised land). The example would help us understand what Paul is doing, but one would still need to justify the hermeneutics.

on the basis of what they do, which is the natural contrast to faith. Wright is correct in his explanation of the terms of membership in the people of God, but incorrect in his analysis of the wrong path Israel was taking.

Third, since 4QMMT does not actually cite Deut 30:12–14, it lacks complete relevance to our understanding of Rom 10:6–8. There are parallels, the most important being the focus on what one must do in order to enjoy God's blessing. However, we are not as interested in a similar discussion about works and righteousness as we are about specific uses of Deut 30:12–14 in intertestamental literature.

Targum Neofiti

Targum Neofiti contains an expansion on Deut 30:13 that helps explain Paul's citation in Rom 10:7. The text reads, "Nor is *the Law* beyond the *Great Sea*, that one should say: '*Would that* we *had one like Jonah the prophet* who *would descend into the depths of the Great* Sea *and bring it up* for us, and make us hear *the commandments* that we might do them!'"[53] The Targum's rendering contains the original reference to the sea and adds a reference to descending into the depths. When Paul cites Deut 30:13, he refers only to the descent into the abyss. Since the Targumim postdate the NT, we cannot conclude with certainty that Paul cited *Targ. Neof.* here.[54] A more likely explanation for Paul's alteration is the frequent association between crossing the sea and descending into the abyss in Jewish literature.[55] For example, Job 28:14 LXX, referring to wisdom, reads, "The abyss (ἄβυσσος) says, 'It is not in me,' and the sea says, 'It is not with me.'" Ps 106:25–26 LXX makes the same comparison.[56] The conceptual overlap allows Paul to substitute "abyss" for "sea" without altering the meaning.

---

53. McNamara, *Targum Neofiti 1: Deuteronomy*, 141; emphases original.

54. Evans, *Ancient Texts*, 185–86. The lack of reference to Jonah also constitutes one major difference between Paul's citation and *Targ. Neof.* For additional arguments against Pauline dependence on *Targ. Neof.*, see Seifrid, "Paul's Approach," 24–25.

55. Dunn, *Romans*, 2:606; Schreiner, *Romans*, 559; Seifrid, "Romans," 657; Suggs, "Word," 300. See also the association between the sea, death and Hades reflected in Rev. 20:1 and the references noted in Wright, *Resurrection*, 472n59.

56. Seifrid cites the same association in the rabbinical literature (*m. Pesaḥ.* 7:7; *m. Naz.* 9:2; *m. Parah* 3:2; *b. Pesaḥ.* 81a; *b. Giṭ.* 84a; *b. B. Meṣiʿa* 94a ["Romans," 657]). See Schreiner, *Romans*, 559n18 for additional evidence.

Conclusion

The intertestamental use of Deut 30:12-14 reveals some ideas that may have informed Paul's exegesis of the same passage. The emphasis in the Apocrypha and Pseudepigrapha on human inability to understand the things of God may reflect an implication of Deut 30:12-14 (humans cannot attain divine knowledge on their own so God has graciously revealed it to them) that Paul develops in Rom 10:5-8: since human effort cannot obtain salvation, God has brought his grace near in the gospel of Jesus Christ. However, this connection is tenuous at best since Paul uses Lev 18:5 to express human inability and not Deut 30:12-14.

Philo's use of the text is closer to Paul's and more in line with the original context: in conversion and salvation, God enables humans to do what he demands. While one cannot become righteous by obeying the law (Lev 18:5), God has brought his grace near in the gospel of Jesus Christ (Deut 30:12-14). Just as God revealed his commandment to Israel and regenerated them so that they might obey it, so he has brought the gospel near to Israel so that they might believe it.

PAUL'S USE OF DEUTERONOMY 8:17A, 9:4A, AND 30:12-14 IN ROMANS 10:6-8

We must now determine how Paul interprets a reference to the nearness of the law as a description of righteousness by faith in Christ and the gospel. First, we examine the form of Paul's citation and analyze where it differs from its transmission history. Second, we examine the hermeneutics and theology of Paul's citation.

The Form of Paul's Citations

Rom 10:6-8 contains four citations from the book of Deuteronomy. First, Paul cites a short phrase which occurs identically in LXX Deut 8:17a and 9:4a: μὴ εἴπῃς ἐν τῇ καρδίᾳ σου, "Do not say in your heart" (10:6a). The citation matches the LXX perfectly, and is true to the MT as well.[57] There are no textual variants in the New Testament manuscript tradition for this citation.

---

57. The phrases are not identical in the MT. In 8:17a, the MT reads ואמרת בלבבך, "You may say to yourself." In 9:4a, the MT reads אל־תאמר בלבבך, "do not say to yourself." Since the LXX translates both phrases as μὴ εἴπῃς ἐν τῇ καρδίᾳ σου, we include both verses.

Immediately following this short phrase, Paul cites three longer phrases from Deut 30:12–14: τίς ἀναβήσεται εἰς τὸν οὐρανόν, "Who will ascend into heaven" (Deut 30:12 in Rom 10:6b); τίς καταβήσεται εἰς τὴν ἄβυσσον, "Who will descend into the deep" (Deut 30:13 in Rom 10:7a); and ἐγγύς σου τὸ ῥῆμά ἐστιν ἐν τῷ στόματί σου καὶ ἐν τῇ καρδίᾳ σου, "The word is in near you; it is in your mouth and in your heart" (Deut 30:14 in Rom 10:8a). In the MT, the full phrase from Deut 30:12 reads מי יעלה־לנו השמימה ויקחה לנו וישמענו אתה ונעשנה, "Who will ascend into heaven to get it and proclaim it to us so we may obey it?"[58] The LXX translates this sentence formally as Τίς ἀναβήσεται ἡμῖν εἰς τὸν οὐρανὸν καὶ λήμψεται αὐτὴν ἡμῖν; καὶ ἀκούσαντες αὐτὴν ποιήσομεν, "who will ascend into heaven for us and receive it for us so that we hear and do it." The structure and meaning are essentially the same as the MT. Paul does not cite the entire sentence, but only the first phrase (τίς ἀναβήσεται εἰς τὸν οὐρανόν), from which he also omits ἡμῖν. The discarded phrase contains the material about receiving, hearing, and obeying the law.

Paul's citation from Deut 30:13 involves omissions and alterations. In the MT, the full phrase reads וישמענו אתה ונעשנה מי יעבר־לנו אל־עבר הים ויקחה לנו, "Who will cross the sea to get it and proclaim it to us so we may obey it?" The LXX translates the sentence formally as Τίς διαπεράσει ἡμῖν εἰς τὸ πέραν τῆς θαλάσσης καὶ λήμψεται ἡμῖν αὐτήν; καὶ ἀκουστὴν ἡμῖν ποιήσει αὐτήν, καὶ ποιήσομεν, "Who will go to the other side of the sea for us and receive it for us and make it audible for us and [so that] we will do it?" Once again, Paul only cites a short phrase (τίς καταβήσεται εἰς τὴν ἄβυσσον), and omits all references to receiving, hearing, and obeying the law. He also alters the LXX phrase Τίς διαπεράσει ἡμῖν εἰς τὸ πέραν τῆς θαλάσσης ("Who will go to the other side of the sea for us?") to read τίς καταβήσεται εἰς τὴν ἄβυσσον, "Who will descend into the abyss?" As noted earlier, Paul's justification for altering the text likely rests in the frequent association between crossing the sea and descending into the abyss in Jewish literature. Paul alters the wording of the text but he does not alter its meaning.

Paul's final citation is the longest, including almost all of Deut 30:14: כי־קרוב אליך הדבר מאד בפיך ובלבבך לעשהו, "No, the word is very near you; it is in your mouth and in your heart so that you may obey it." Once again, the LXX translates the verse formally, yet adds a reference to the presence of the word in one's hands: ἔστιν σου ἐγγὺς τὸ ῥῆμα σφόδρα ἐν τῷ στόματί σου καὶ ἐν τῇ καρδίᾳ σου καὶ ἐν ταῖς χερσίν σου αὐτὸ ποιεῖν, "the word is

---

58. According to Deut 30:11, the object pursued in this quest is המצוה הזאת אשר אנכי מצוך היום, "this commandment which I command you today."

near you, in your mouth and in your heart and in your hands to do it." Paul's citation omits the reference to the hands and to obeying the law: ἐγγύς σου τὸ ῥῆμά ἐστιν ἐν τῷ στόματί σου καὶ ἐν τῇ καρδίᾳ σου.[59]

We make four conclusions from this examination of the relevant texts. First, Paul does cite the Old Testament here. His wording corresponds closely, at times perfectly, to that of the LXX, which accurately translates the MT. Second, the textual history of these texts is quite stable. There are no variants that greatly affect the sense of the passage. Third, Paul's alteration of Deut 30:13 in Rom 10:7 does not affect the meaning of the passage. The different words employed communicate the same idea. Fourth, Paul deliberately omits references to obeying the law. His threefold omission of references to doing the law in the Deuteronomic passages is too consistent to be coincidental.

The Interpretation of Paul's Citations

Romans 10:6–8 gives a threefold description of the righteousness of faith, which serves as a counterpart to the righteousness of the law in Rom 10:5. Whereas Moses describes the righteousness of the law in Lev 18:5 (Μωϋσῆς γὰρ γράφει τὴν δικαιοσύνην τὴν ἐκ τοῦ νόμου), the personified righteousness of faith describes itself using Deut 8:17a; 9:4a; 30:12–14 (ἡ δὲ ἐκ πίστεως δικαιοσύνη οὕτως λέγει).[60] Ironically, the first thing that righteousness by faith says is something that humans seeking salvation must not say: "Do not say in your heart" (μὴ εἴπῃς ἐν τῇ καρδίᾳ σου [Rom 10:6a citing Deut 8:17a; 9:4a]). Paul then supplies the content of what one must not say in Rom 10:6b-7: "'Who will ascend into heaven?' that is, to bring Christ down; or, 'Who will ascend into the abyss?' that is, to bring Christ up from the dead" (τίς ἀναβήσεται εἰς τὸν οὐρανόν; τοῦτ' ἔστιν Χριστὸν καταγαγεῖν· ἤ· τίς καταβήσεται εἰς τὴν ἄβυσσον; τοῦτ' ἔστιν Χριστὸν ἐκ νεκρῶν ἀναγαγεῖν [citing Deut 30:12–13]).

Many interpreters read these phrases as a reference to the incarnation and resurrection of Christ.[61] One does not need to ascend into heaven in

---

59. Rom 10:8 contains the only variant worth noting in the passage, the addition of η γραφη after λέγει by D (˙ F G) 33. 104. 365. 629. *l* 249 *al* (ar vgcl) bo; (Ambst). According to Jewett the variant "has an explanatory function and appears to be clearly secondary, a conclusion confirmed by the varying placement before and after the verb" (*Romans*, 622).

60. Moo notes that personifying activities and concepts that are closely related to God is a common biblical pattern (Ps 85:10–13; Prov 8:21ff; Isa 45:8; 55:10–11 [*Epistle to the Romans*, 650]).

61. Cranfield, *Romans*, 2:524–25; Moo, *Epistle to the Romans*, 654; Schreiner, *Romans*, 558.

order to bring Christ down because the incarnation has already taken place. Likewise, one does not need to descend into the abyss and bring Christ up from the dead because the resurrection has already taken place.⁶² Jewett describes the first phrase as "a historically apt description of the goals of some of the Jewish parties in Paul's time. They sought to hasten the coming of the divinely appointed Χριστός (= "anointed one, king") by religious programs associated with the law."⁶³ Paul counters such efforts to assist the Divine by stating that God has already done in Christ all that humans need for their salvation.

However, James Dunn and Tom Holland interpret the image of ascending as a reference to Christ's post-resurrection ascension: it is unnecessary for a person to go into heaven and bring Christ down because he has already ascended into heaven and is dispensing New Covenant blessings.⁶⁴ Paul refers to Christ's ascension before his resurrection because he is referring to historical events retrospectively (a similar pattern occurs in Rom 10:14–15). The idea has some merit, and would correspond in a chiastic fashion to the way of salvation outlined in 10:9: confess with your mouth that "Jesus is Lord" (the ascended and enthroned Messiah, cf. v. 6) and believe in your heart that God raised him from the dead (the resurrected savior, cf. v. 7). However, Paul usually refers to the work of Christ in a manner consistent with the salvation-historical order of events (incarnation then resurrection [Rom 1:3–4; Phil 2:6–11; 1 Tim 3:16]).⁶⁵ Without other qualifiers to indicate a reference to the ascension, we think that Paul follows the pattern of incarnation then resurrection in Rom 10:6–7.

Romans 10:8 provides the positive content of what the righteousness of faith actually says: "But what does it say? 'The word is near you, in your mouth and in your heart,' that is, the word of faith which we preach." (ἀλλὰ τί λέγει; ἐγγύς σου τὸ ῥῆμά ἐστιν ἐν τῷ στόματί σου καὶ ἐν τῇ καρδίᾳ σου, τοῦτ' ἔστιν τὸ ῥῆμα τῆς πίστεως ὃ κηρύσσομεν [citing Deut 30:14]). The righteousness of faith reveals that the way of salvation lies not in the path of superhuman quests into the heavens or abyss, but is near at hand, in one's mouth and in one's heart. The gospel which Paul preaches contains this near word and brings this word near to human brings.

Paul's use of Deut 8:17a and 9:4a in Rom 10:6a is not controversial. In Deut 8:17a and 9:4a, Moses warns the people of Israel against presuming

---

62. Porter notes that these are the only occurrences of καταγαγεῖν and ἀναγαγεῖν in Paul (*Romans*, 197).

63. Jewett, *Romans*, 626–27.

64. Dunn, *Romans*, 2:605, and Holland, *Romans*, 346–48.

65. Seifrid, "Paul's Approach," 26–27.

that their righteousness has procured God's blessing.[66] In Romans 9:30—10:3, Paul faults Israel for pursuing her own righteousness instead of submitting to the righteousness which God provides (see esp. Rom 9:32; 10:3). They are presuming a righteous status instead of recognizing God's grace (cf. Deut 8:18; 9:5). Therefore, Paul begins his description of righteousness by faith with a reminder that sinful humans ought not to presume that they can merit salvation by their own power or goodness.[67] Paul interprets the verses in accordance with their contextual meaning and utilizes them in the same manner as Moses did in Deuteronomy.[68]

The use of Deut 30:12-14 in Rom 10:6b-8 is unfortunately not so straightforward. Gone from Deut 30:12-14 is any reference to the law and one's obedience to it. Instead, Paul uses the formula τοῦτ' ἔστιν to relate the three citations from Deut 30:12-14 to particular aspects of Christ's work and the gospel. Commentators agree that Paul is using Deut 30:12-14 to describe righteousness by faith. The question is, *How* does he do this? In the attempt to answer that question, six major positions have emerged. Like the explanations of Lev 18:5 in Rom 10:5, some of these views correspond directly to the main critiques of Israel's error in Rom 9:30—10:13.

Bad Exegesis

The first position simply claims that Paul utilizes the text to say what he wants to say and shows no respect for the original meaning. C. H. Dodd remarks, "As an interpretation of Scripture this is purely fanciful. Its interest for us is confined to the light it throws on Paul's conception of the Christian faith."[69] While we can perhaps commend Dodd for trying to wrestle honestly with this text and not force his preconceptions on it, nonetheless this explanation will not do. First, Dodd's explanation puts Paul in a very awkward

---

66. Dunn overemphasizes the military context of Deut 8:17a and argues that they warn against assuming that Israel's righteousness establishes the covenant ("Righteousness," 224). But Deut 8:17a speaks of prosperity in the land, and therefore fits this assessment of a warning against assuming that one's righteousness merits divine blessing.

67. Badenas, *Christ*, 129; Moo, *Epistle to the Romans*, 651; Seifrid, "Romans," 657. This further reinforces the idea that Lev 18:5 in Rom 10:5 functions to highlight human inability to obtain righteousness by means of the law.

68. Moo, *Epistle to the Romans*, 651. Hays remarks, "The message is so apt for Paul's argument in Romans that we are left wondering why he did not go ahead and quote these words rather than delving into his problematic exegesis of Deut. 30:12-14" (*Echoes*, 79).

69. Dodd, *Romans*, 166. Black also writes, "The Old Testament text serves as little more than a scriptural base for Christological doctrine" ("Christological Use," 9). See also Kirk who calls it a "drastic and unwarrantable allegorizing" (*Romans*, 225).

position. If Paul is trying to use the OT to convince unbelieving Jews of the necessity of faith in Christ, then he is seriously jeopardizing his goal if he is using the OT in a careless and convenient manner.[70] Second, Dodd's position cannot be harmonized with a high view of Scripture. If Scripture has ultimately one author, then some explanation exists that makes sense of Paul's hermeneutics.[71] Third, even if we stepped back from such a view of Scripture and reasoned on Dodd's terms, we do not need to retreat to his explanation. Such a position should be utilized only as a last resort when no other explanation makes sense.[72] As we see throughout this examination, other positions give a competent account of Paul's hermeneutics.

Use of Biblical Language

The second position argues that Paul is not citing the Old Testament, but is merely using biblical language to describe righteousness by faith.[73] Sanday and Headlam explain: "the Apostle does not intend to base any argument on the quotation from the O. T., but only selects the language as being familiar, suitable, and proverbial, in order to express what he wishes to say."[74] As proof, they offer five arguments: (1) the context does not emphasize how righteousness by faith can be proven from the OT, but only describes its characteristics; (2) Paul alters the citation; (3) the citation is incomplete; (4) intertestamental literature often uses Deut 30:12–14 proverbially (Philo; 4 Ezra 4:8; Bar 3:29–30; Jub 24:32); and (5) Paul uses the OT proverbially in other passages (Rom 10:18; 11:1).[75]

These arguments do not adequately explain Paul's use of the OT here. First, as this dissertation shows, Rom 9:30—10:13 contains many OT proofs of the necessity of righteousness by faith.[76] One does not expect Paul to

---

70. Suggs, "Word," 299; Toews, "Law," 289.

71. Räisänen maintains that Paul is theologically inconsistent, even in the space of a single letter such as Romans (*Paul*).

72. Authors who offer an explanation for Paul's varying modes of expression while maintaining his theological consistency include Beker, *Paul*; Spanje, *Inconsistency*; Woodbridge, "Paul," 5–18.

73. Barrett, *Romans*, 199; Kalland, "Deuteronomy," 190; Longenecker, *Biblical Exegesis*, 104–6; Longenecker, *Romans*, 852–54; Sanday and Headlam, *Romans*, 288–90; Str-B 3:281.

74. Sanday and Headlam, *Romans*, 289.

75. Sanday and Headlam, *Romans*, 289.

76. We have already seen that Paul cites Isa 8:14; 28:16 to prove the necessity of basing one's relationship with God on faith, and Lev 18:5 to prove the impossibility of earning a right standing before God by obeying the law. In the next section, we will see

merely use the language of the OT here when his *modus operandi* thus far has been to cite the OT to prove his point. Second, Sanday and Headlam note that Paul alters Lev 18:5 in Rom 10:5 slightly, but they do not dispute that as an OT citation.[77] The alterations to Deut 30:12–14 then do not constitute proof that Paul is not citing the text. Third, while we grant Sanday and Headlam's point that intertestamental literature uses Deut 30:12–14 proverbially, Paul's citation is introduced by ἀλλὰ τί λέγει, a formula used elsewhere to introduce scriptural citations (Gal 4:30; Rom 4:3; 11:2, 4).[78] Finally, the explanatory phrase τοῦτ' ἔστιν is used elsewhere to introduce commentary on cited biblical material (Rom 9:7–8; Heb 7:5; 1 Pet 3:20).[79] Paul does not utilize such language when he uses Scripture illustratively (e.g., Rom 10:18). Paul's use of this text therefore indicates Scriptural citation and exposition.[80]

Jewish Exegetical Methods

The third view reasons that Paul follows the Jewish exegetical methods of his day while reading the text on the basis of Christian presuppositions. This allows him to discern additional meanings in the text which go beyond its original sense. For Paul, Christ is the τέλος of the law (Rom 10:4), and thus all Scripture finds its meaning in him.[81]

Paul once again citing Isa 28:16 to emphasize the necessity of faith, and introducing Joel 2:32 to encourage his unbelieving readers to call on Christ for salvation. Toews, "Law," 288, notes that the ten verses which precede Rom 10:6–8 and the twelve which follow contain eleven OT citations, and that none of these are used allusively.

77. Sanday and Headlam, *Romans*, 285. Dunn, "Righteousness," 217, also notes that the text Paul cites is very close to the original wording, too close to be accidental.

78. Dunn, "Righteousness," 218; Moo, *Epistle to the Romans*, 651; Schreiner, *Romans*, 556; Suggs, "Word," 301–2; Toews, "Law," 288. Note again the addition of ἡ γραπή to Rom 10:6 by D (F G) 33. 104. 365. 629. *l* 249 *al* (ar vgcl) bo; (Ambst). These additions reflect the understanding that Paul is citing the OT here.

79. Dunn, "Righteousness," 217–18; Schreiner, *Romans*, 556; Suggs, "Word," 301–2.

80. Moo, *Epistle to the Romans*, 651.

81. Bekken, *Word*, 53–81; Bruce, *Romans*, 203–4; Hays, *Echoes*, 79–82; Humphrey, "Rhetoric," 131–38; Jewett, *Romans*, 626–29; Johnson, "Romans 9–11," 228–29; Haacker, *Römer*, 235–37; Southall, *Rediscovering Righteousness*, 258–59; Suggs, "Word," 308–12; Vincent, "Derash Homiletico," 751–88; Wilckens, *Römer*, 2:225; Witherington, *Romans*, 261–62. Luther, *Lecures on Romans*, 405, comes closest to this view because he argues that Christ is the key to the OT scriptures, but he does not credit Paul with using Jewish exegetical methods.

This position has several subgroups because its advocates see different background literature informing Paul's exegesis.[82] First, some argue that Paul's threefold use of τοῦτ' ἔστιν in Rom 10:6–8 resembles the line-by-line *pesher* commentary found in the Qumran biblical commentaries.[83] Paul interprets the references to the law as references to Christ, thus identifying the word that was near to Israel in the law with the word that is now near in the Christian kerygma. Second, others see the Wisdom tradition behind Paul's exegesis.[84] Suggs states the position well: "In Rom. 10:6–10 Paul has taken up the familiar identification of Wisdom and Torah and added a third term: Jesus Christ. The tension between Gospel and Law is resolved by the identification of Christ with Wisdom-Torah."[85]

Perle Jar Bekken represents a third subgroup and highlights the similarities between Paul and Philo's exegetical method.[86] Bekken describes their method as "exegetical paraphrase," which consists of "adapting and conforming a biblical text to various themes and contexts, including the practice of selective citation, omissions, additions, alteration, rephrasing and substitution of words of the citation with other words."[87] Paul and Philo apply their method to Deut 30:11–14 and use it to explain the conditions that one must fulfill in order to participate in the eschatological people of God.[88]

These explanations give good attention to the historical and literary background of Paul's thought and try to discern what may have shaped his hermeneutics. Paul's encounter with Christ on the Damascus Road certainly opened his mind to read the OT in a new light. As D. A. Carson writes, "if Jesus was truly alive and vindicated, Saul/Paul had a lot of re-thinking to do, a lot of re-reading of ancient scriptural texts."[89]

However, the position as a whole suffers two weaknesses. First, we question Paul's dependence on the interpretive traditions suggested by this

---

82. These subgroups can overlap as well.

83. Bruce, *Romans*, 203–4; Hays, *Echoes*, 79–82; Jewett, *Romans*, 626–29; Vincent, "Derash Homiletico," 751–88.

84. Johnson, "Romans 9–11," 228–29; Southall, *Rediscovering Righteousness*, 258–259; Suggs, "Word," 308–12; Witherington, *Romans*, 261–62. Hays, while arguing for a *pesher* methodology on Paul's part, also believes that his method is informed by the Wisdom tradition in Baruch 3:29–30 (*Echoes*, 82).

85. Suggs, "Word," 311.

86. Bekken, *Word*.

87. Bekken, *Word*, 54–55.

88. Bekken, *Word*, 154. When Paul employs the text, he does not distinguish between Jews and gentiles as Philo does. Paul uses Deut 30:12–14 "to redraw the boundary between Jews and Gentiles by reclaiming what he considers to be the proper meaning of the Law and thus the criteria for belonging to the people of God."

89. Carson, "Mystery," 411n48.

explanation. We noted above our objections to Sugg's equation of Christ with Wisdom and Torah. Regarding Qumran, Mark Seifrid has surveyed the use of the phrase in the LXX and other Greek versions, Philo, Josephus, literary Greek, the papyri, Qumran, and the NT.[90] He concludes that Paul's use of the phrase does not match the *pesher* technique of Qumran, but functions rather in an explanatory manner.[91] Philo's use of the phrase comes the closest to Paul's, but since Philo utilizes the main idea of Deut 30:12–14 (though with some reinterpretation of the referents), we are safer connecting Paul's use to the original meaning than to Philo's interpretation of the passage.[92]

Second, this explanation of Paul's hermeneutics is incomplete, for it does not connect Paul's exegesis to a larger doctrine of Scripture, nor does it answer the question, Is the meaning that Paul finds in the OT *really there*?[93] A historical description is not the same thing as historical legitimation.[94] The explanation is not wrong as much as it is incomplete.[95]

New Covenant (Eschatological) Fulfillment

The fourth position argues that Paul reads Deut 30:11–14 as a prediction of the New Covenant (or eschatological) age, and that he cites these verses to demonstrate that in Christ that age has dawned. Moses' age was

---

90. Seifrid, "Paul's Approach," 29–34.

91. Seifrid, "Paul's Approach," 34. Hays notes that the resemblance to Qumran is formal and not material (*Echoes*, 79).

92. Badenas argues that an understanding of the context of Deut 30:12–14 is more valuable for understanding Paul's exegesis here than knowledge of the possible exegetical parallels he might have used (*Christ*, 129).

93. Moo writes, "while dependence on this Jewish tradition may help explain why Paul uses Deuteronomy in the way that he does, it does not help us at all with the 'legitimacy' question" ("Paul's Reading," 409).

94. Though offering a different explanation from the view discussed here, Hays highlights the difference between explanation and legitimation when he writes, "This account of intertextual echo in Rom. 10:5–10 should not be read as a defense of Paul's exegesis. It is, rather, an account of the devices whereby a historically outrageous reading gains poetic plausibility. (Whether this intertextual plausibility ought, normatively speaking, to confer upon the reading theological legitimacy is a question beyond the scope of our present deliberations. Readers interested in this issue are referred to the final chapter of this book.)" (*Echoes*, 82).

95. We could include here the analysis of Nygren, *Romans*, 381–82. He does not directly appeal to Jewish exegetical methods, but claims that Paul sees a deeper meaning of the text here, a meaning God intended all along. While Duet 30:12–14 literally refers to the law, on a deeper level it refers to Christ. However, Nygren offers no justification for this explanation apart from an appeal to *sensus plenior* (though he does not use that term).

characterized by the righteousness of the law (Lev 18:5); the future age will be characterized by the righteousness of faith (Deut 30:12–14). Paul cites Deut 30:12–14 because his day is that time.[96]

The biggest objection to this position is the exegesis it proposes for Deut 30:12–14. We have already demonstrated that this passage most likely refers to Moses' day ("today" in Deut 30:11), not a future time period.[97] Furthermore, the tension between works and faith is not limited to the tension between the old and new covenants, but rather runs throughout the scriptures as a whole. Moses faithfully records the description of Abraham's justification by faith (Gen 15:6), and at the same time records YHWH's statement that one must do the commandments in order to live (Lev 18:5). Moses sets before the people of Israel the law and commands them to obey it (Deut 10:12–13; 29:29), but recognizes that such obedience is impossible without the inward, regenerating work of God (Deut 10:16; 30:11–14). These principles operate simultaneously in salvation history; they are not identified solely with the old and new ages, or old and new covenants.[98]

Describing the True Nature of the Law

Fifth, many argue that Paul uses Deut 30:12–14 to describe the true nature of obedience to the law. Lev 18:5 brings together doing and living, and Deut 30:12–14 explains what doing and living actually mean: faith in Christ. Those who believe in Christ are obeying the law in the way Deuteronomy intended. This idea was latent in the Torah, and is now brought to full light in the Gospel.[99]

---

96. Barker, *Triumph*, 194–98; Bock, "Single Meaning," 132–40; Coxhead, "Deuteronomy 30:11–14," 311–19; Dunn, *Romans*, 2:612–15; Dunn, "Righteousness," 225–26; Estelle, "Leviticus 18:5," 141–45; McConville, *Deuteronomy*, 432–33; Michel, *Römer*, 328–29; Käsemann, *Romans*, 284–87 (though he argues more from a γράμμα/πνεῦμα distinction à la 2 Cor 3); Sailhamer, *Pentateuch*, 474; Schreiner, *Romans*, 557–58; Strickland, "Inauguration," 250–53; Thielman, *Plight*, 113–14; Viard, *Romains*, 226.

97. Bock agrees that Deut 30:11–14 is not a prophetic text ("Single Meaning," 136n32). However, he argues that Deut 30:11–20 contains an expectation for how Israel will respond to God in the future, and that Paul's reading of Deut 30:11–14 is justified by him putting it "into the appropriate temporal perspective" (138; so also Schreiner, *Romans*, 558n17). We argue that it is not a temporal shift that drives Paul's argument here and throughout Rom 9:30—10:13, but rather a contrast of two principles present in the OT (works and faith). One must read the flow of redemptive history (even redemptive history prior to the NT) properly in order to discern which principle takes precedence.

98. Moo, *Epistle to the Romans*, 654.

99. Badenas, *Christ*, 130; Fuller, *Gospel*, 85–86; Davies, *Faith*, 201; Kaiser, "Leviticus 18:5," 27; Suggs, "Word," 311; Toews, "Law," 315–20; Wright, *Paul*, 1173; Wright, *Romans*, 658–63 (like the New Covenant Fulfillment view, Wright's interpretation is

Advocates of this view appeal to the larger context of Rom 9:30—10:13 to justify this understanding of Paul and the law. Special attention is given to Paul's criticism of Israel for seeking the law by works instead of by faith (9:31–32a). This language supposedly indicates that the law never demanded perfect obedience but rather faith in Christ.[100] One must first accept this interpretation of the law as a whole in order to read Lev 18:5 and Deut 30:12-14 in this light.

Rom 9:30—10:13 does not support this approach to the law. Rom 10:5-8 contain the third contrast between righteousness by faith and righteousness by works in this passage.[101] The first contrast uses the language of Israel seeking the law and perhaps offers the best chance for justifying this approach to the law. However, the entire proposal is based on a dubious interpretation of an ambiguous phrase (νόμον δικαιοσύνης). Rather than recasting Paul's approach to the law by suggesting that the law actually calls for faith, we have suggested that the difficult phrase in Rom 9:31 communicates the idea that Israel sought the law for the purpose of being righteous, and that their works were insufficient to obtain that goal. Paul supports this line of interpretation in his second contrast when he notes that Israel, out of ignorance, tries to establish her own righteousness because she does not understand where righteousness really comes from: faith in Christ (Rom 10:3-4). Paul then makes the same point when he contrasts Lev 18:5 and Deut 30:12-14 in Rom 10:5-8.

Advocates of this view oppose a contrast between these two texts by reinterpreting them in a manner different from their original contexts and history of interpretation. The previous chapter noted how Lev 18:5 is reread as a summons to a particular type of obedience, namely, faith. Deut 30:12-14 suffers the same treatment as well. Rather than seeing some unifying principle between Romans and Deuteronomy, advocates of this interpretation

---

predicated on the idea that the new covenant is now in effect; however, his explanation of the function of Deut 30:12-14 here warrants his placement here). Davies, Fuller, and Kaiser comprise a subgroup of this position. They argue that both Lev 18:5 and Deut 30:12-14 refer to the obedience which springs from faith, and that Paul uses both texts harmoniously to show the Jews what has always been God's way of salvation. Rather than viewing both texts as a witness to salvation by faith, they view both texts as a witness to the necessity of faith and works in the believer (Kaiser emphasizes the priority of faith while Davies and Fuller speak of faith and works as a whole). We place them here because they see Deut 30:12-14 functioning as an explanation of the true nature of the law.

100. Fuller, *Gospel*, 71–79 (discussion of Rom 9:31–32a is interwoven throughout Fuller's entire treatment of Rom 10:5–8); Hays, *Echoes*, 75–76; Wright, *Romans*, 648–49, 656–57.

101. Moo, *Epistle to the Romans*, 646.

argue that Paul really did change the meaning of Deut 30:12-14 when he cited it in Rom 10:6-8.[102] They attempt to solve the riddle of Paul's interpretation by highlighting just how radical it supposedly is. This does not solve the problem, but rather amplifies it.[103]

---

102. Toews acknowledges that "The original intention of the passage to stress the fulfillability of the law is transformed in Paul's exegesis. Christ replaces the 'commandment' of the Deuteronomic text. The 'righteousness of faith' interpreter via the pesher on Deut. 30:11-14 renounces one's own efforts in doing 'the righteousness of the law' and fulfills the law by faith in and confession of the near word" ("Law," 316).

103. Pattee presents another variant on this position worth noting ("Stumbling Stone," 290–93). He believes that Paul uses Deut 30:12-14 to argue that the law can be kept and that Israel's problem is their failure to practice the most fundamental requirement of the law as expressed in Lev 19:18 (love for neighbor, referring to the gentiles). We noted in the previous chapter the weakness of defining the obedience of Lev 18:5 solely in terms of Lev 19:18. Here we note Pattee's attempt to find this theme in Paul's use of Deut 30:12-14. Pattee argues that Paul's reference to the abyss in Rom 10:7 comes primarily from Sirach 24:5-6, which juxtaposes a reference to the depth of the abyss with a reference to the waves of the sea (essentially the conceptual overlap between the abyss and the sea noted in our examination of the intertestamental use of Deut 30:12-14). Pattee, however, believes that Sirach 24 is the chief text Paul is utilizing because this passage also allegedly teaches that the wisdom of God is universally accessible to all in creation through the Torah. This informs Paul's argument and supports Pattee's thesis because it is supposedly another example of Paul arguing that the goal of the law is to incorporate gentiles into the people of God and that the chief commandment of the law (and the way in which this goal is accomplished) is for Israel to love their neighbor (gentiles) as they love themselves (i.e., incorporating them into the people of God).

We note two problems with Pattee's thesis. First, he falls prey to some circular reasoning here: Paul is supposedly countering the sin of partiality, and Sirach supposedly implies that partiality is wrong (though Pattee himself admits that Sirach 24 does not specifically mention the sin of partiality [289]). Therefore, Pattee argues that Paul leans primarily on Sirach 24 here. Pattee has found exactly what he was looking for in Rom 10:7, though other exegetes do not elevate Sirach 24 to this level of importance, nor do they attempt to incorporate all of these additional themes into Rom 10:6-8 (and rightly so, for the connections between Sirach 24 and Rom 9:30—10:13 are far too tenuous to allow the wider themes of Sirach 24 to interpret the direct statements of Rom 9:30—10:13).

Second, Pattee frankly gets it wrong when he analyzes Paul's critique of Israel. Paul does not in this passage directly mention impartiality towards gentiles. Pattee suggests such themes by a long and complicated trail of supposed allusions to a plethora of OT texts, none of which are directly cited. Paul, however, clearly states Israel's problem: they have missed the righteousness of faith because they have pursued righteousness by works (Rom 9:30-32a). They have not kept gentiles out of the people of God. In fact, the gentiles have gained access to a right standing with God by faith (9:30)! Rather, Israel has kept themselves out because they seek the law of righteousness by works instead of by faith (9:31-32a).

Theological Correspondence

The sixth view justifies Paul's reading of Deut 30 on the basis of a theological correspondence between God's gracious revelations in the Old and the New Testaments.[104] Deuteronomy 30:11–14 expresses the principle that God's grace establishes a relationship with his people. Israel did not need to ascend into heaven or cross the sea in order to find God's commandment, for God's grace had brought it to them and enabled them to obey. In the same way, God's grace has now brought the word of the Gospel near in order that all may believe it and receive the righteousness of God by faith. There is no need for one to ascend into heaven now and bring Christ down, or to ascend into the grave and bring Christ up. Christ has finished his work, and calls people to believe in his gospel. Since Deut 30:12–14 reflects this gracious work of God, it serves as an ideal text to express the same grace operative in the righteousness of faith.[105]

This explanation does not succumb to the charge that Paul was pitting Moses against Moses in the two citations of Rom 10:5–8.[106] Rather, the two

---

104. Calvin, *Romans*, 388–92; Calvin, *Four Last Books of Moses*, 412–14; Ciampa, "Deuteronomy," 109–10; Boor, *Römer*, 246; Haldane, *Romans*, 504–6; Harrison, "Romans," 111–12; Hendriksen, *Romans*, 343–44; Keener, *Romans*, 126–27; Lagrange, *Romains*, 257–58; Leitzmann, *Römer*, 96; Moo, *Epistle to the Romans*, 653–57; Moo, "Paul's Reading," 409–12 (this essay elaborates and *strengthens* the view put forth in Moo, *Epistle to the Romans*); Murray, *Romans*, 2:52–53; Seifrid, "Paul's Approach," 34–37; Seifrid, "Romans," 657–59. Mohrmann argues that Paul utilizes Deut 30 as an expression of God's nearness in Christ, yet insists that Paul is supplanting the original message of Lev 18:5 and Deut 30:12–14 by applying them to righteousness in Christ versus righteousness by the law ("Semantic Collisions," 259–60). The explanation of Paul's use of Scripture set forth here does better justice to the unity of Scripture than Mohrmann's suggestions. Throughout Rom 9:30—10:13, Paul cites Scripture to support his point: "just as it is written" (9:33); "Moses describes the righteousness of the law" (Rom 10:5); "the righteousness of faith speaks thus" (10:6); "for the Scripture says" (10:11). He does not cite Scripture in order to supplant it.

105. Ironically, this view of the law in Deuteronomy and Paul's use of Deut 30:12–14 agrees with the conclusion set forth in Hays: "From Deuteronomy, Paul echoes the idea that the covenant depends on grace from start to finish rather than on Israel's own righteousness" (*Echoes*, 82). Hays (and others such as Wright) are zealous to promote a more gracious view of Torah, but they do so at expense of Torah's role in revealing guilt and bringing people to a knowledge of sinfulness. By reading Torah in the light of a law-gospel paradigm, one can discern elements of law and gospel without resorting to the new interpretation of the law proposed by Hays, Wright, and others.

106. Pattee argues that a contrast between Rom 10:5 and 10:6–8 means that "Paul violates one of Israel's basic assumptions about scripture," namely, that Scripture is indivisible and cannot contradict itself ("Stumbling Stone," 258; Wright implies a similar charge [*Romans*, 660]). However, Paul is not creating a contradiction so much as resolving a natural tension within the Scriptures themselves. The principle of works salvation must be subordinated to the principle of salvation by grace alone through faith alone.

themes of law and gospel coexist within Moses' own writings. Paul sees the proper relationship between the two because he understands the salvation-historical dimensions of the OT (Abraham's salvation by faith before the law shows that law was not given to justify).[107] Paul develops this contrast between law and gospel in Rom 9:30—10:13 by continually contrasting two kinds of righteousness.

This position also demonstrates that Paul's exegesis is not arbitrary and forced, but rather utilizes a specific area of correspondence between the message of Deut 30:12–14 and the argument of Rom 10:6-8: God graciously brings his revelation near. Likewise, Paul does not employ τοῦτ' ἔστιν in order to offer a specific interpretation of Deut 30:12–14, but to reveal the reference point for his application of the text.[108] It answers the question, How is God revealing his grace now as he did then? Paul's answer is Christ: just as God manifested his grace in giving Israel the law and enabling them to obey it, so God has done that again in the work of Christ and the gospel.

CONCLUSION

We conclude that Paul cites Lev 18:5 and Deut 30:12–14 in Rom 10:5–8 in order to contrast the two principles he views as operative within the OT Scriptures.[109] On the one hand, the Scriptures bear witness to the principle that if a person can keep the law, then he will have eternal life (Lev 18:5). However, human sinfulness prevents any person from performing this obedience. On the other hand, the Scriptures bear witness to God's grace that transforms sinful people on the inside, makes them willing and able to believe in him, and to obey his law (Deut 30:12–14). God has manifested the necessary priority of this grace in saving Abraham prior to his circumcision (Gen 15:6; 17:1; so the argument of Rom 4:1–12) and prior to the giving of the law (Rom 4:13–25; Gal 3:1–29). God has also manifested this priority in the call to Israel to circumcise their hearts before they can obey his law (Deut 10:16; 30:11–14).

Dodd comments that Paul's use of Scripture in Rom 10:5–8 "shows real spiritual insight on Paul's part that he should have recognized (without the aid of modern criticism) that there is a *stratum* in the Pentateuch which goes deeper than the bald legalism of other parts, and comes very near in spirit to Christianity" (*Romans*, 165–66). We believe the explanation of Paul's use of Scripture presented here is a better solution to that tension than Dodd's.

107. Carson, "Mystery," 411.

108. Moo, *Epistle to the Romans*, 654; Seifrid, "Paul's Approach," 34. Seifrid suggests rendering the phrase as "that is to say" or "that means."

109. Moo, *Epistle to the Romans*, 654.

Paul utilizes these theological principles in his scriptural defense of the assertion that Christ ends using the law to obtain a right standing with God for those who believe (Rom 10:4). Since the law cannot justify (10:5), one must obtain righteousness by means of faith in Christ (10:6–8). Israel ought to know this since this has always been God's approach to his people: the same grace that brought the law to them and enabled them to obey it has now brought the gospel near to them.[110]

We also conclude that Paul respects the context of these Old Testament citations. He does not utilize them merely to add scripturally-disguised support to his doctrine, but because they teach the very ideas he is trying to communicate. He employs these texts in order to add powerful support to his argument that Israel must stop trying to obtain a right standing with God by obeying the law, and instead seek righteousness by faith in Christ.

---

110. Moo writes, "If the Jews would only see the message of the OT as Paul sees it, they would recognize that the OT itself proclaims the indispensability of faith—the very message that Paul and the other apostles are preaching" ("Paul's Reading," 402).

Chapter 6

Romans 10:9–13

INTRODUCTION

The final section of Rom 9:30—10:13 (10:9–13) picks up the earlier strands of 9:30–10:8 and ties them together into a powerful conclusion. Previous chapters in this dissertation emphasized Paul's critique of Israel's pursuit of righteousness by means of works. In this final paragraph, Paul emphasizes the universal availability of righteousness by faith. This does not mean that faith has been absent from Paul's critique of Israel's error with reference to the law (9:30, 32a, 33; 10:3, 4, 6–8). However, while the previous paragraphs focus on the inability of works to justify in contrast to faith, the final paragraph focuses on the necessity and accessibility of righteousness by faith.

Paul makes several connections between 10:9–13 and 9:30–10:8. The ὅτι that begins 10:9 establishes the first connection. In 10:6–8, Paul gives his threefold description of what the righteousness of faith does and does not say: it does not say, "Who will ascend into heaven in order to bring Christ down," or, "who will descend into the abyss in order to bring Christ up from the dead," but it says, "the word is near you, in your mouth and in your heart." The last description is the most explicit: the near word corresponds to "the word of faith which we preach" (τὸ ῥῆμα τῆς πίστεως ὃ κηρύσσομεν [10:8]). When Paul introduces 10:9 with ὅτι, he signals that what follows provides the specific contents of that word of faith.[1] Furthermore, ὅτι

---

1. Käsemann, *Romans*, 291; Porter, *Romans*, 198; Schreiner, *Romans*, 559; Toews,

plays the important dual function of demonstrating that 10:9–13 is both a new section (ὅτι breaks up the successive occurrences of γὰρ in 10:2–5 and 10:10–13) and the essential completion of the previous argument (10:9–13 develops the nature of the faith presented in 10:6–8 as a contrast to righteousness based on the law [10:5]).

The second connection between 9:30—10:8 and 10:9–13 emerges from the language of 10:8–10. The references to the heart and mouth in 10:9–10 parallel those in 10:8.[2] In fact, the very order of words in the citation of Deut 30:14 in Rom 10:8 (first mouth then heart) influences the order in which Paul discusses the terms of salvation in 10:9 (confess with the mouth, believe in the heart).[3] Logically, belief in the heart precedes confession with the mouth, and Paul returns to this order in 10:10 (the heart believes unto righteousness, confession is made unto salvation). The order of mouth and heart in 10:9 provide a link to the previous discussion.

Several other smaller connections help unite 10:9–13 to the larger argument of 9:30—10:8. The reference to Christ's resurrection (10:9) corresponds to one of the things that righteousness by faith does not say: "who will descend into the abyss, that is, to bring Christ up from the dead?" (10:7)[4] The reference to "righteousness" in 10:10 echoes 9:30–31; 10:3–6.[5] The citation of Isa 28:16 in 10:11 forms an inclusio with 9:33 and indicates that 9:30—10:13 is one unit.[6] Finally, Paul grabs the thread of faith and refers to it directly three times in this final paragraph: πιστεύσῃς in 10:9, πιστεύεται in 10:10, and πᾶς ὁ πιστεύων in 10:11.[7]

"Law," 260; see also KJV, NKJV, NASB, NIV. Moo favors cause because it would be awkward to have two content clauses (10:8b and 9) in a row (*Epistle to the Romans*, 657; see also Cranfield, *Romans*, 2:526–27, and RSV, NRSV). However, it makes less sense to argue that 10:9 gives the reason for 10:8 (the near word is the word which Paul preaches because confession and faith lead to salvation?). Two content clauses make sense if the second is more specific than the first. Early scribes also may have read the grammar this way as indicated by the addition of το ρημα prior to εν τω στοματι in B cop^sa. These mss also read οτι κυριος Ιησους as opposed to κυριον Ιησουν which also reflects a view of the verse as an early Christian confession (see Longenecker, *Romans*, 831).

2. Moo, *Epistle to the Romans*, 657.
3. Cranfield, *Romans*, 2:527; Keck, *Romans*, 254.
4. Moo, *Epistle to the Romans*, 658.
5. Schreiner, *Romans*, 560.
6. Dunn, *Romans*, 2:616.
7. Toews, "Law," 327–28. Badenas also notes the following corresponding ideas: τέλος νόμου (10:4), λέγει ἡ γραφὴ (10:11), λέγει ἡ γραφὴ (10:13 and 9:33); παντὶ (10:4), πᾶς (10:11), πᾶς ὃς ἂν (10:13 and 9:33); Χριστὸς (10:4), ἐπ᾽ αὐτῷ (10:11), τὸ ὄνομα κυρίου (10:13 and 9:33); εἰς δικαιοσύνη (10:4), οὐ καταισχυνθήσεται (10:11), σωθήσεται (10:13 and 9:33 [*Christ*, 135]). The reference to the heart (10:9–10) may also reflect the New Covenant promise of a new heart (Ezek 36:26), which is not far

These connections demonstrate that Romans 10:9–13 plays an important role in Paul's critique of Israel's error with reference to the law. While Paul does not employ the terms νόμος or ἔργον, he concludes the discussion relevant to those terms. Romans 10:9–13 presents the solution to Israel's plight: faith in Jesus, the resurrected Lord.[8] Paul's presentation also contains an implicit invitation to Israel to embrace her Messiah, to stop trusting in her own works, and to receive the righteousness of faith.

Paul communicates this message in three ways. First, he carefully constructs the argument of Rom 10:9–13 to highlight the central role of faith in obtaining righteousness and salvation. Second, he uses the confession "Jesus is Lord" to present a high Christology that directs Israel's attention away from the law and unto Christ. Third, he once again uses the OT (Isa 28:16 in 10:11; Joel 3:5 [MT, LXX] in 10:13) to show that Israel's scriptures present faith as the sole means of justification.[9]

THE MESSAGE OF ROM 10:9–13

Paul carefully constructs the final phase of the argument of Rom 9:30—10:13. Rom 10:9–13 contains five occurrences of the conjunction γάρ (10:10, 11, 12a, 12b, 13). The conjunction can communicate clarification or reason, and Paul appears to use both here.[10] In Rom 10:9, Paul gives the conditions of salvation: "if you confess with your mouth, 'Jesus is Lord,' and believe in your heart that God raised him from the dead, you will be saved." Paul then uses the first γάρ to further develop the nature of faith and confession: "*for with the heart one believes unto righteousness, and with the mouth one*

---

from Paul's thinking in his OT citations in Rom 10:5–8. The reference to Lev 18:5 in Rom 10:5 does connect to Ezek 20:11, 13, 21, which we observed contributes to the negative side of Ezekiel's theology of obedience (people are incapable of keeping the law and obtaining life thereby). The movement of Ezekiel culminates in God's promise to enable his people to obey him from the heart and to live (Ezek 36:25–27; 37:1–14). The use of Deut 30:12–14 to describe the proper response to the gospel is predicated on Moses' understanding of Israel possessing a new heart. The citation of Joel 3:5 [MT, LXX] which is coming in Rom 10:13 connects to another context where God ties the eschatological work of salvation to the work of the Spirit. Saving faith and the possession of the Spirit characterize the people of God in the eschatological age (cf. Rom 2:25–29).

8. The change in focus in 10:9–13 ironically highlights the continuity between 9:30—10:8. As Longenecker observes, Paul uses this final section to show that the focus of the Christian message is on the person and work of Christ, not the Mosaic law (*Romans*, 854). This is the culmination towards which Paul has been moving all along.

9. Throughout this chapter the references to the book of Joel follow the MT and LXX versification.

10. See BDAG, 189, for options.

confesses unto salvation" (10:10).¹¹ The next γάρ then gives the reason why faith and confession bring salvation: "*for* the Scripture says, 'everyone who believes in him will not be put to shame'" (10:11).¹² After this scriptural citation, Paul employs two explanatory uses of γάρ to clarify why everyone who believes will not suffer shame: "*for* there is no difference between Jew and Greek, *for* the same Lord is over all, rich unto all who call upon him" (10:12). The final occurrence of γάρ then gives the reason why the Lord is rich to all who call upon him: "*for* [the Scriptures promise that] 'whoever calls upon the name of the Lord will be saved'" (10:13).¹³ The significance of these five successive occurrences of γάρ is that they not only tightly tie the paragraph together, but that they pull the reader towards an expected end. Rowe notes that they deepen σωθήσῃ in 10:9, and press forward toward the climactic quotation of Joel 3:5 in 10:13.¹⁴ The structure of the paragraph focuses the reader's attention on the declaration that all who call upon the name of the Lord will be saved.

The content of the paragraph especially highlights the centrality of faith. In sum, the section presents "*Jesus* as the one in whom *all* must believe to avoid eschatological shame and to receive *salvation*."¹⁵ Here Paul defines exactly what Christian faith consists of: "the confession of Jesus as Lord and the belief that God raised him from the dead."¹⁶ Although Paul employs a conditional sentence, he does so not to emphasize deeds, but because "the one essential condition of salvation is faith."¹⁷

Paul's emphasis on faith is not damaged by the fact that he refers to confession with the mouth before faith in the heart (10:9). As noted earlier,

---

11. The verbs πιστεύεται and ὁμολογεῖται are both present passive indicatives in 10:10 (they are both aorist active subjunctives in 10:9). Jewett, *Romans*, 631, translates them as "faith is evoked" and "confession is evoked." Moo suggests that "Paul uses the passive to connote an impersonal nuance: 'one believes,' 'one confesses'" (*Epistle to the Romans*, 658n62; see Blass and Debrunner, *Greek Grammar*, 72).

12. Cranfield, *Romans*, 2:531; Dunn, *Romans*, 2:609.

13. Dunn takes this final occurrence of γάρ as explanatory as well, which does work. We prefer reason because of the parallel with 10:11 (*Romans*, 2:616).

14. Rowe, "Romans 10:13," 141. We also see in this paragraph the same strategy that characterized 9:30—10:8: a theological argument driven home by citations from the OT.

15. Rowe, "Romans 10:13," 145, emphasis original.

16. Wright, *Romans*, 664. Rom 1:4 anticipates 10:9–10 by uniting Jesus' resurrection to his status as Lord. Porter notes, "This proclamation was very likely an early creedal formulation that contains the faith-confession that Christians were expected to make" (*Romans*, 198).

17. Dunn, *Romans*, 2:616. The sentence is a third-class conditional sentence, emphasizing the logical if-then sequence (see Wallace, *Greek Grammar*, 696).

Paul's order intentionally parallels the citation of Deut 30:14 in Rom 10:7. Furthermore, the references to mouth and heart in 10:9–10 are arranged as a chiasm, thus putting faith in the center.[18] Confession is the outward manifestation of faith, which receives much emphasis in 9:30—10:13 (9:30, 32a, 33; 10:3–4, 6–8).[19]

Faith is directed towards God and what he has done (10:9).[20] Paul does not advocate generic faith, but faith that God raised Christ from the dead. Christ's resurrection rests at the heart of the Christian confession.[21] This contrasts with the Jewish approach to the law that emphasized works of obedience. Christ, not the law, must be the proper object of Israel's pursuit (cf. Rom 9:31; 10:3).

The reference to the heart (10:9–10) links back to 2:29: genuine Christian faith comes about through the work of the Spirit within.[22] Dunn suggests that καρδία indicates "an affective and deeply motivating belief," and "not merely a recitation of creedal form."[23] Aquinas interprets the reference to the heart as a reference to the will.[24] Käsemann writes, "Here again faith should not be interpreted merely as inner understanding. For the heart as the center of personality means existence in its totality. It is as such defined by faith and manifests that in the confession."[25] Paul's point here, as it has been throughout 9:30—10:8, is that only faith will lead to justification. Heartless confession cannot become a new work that will substitute for

---

18. The poetic arrangement of 10:10 indicates that Paul does not intend a substantial distinction between δικαιοσύνην and σωτηρίαν here. However, Dunn believes that both have a future orientation, and explains δικαιοσύνη as "God's righteousness not just as his initial acceptance of the believer, but also his ongoing sustaining power and final vindication" (*Romans*, 2:609). On the basis of the references to righteousness in 10:6 and 10, I would suggest that Paul here defines the broader word σωτηρίαν in terms of δικαιοσύνην. Salvation as a whole is not in view, but rather the obtaining of a right standing before God (9:30–31; 10:3–8). Royster, on the basis of the distinction between righteousness and salvation, argues that faith puts the believer on the path of righteousness so that he can obtain the end of his faith, the salvation of his soul (*Romans*, 264). Although the two terms refer to different things, Paul's parallel usage indicates that they are both obtained by faith, not that one leads to another.
19. Moo, *Epistle to the Romans*, 657.
20. Rowe, "Name," 143.
21. Osborne, *Romans*, 271.
22. Wright, *Romans*, 664.
23. Dunn, *Romans*, 2:608.
24. Aquinas, *Romans*, 284.
25. Käsemann, *Romans*, 291.

obedience to the law, nor can faith be viewed as something that the believer *does*, for it is the work of God's Spirit.[26]

Paul emphasizes the connection between faith in the heart and confession with the mouth. Dunn defines ὁμολογήσῃς as "a public confession of a solemn nature."[27] Michel defines ὁμολογέω as "to make solemn statements of faith," "to confess something in faith."[28] Dunn notes that the content of the confession is "an (or the) equivalent of the Shema (Deut 6:4): as he who says the Shema identifies himself as belonging to Israel, so he who says κύριον Ἰησοῦν identifies himself as belonging to Jesus."[29] Just as faith has a specific object (the resurrection of Christ), so does the believer's confession (the lordship of Christ).

We discuss the Christology implied in identifying Jesus as κύριος in the next section. For now, the personal significance of such a confession helps reinforce Paul's emphasis on faith in Christ for salvation. According to Dunn, "κύριος was widely used to denote an asserted or acknowledged dominance and right of disposal of superior over inferior."[30] Furthermore, "to confess someone as 'lord' denotes an attitude of subserviency and sense of belonging or devotion to the one so named."[31] Finally, "if the confession here was used in baptism, as again is widely agreed to be very likely, it would also indicate a transfer of allegiance, a change in acknowledged ownership."[32] Jewett says it "affirms Jesus as authoritative and identifies the confessor as his follower."[33]

---

26. The believer is active in the exercise of faith, but does not view it as a work performed to satisfy divine requirements. Faith involves actively resting and trusting in the merits of Christ's death and resurrection. Moo observes that Paul rhetorically employs the reference to confession with the mouth (along with the reference to belief in the heart) in order to show how the quotation of Deut 30:14 in Rom 10:8 finds fulfillment in the preaching of the gospel (*Romans*, 336). The purpose is not to present confession as something that one must *do* in order to obtain salvation. That runs counter to the thurst of the whole argument of 9:30—10:13.

27. Dunn, *Romans*, 2:607.
28. Michel, "ὁμολογέω," 209.
29. Dunn, *Romans*, 2:607.
30. Dunn, *Romans*, 2:608.
31. Dunn, *Romans*, 2:608.
32. Dunn, *Romans*, 2:608.
33. Jewett, *Romans*, 629. Bultmann is similar: "Kyrios indicates the respective deity not primarily in his divine majesty and power, but in his 'master' relation to the speaker (the corresponding term for the worshiper is 'slave,' δοῦλος)" (*Theology*, 125). Porter helpfully notes that the confession that Jesus is Lord highlights Jesus' divinity while the confession that God raised him from the dead highlights his humanity (*Romans*, 199).

The emphasis on faith continues in Paul's OT citations in 10:11 and 10:13. The reference to faith is explicit in 10:11: "all who believe in him will not be put to shame."[34] In 10:13, Paul emphasizes faith using the words of Joel 3:5: "whoever calls upon the name of the Lord will be saved." The phrase "call upon the name of the Lord" has its roots in the OT and functions to identify YHWH as one's own God (Gen 4:26; 12:8; 1 Kgs 18:24; 2 Kgs 5:11; 1 Chr 16:8; Pss 79:6; 80:18; 116:13, 17; Isa 41:25; 64:7; 65:1; Jer 10:25; Zeph 3:9).[35] The phrase does not refer generically to prayer,[36] but identifies those who worship YHWH consistently and exclusively.[37] To call on the Lord is a cry of allegiance and a declaration of commitment.[38]

The phrase continues into the NT and identifies those who belong to the people of God through faith in Jesus Christ (Acts 9:14, 21; Rom 10:13; 1 Cor 1:2).[39] Aquinas describes it as recognizing Christ as Lord and submitting one's will to him.[40] Osborne writes, "it should not be narrowed to prayer but includes prayer, worship and a general dependence on Christ for grace and mercy in every area of life . . . Here it begins with calling on the Lord in faith for salvation (as in v. 13) and continues with the lifelong calling on the Lord that results."[41] Daniel Estes highlights the cultic significance of the term: "to 'call on the name of the Lord' (ἐπικαλεῖν τὸ ὄνομα κυρίου) means more than to invoke the Lord, but expresses a prayer for deliverance with cultic connotations, that is, 'to worship Jesus as Lord.'"[42] Christian faith has a specific object (Jesus Christ), it serves as the proper alternative

---

34. We discuss the identification of "him" in the section addressing the use of the OT in Rom 10:9–13.

35. Garrett, *Hosea, Joel*, 375.

36. *Contra* Capes, "YHWH," 134.

37. Stuart, *Hosea–Jonah*, 261. Allen suggests that the Hebrew phrase קרא בשם יהוה literally means, "'call (upon God) by the name Yahweh,' i.e., by calling out the name" (*Joel, Obadiah, Jonah and Micah*, 101n25).

38. Block, "Romans 10:13," 185.

39. Dunn, *Romans*, 2:610–11. So also Fitzmyer, *Romans*, 593; Wright, *Romans*, 665n400.

40. Aquinas, *Romans*, 282.

41. Osborne, *Romans*, 273. Also Black: "The original Hebrews means, not simply 'make appeal to Yahweh,' 'invoke Yahweh,' but implies that the Israelite, in so doing, places himself on Yahweh's side, professes allegiance to Yahweh, and so for Paul, the words mean 'to profess oneself a Christian'" (*Romans*, 139).

42. Estes, "Calling," 21. Estes also argues that ἐπικαλέω "draws on a long OT tradition of employing such language in cultic settings, it parallels closely other NT texts that are cultic in orientation, and it coheres with our earliest evidence about the worship practices of the early church." Cf. Dunn (cited earlier): "as he who says the Shema identifies himself as belonging to Israel, so he who says κύριον Ἰησοῦν identifies himself as belonging to Jesus" (*Romans*, 2:607).

to pursuing righteousness through the law, and identifies those who belong to God's people.

Now that we have seen the message of the paragraph, we can make one final structural observation. Paul drives home the emphasis on faith and salvation by highlighting similar themes at the beginning and end. The injunction to faith in 10:9 connects directly with the implied injunction to call on the name of the Lord in 10:13. According to Seifrid, calling upon the Lord (10:12–13) explains what it means to confess Jesus as Lord (10:9–10).[43] Paul's point is not to muddy the emphasis on faith by referring to an action like confession, but rather to describe faith in terms of calling upon the name of the Lord, that is, confessing Jesus as Lord (one's God and Savior).[44]

Paul also begins and ends this paragraph with references to the verb σῴζω in the future tense (σωθήσῃ in 10:9, σωθήσεται in 10:13). On the nature of the future tense, Moo suggests a "logical" future: salvation as the result of and therefore future to believing and confessing.[45] Porter describes such a future as follows: "timeless Futures are not specific in their deictic reference but implicate general, conditional or logical expected processes."[46] Wallace argues that the future indicative can stand in for the aorist subjunctive.[47] If so, then this future may simply be functioning as the subjunctive in conditional sentences.[48] Dunn and Wright refer salvation to the future temporally,[49] but this probably makes too much of the future tense. We favor the logical future approach: salvation is the immediate result of believing and confessing.[50] The larger biblical idea of salvation certainly contains a major eschatological component, but that is not the main idea here.[51] Here

---

43. Seifrid, "Romans," 660. Also Bultmann, *Theology*, 126.

44. Barrett suggest no distinction between confession and faith: "the confession is believed and the faith confessed" (*Romans*, 200).

45. Moo, *Epistle to the Romans*, 658n61. Also Jewett, *Romans*, 630; Osborne, *Romans*, 270.

46. Porter, *Verbal Aspect*, 421.

47. Wallace, *Greek Grammar*, 571.

48. Wallace, *Greek Grammar*, 469–70; also Porter, *Verbal Aspect*, 421–23.

49. Dunn, *Romans*, 2:609; Wright, *Romans*, 664. Schreiner also asserts that Paul typically intends a genuine future when he uses σῴζειν in the future tense (*Romans*, 560).

50. This may be what Blass and Debrunner are indicating when they describe the use of the future indicative "*relatively* in declarative sentences after verbs of believing to denote a time subsequent to the acquisition of belief" (*Greek Grammar*, 178, emphasis original).

51. Oropeza argues that Paul consistently uses σῴζω to refer to humans being saved in relationsip to the eschaton (*Jews*, 79). We cannot divorce the eschatological dimension from Paul's thought, but the overall focus is on salvation in the present, which anticipates the verdict of the eschaton.

Paul identifies the conditions of salvation (faith and confession); those who fulfill the conditions have salvation.[52]

THE SIGNIFICANCE OF THE CONFESSION ΚΎΡΙΟΝ ἸΗΣΟΥΝ

Romans 10:9–13 contains four occurrences of the noun κύριος (10:9, 12 [2x], 13). The confession κύριον Ἰησοῦν forms an integral part of the Christian confession that leads to salvation (10:9, 13).[53] This confession presents a high Christology that directs Israel's attention away from the law and unto Jesus.

Origin and Christology of the Confession Κύριον Ἰησοῦν

Much debate has taken place regarding the origin of the κύριος title.[54] Vos argues, "from the beginning onward and uninterruptedly ever after Jesus called Himself or was called Kyrios."[55] The preservation of the Aramaic μαράνα θά in 1 Cor 16:22 does lend credence to this suggestion, or at least indicates that the designation of Christ as Lord was a very early liturgical formula.[56] Fitzmyer presents evidence which suggests that Palestinian Jews could refer to YHWH as κύριος, and that those who joined the Christian community did apply the title to Jesus.[57]

---

52. Pelagius states that salvation here refers to past transgressions, not future. There is no basis in the text for this distinction (*Romans*, 123).

53. κύριον Ἰησοῦν (10:9) is a double accusative governed by ὁμολογήσῃς (see Blass and Debrunner, *Greek Grammar*, 86; cf. John 9:22; 1 Cor 12:3). Believers confess that Jesus is Lord (so ESV, NASB, NIV, RSV, NRSV, NLT, HCSB, NET).

54. For a starting point, see Bultmann, *Theology*, 125; Fitzmyer, "Semitic Background"; Hurtado, *Lord Jesus Christ*, 197–200, Neufeld, *Earliest Christian Confessions*, 42–68; Vos, "Continuity," 161–89.

55. Vos, "Continuity," 161.

56. Cranfield, *Romans*, 2:528; Neufeld, *Earliest Christian Confessions*, 55.

57. Fitzmyer, "Semitic Background," 126; also Block, "Romans 10:13," 182; Dunn, *Romans*, 2:608; Hurtado, *Lord Jesus Christ*, 199. Hultgren suggests it is perhaps the earliest of all confessional formulations (*Romans*, 388). Howard argues that the divine name, יהוה, was not rendered by κύριος in the pre-Christian Greek Bible, but was written out in Aramaic or in paleo-Hebrew letters or was transliterated into Greek letters ("Tetragram," 65). He also suggests that Jewish Christians continued to write the Tetragram in their copies of the LXX ("Tetragram," 76). In the late first century gentile Christians began to substitute κύριος and θεός for the Tetragram ("Tetragram," 76–77). Based on this, Howard conjectures that the NT writers also used the Tetragram when citing the OT ("Tetragram," 77). While Howard's work presents helpful evidence

The more significant point of the debate concerns the christological implications of Paul's application of κύριος to Jesus. Dunn argues that while the title shows that Jesus shares in the one God's lordship, it does not indicate preexistence and incarnation.[58] Likewise, Fitzmyer does not think that the title identifies Jesus with YHWH, but identifies Jesus as sharing in some sense in YHWH's transcendence (Jesus is more than merely human; Jesus is King over his people).[59]

Hurtado, however, argues that the application of κύριος to Jesus equates him with God.[60] As noted above, the phrase "call upon the name of the Lord" communicates notions of worship and devotion; calling upon the name of the Lord is a cultic act.[61] When the early Christians called Jesus Lord, they were equating his name with the name of the Lord, and viewing such an equation as "the proper liturgical expression of the biblical phrase, to 'call upon the name of the Lord.'"[62] Such use identifies Jesus as the appropriate recipient of cultic devotion.[63] Knowing the sensitivity of Jewish monotheism, such identification means one thing: early Christians identified Jesus as God.[64]

Cranfield offers four points to support such an identification: (1) Paul applies to Christ the κύριος title of the LXX when the OT referent is God (10:13; 1 Thess 5:2; 2 Thess 2:2); (2) Phil 2:9–11 connects the κύριος title with τὸ ὄνομα τὸ ὑπὲρ πᾶν ὄνομα ("the name which is above every name" [2:9]), a reference to the name of God himself;[65] (3) Paul invokes Christ in prayer (10:12–14; 1 Cor 1:2; 16:22); (4) Paul often tightly associates God

---

for the early application of κύριος to יהוה, he does not have the support of any extant witnesses that would justify extending his theory into the NT documents. The best he can do is examine certain NT passage which cite the OT and then contain a textual variant regarding God and Christ as a reflection of the supposed ambiguity created by the removal of the Tetragram ("Tetragram," 78–82).

58. Dunn, *Romans*, 2:608, 610.

59. Fitzmyer, "Semitic Background," 130–32. Howard uses his research to suggest that the removal of the Tetragram from the NT citations of the OT created considerable ambiguity regarding whether a writer was referring to God or Christ ("Tetragram," 77). The presence of the Tetragram would have guaranteed less "functional identity" between God and Christ (78n72).

60. Hurtado, *Lord Jesus Christ*, 197–200.

61. *Inter alios*, Estes, "Calling," 26–33.

62. Hurtado, *Lord Jesus Christ*, 198.

63. Hurtado, *Lord Jesus Christ*, 198.

64. Hurtado, *Lord Jesus Christ*, 199. Hurtado also notes that Jewish literature recognizes certain divine agents, but does not give them such cultic veneration.

65. Dodd, *Romans*, 168, notes the same.

and Christ (1:7; 8:35, 39; 1 Cor 1:3; 2 Cor 1:2).⁶⁶ He concludes that such a confession "meant the acknowledgement that Jesus shares the name and the nature, the holiness, the authority, power, majesty and eternity of the one and only true God."⁶⁷

From a grammatical perspectice, Daniel Wallace identifies κύριον Ἰησοῦν as a possible double accusative of the object-complement.⁶⁸ In this construction, Ἰησοῦν is a proper name and thus the object, and κύριον is complement ("Jesus is Lord").⁶⁹ The significance of this is that "Since the complement *κύριον precedes* the object, it is possible that it is definite though anarthrous. Thus, the confession would be that Jesus is *the* Lord, that is, *Yahweh*."⁷⁰

Other lines of evidence in the passage point in this direction. The title "Lord of all" (10:12) is a Jewish formula that refers to YHWH. 1QapGen 20:12b–13a reads, "'Blessed are You, O God Most High, Eternal Lord, for you are Lord and Master over all."⁷¹ 4Q409 1:6 reads, "Bless the Lord of all."⁷² Josephus (*Ant.* 20:90) states, "Thou art the first and only rightful Lord of all."⁷³ The application of this title to Christ is consistent with Acts 10:36 (Ἰησοῦ Χριστοῦ, οὗτός ἐστιν πάντων κύριος).

The parallel thoughts between Rom 3:29–30 and 10:12 also indicate a high Christology. In 3:29–30, the one God justifies Jew and gentile alike. In 10:9–13, the one Lord gives righteousness and salvation to Jew and gentile alike. The monotheism of 3:29–30 is expanded by the parallel language of Rom 10:12 and the identification of Jesus as YHWH (10:13).⁷⁴

---

66. Cranfield, *Romans*, 2:529.

67. Cranfield, *Romans*, 2:529.

68. Wallace, *Greek Grammar*, 187–88. See also earlier discussion of this construction.

69. Wallace, *Greek Grammar*, 188.

70. Wallace, *Greek Grammar*, 188, emphasis original. For more discussion, see Wallace, "Semantics," 108–11.

71. Wise et al., *Dead Sea Scrolls*, 100.

72. Wise et al., *Dead Sea Scrolls*, 476.

73. Feldman, *Josephus*, 9:435.

74. Block, "Roman 10:13," 189–90. This indicates that there is no problem in translating Rom 9:5 in a way that identifies Christ as God. Toews argues that κύριος in 10:12 refers to God, not Jesus ("Law," 328). He bases this on three ideas: (1) the antecedent of ἐπ' αὐτῷ (10:11), (2) the interpretation of τοὺς ἐπικαλουμένους αὐτόν (10:12) as a reference to prayer, and (3) the original reference of Joel 3:5 to YHWH. However, one could also read this evidence as indicating that Paul was attributing divinity to Jesus. Rowe notes that the confession κύριον Ἰησοῦν in 10:9 indicates that the references to κύριος in 10:12–13 refer to Jesus as well ("Name," 146).

Finally, that Paul commends calling on Christ for salvation (10:13) also reflects a high Christology.[75] BDAG notes that ἐπικαλέω is often used for calling upon a deity.[76] Rowe notes, "The act of 'calling upon' varies from worship (e.g., Gen 13:4; 21:33), to prayer for deliverance (e.g., 2 Sam 22 [Ps 18]), to apocalyptic or eschatological vision (Zech 13:9; Joel 3:5), but in each case, the one upon whom the people call is *YHWH*, the one God of Israel."[77] Rowe concludes that the citation of Joel 3:5 in Rom 10:13 "makes an unreserved identification of Jesus with YHWH, the unique Lord and only God of Israel."[78]

While Christian claims to Jesus' divinity are considered blasphemous to Jewish interpreters,[79] Paul's identification of Jesus as Lord points in that direction. This identification serves the purpose of directing Israel's attention away from the law and unto Christ, the only suitable object of saving faith. The confession "Jesus is Lord" is not only a declaration of commitment, but a confession of Jesus as a divine person.

Gospel and Empire?

Some NT scholars argue that Paul employs the confession of Jesus' Lordship as a polemic against the cult of Caesar. Evidence exists showing that the Caesars were viewed in terms of lordship and sovereign authority. Dio Cassius refers to Augustus as μόνος ἀναμφιλόγως κύριος ἁπάντων.[80] Josephus records that the Sicarii could not be compelled to confess Caesar as Lord (Καίσαρα δεσπότην ὁμολογήσωσιν), neither could their children (Καίσαρα δεσπότην).[81] Polycarp was urged to confess Κύριος καῖσαρ.[82]

---

75. Schreiner, *Romans*, 562.

76. BDAG, 373. See also the LXX and NT evidence in Estes, "Calling," 26–33.

77. Rowe, "Name," 151.

78. Rowe, "Name," 160. Campbell adds that Paul's identification "is quite consistent with the broader apologetic that we have seen Paul developing through this chapter of Romans. His point is that *God has come to Israel in person*, so any rejection of this gracious drawing-near is the more incomprehensible" (*Deliverance*, 804, emphasis original). Wright notes, "when the early Christians called Jesus *kyrios*, one of the overtones that word quickly acquired, astonishing and even shocking though this must have been, was that texts in the Greek Bible which used *kyrios* to translate the divine name yhwh were now used to denote Jesus himself, with a subtlety and theological sophistication that seems to go back to the earliest days of the Christian movement" (*Resurrection*, 571).

79. See Schoeps, *Paul*, 160–67.

80. Dio Cassius, *Hist. Rom.* 56.39.

81. Josephus, *J.W.* 7.418–19.

82. Polycarp, *Mart. Pol.* 8:2.

Building on these identifications and more, Jewett argues, "The formulation of this verse proclaims Christ as the one replacing the emperor in establishing a new realm of plentitude in which all are treated equally."[83] Similarly, Wright argues that the proclamation of Messiah Jesus as the resurrected ruler of the nations "cannot, I suppose, be other than a direct challenge to the present ruler of the nations, Caesar himself."[84] According to Wright, many of Paul's statements echo and parody the imperial ideology.[85] For example, Rom 1:18—4:25 teaches that God overthrows the powers of the world and creates the true family of God; Rom 8:31–39 shows that God works by love whereas Caesar works by violence and terror; Rom 9–11 shows that God's people have a more ancient story than Rome; Rom 13:1–7 teaches that Caesar is responsible to the true God.[86] Wright also argues that shared terminology between Paul's gospel and imperial slogans (terms such as gospel, Son of God, salvation, righteousness) would have directly challenged Rome's interpretation and ownership of such concepts.[87]

Wright's evidence is not convincing. The key missing ingredient is any specific challenge of Rome in Paul's letters.[88] The most Wright can offer are terminological parallels, but parallel terminology does not constitute direct challenge or identity of referent.[89] Paul makes his real challenge to Rome clear: he denies the validity of their gods.[90] Paul criticizes Rome because they are one manifestation of the present evil age doomed to destruction.[91]

---

83. Jewett, *Romans*, 632–33.

84. Wright, "Paul and Caesar," 177.

85. Wright, *Resurrection*, 568–69.

86. Wright, "Paul and Caesar," 188–91. See also Elliott, "Anti-Imperial Message," 180–82.

87. Wright, *Resurrection*, 568–70.

88. Barclay notes that there is "no specification [in Paul] of Rome on the countless occasions where Paul *could have* spoken of her empire, her rulers and her cult" ("Roman Empire," 375). Burk uses Hirsch's hermeneutical concepts and identifies this weakness as a substitution of implication for meaning ("Paul's Gospel," 319–22).

89. Barclay, "Roman Empire," 376. The same critique appears in Burk, "Paul's Gospel," 315–19.

90. Barclay, "Roman Empire," 381; Barclay, "Paul," 358; Dunn, *Romans*, 2:608. See also Revelation 13:1–18; 17:1–18, where elements of Roman culture function symbolically for any pagan, oppressive government or institution that fits the description (according the interpretation advanced in Beale, *Revelation*).

91. Barclay, "Roman Empire," 383–87. Neufeld takes a similar approach by arguing that the confession κύριος Ἰησοῦς is not a direct polemic against the cult of Caesar, but did remind gentile Christians that their loyalty did not ultimately belong to Caesar (*Earliest Christian Confessions*, 65–66). The confession opposed loyalty to Caesar as well as loyalty to other gods. Hultgren writes, "Its origins need not be traced to an opposition to the imperial cult, in which 'Caesar is Lord,' but to a prior conviction already

Paul's critique of Rome is the same as his critique of Judaism: it trusts human achievement rather than the work of Christ.

THE USE OF THE OT IN ROM 10:11, 13

Romans 10:9–13 once again finds Paul using the OT to prove his theological argument. Here he cites Isa 28:16 in 10:11 and Joel 3:5 in 10:13 to show that Israel's scriptures present faith as the only way of salvation. The citation of Isa 28:16 in 10:11 links back to the beginning of the argument (Paul previously cited Isa 28:16 in Rom 9:33) and further reinforces the idea that Rom 10:9–13 are devoted to presenting the solution to Israel's plight. The citation of Joel 3:5 in 10:13 makes this explicit.

The Use of Isa 28:16 in Rom 10:11

Our previous discussion of Rom 9:30–33 addresses the relevant questions concerning Paul's use of Isa 28:16. Therefore, we can summarize our findings there and focus on the significance of Paul's use of the text in Rom 10:11. Isaiah 28–33 demonstrate the foolishness of Israel trusting the nations for military deliverance instead of the Lord.[92] Faced with the threat of Assyrian invasion, Judah is considering an alliance with Egypt to deliver them from the judgment threatened in Isa 8:6, 8, 14 (a judgment threatened, ironically, for trusting the nations [Isa 30:1–7; 31:1–5]).[93] In 28:16, Isaiah admonishes the people to put their trust in God, depicted metaphorically using the imagery of the stone: "Therefore, thus says YHWH the Lord, 'Behold, I establish in Zion a stone, a stone of testing, a corner, precious, established as a foundation, the one who trusts will not show haste.'" Paul cites the final phrase of this verse (המאמין לא יחיש) in Rom 9:33; 10:11.

Two points are worth noting concerning the LXX translation. First, the LXX adds the words ἐπ' αὐτῷ (καὶ ὁ πιστεύων ἐπ' αὐτῷ οὐ μὴ

---

in Palestinian Christianity that Jesus is the one appointed by God to reign. But the confession could hardly avoid taking on additional significance as a counterconfession to emperor worship. At least that is how it would have been understood in Rome. But Paul does not seem interested at this point in engaging in polemics against the imperial cult. He is concerned rather about the way of righteousness for all people in the presence of God" (*Romans*, 388). For detailed critiques, see Burk, "Paul's Gospel," 309–37; Kim, *Christ*, 28–64.

92. Oswalt, *Isaiah, Chapters 1–39*, 504.

93. Oswalt, *Isaiah, Chapters 1–39*, 504; Webb, *Isaiah*, 116. Snodgrass notes verbal parallels between 8:8 and 28:15, 18, and 8:15 and 28:13 ("Christological Stone Testimonia," 33).

καταισχυνθῇ), which is missing from some important Septuagint witnesses, but well-established by others.[94] The Targumim translate this verse as, "*and the righteous* who believe *in these things* will not be *shaken when distress comes.*"[95] The presence of באלין ("in these things") in the Targumim indicates that ἐπ' αὐτῷ is original to the LXX and not added because of Rom 9:33.[96]

Second, the LXX translates חוש ("to hurry, to hasten, to give way"[97]) with καταισχύνω ("be disappointed"[98]). The LXX never uses καταισχύνω to translate חוש except here. Since Isaiah 28:16 describes the stone as "a stone of testing" and a precious cornerstone that serves as a foundation, the LXX translator may have chosen a word that conveyed the idea that those who trusted this reliable stone would not be disappointed with their choice. The two ideas overlap: those who trust God are not in haste but rather have peace (MT); they are not disappointed because they have put their trust in God (LXX). Perhaps Paul cites the LXX here instead of the MT in order to make use of the second emphasis in his argument.

When Paul cites Isa 28:16 in Rom 9:33; 10:11, he uses the future passive with a single negative (οὐ καταισχυνθήσεται) instead of the aorist passive with double negative of the LXX (οὐ μὴ καταισχυνθῇ). Kruse suggests, "This lessens the emphatic nature of the Isa 28:16 text, and also implies a future reference in the text, affirming that on the last day those who put their trust in the Lord will never be put to shame; their trust in him will be fully honored."[99] Stanley suggests that the lack of a clear reason for the change indicates that Paul's source read this way.[100] The difference could also be stylistic. The change does not affect the meaning of the passage. Paul also omits the introductory καί, but according to Stanley, such an omission is consistent with "Paul's regular practice of omitting introductory particles that would impede a smooth transition from text to quotation."[101]

The most significant change (and here Paul even differs from his previous citation in 9:33) is the addition of πᾶς.[102] The addition is interpretative,[103]

---

94. Stanley, *Paul*, 124; Ziegler, *Isaias*, 218.
95. Chilton, *Isaiah Targum*, 56. "These things" likely refers to God's promise to appoint a King in Zion.
96. Snodgrass, "Stone Testimonia," 51–52.
97. HALOT, 300.
98. BDAG, 517.
99. Kruse, *Romans*, 411n122.
100. Stanley, *Paul*, 125.
101. Stanley, *Paul*, 133.
102. A few minuscules add ὅτι before the citation but this is obviously secondary.
103. Toews, "Law," 327.

and a number of factors could have influenced Paul's decision. Perhaps he is picking up the universal element of Rom 10:4b,[104] or perhaps he is influenced by the "all" of Joel 3:5 in 10:13.[105] Seifrid even suggests that universalism is implicit in the Isaianic text.[106] The tight connection between Rom 10:11 and 10:13 indicates that the addition of πᾶς in Rom 10:11 is influenced by and preparing for Rom 10:13.

As we observed in our discussion of the use of this text in Rom 9:33, Paul uses Isa 28:16 analogically. Just as the Israel of Isaiah's day was foolishly trusting human resources to deliver them from death when they should have trusted YHWH, so Paul's contemporary Israelites rely on their efforts to keep the law instead of trusting God's promise of salvation in Christ. In 10:11, Paul emphasizes the other side of that equation: salvation is available to all who believe, and Israel should put their trust in Christ because no one who exercises faith will be disappointed.[107] The citation communicates the timeless truth that salvation comes from faith not works.

The citation also plays an important structural role. It supports the assertion of 10:9–10 that those who believe will be saved, and provides the vital link to the universality of 10:12.[108] In fact, 10:11 is the linchpin of the paragraph: it grounds 10:9–10 and introduces the universal focus of 10:12–13.[109] Since Isaiah does not preclude gentiles from participating in salvation by faith, Paul's interpretative addition is not only justified, but demanded by the trajectory of his argument.[110]

---

104. Moo, *Epistle to the Romans*, 659.

105. Wright, *Romans*, 666.

106. Seifrid, "Romans," 659.

107. Rowe presents the following as evidence that ἐπ' αὐτῷ (10:11) refers to Jesus: (1) αὐτόν in 10:9 refers to Jesus and is the clearest antecedent of αὐτῷ in 10:11; (2) both God and Christ are in focus in 10:9 (Jesus is Lord because God raised him from the dead), so an either-or decision is not necessary; (3) Isa 28:16 in Rom 9:33 refers to Christ; (4) the identification of κύριος in 10:12–13 as Jesus indicates that 10:11 also refers to Jesus ("Name," 143–44).

108. Schreiner, *Romans*, 561.

109. Rowe notes that πᾶς also looks ahead to 11:26: πᾶς Ἰσραὴλ σωθήσεται ("Name," 152n58).

110. Stanley concludes from the difference in citation between 9:33 and 10:11 "shows how little Paul was concerned to hide from his readers the freedom with which he could handle the wording of the biblical text" (*Paul*, 134). This exaggerates the significance of the addition of one word.

The Use of Joel 3:5 in Rom 10:13

Original OT Context of Joel 3:5

Paul's universal trajectory culminates in the citation of Joel 3:5 in Rom 10:13. The book of Joel develops the idea of the Day of the Lord.[111] The book begins by declaring that Israel has suffered a devastating locust plague as chastisement from YHWH (Joel compares this plague to the coming day of the Lord [1:1–20, esp. 1:15]). Joel then announces that this coming day of the Lord is near (2:1), and warns Israel that they are in danger of suffering another judgment, this time a coming invasion depicted in terms of an army (2:1–11). What follows is a call to repentance to avoid the day of the Lord (2:12–17), and the Lord's promise to restore his people and their land (2:18–27).[112] The next section (3:1–5) begins with the prediction of the outpouring of the Spirit (3:1), and concludes with the promise that "all who call upon the name of YHWH will be saved" (3:5). The final chapter (4:1–21) continues the narrative of what God will do "at that time, when I restore the fortunes of Judah and Jerusalem" (3:1) and "gather nations" for judgment (3:2).

Paul cites the last verse (3:5) of the passage which describes the outpouring of the Spirit (3:1–5).[113] This outpouring of the Spirit will take place "after these things" (והיה אחרי־כן, 3:1), referring to the blessings of 2:18–27.[114] First, God will pour out the rain on Israel's depleted land (2:23), then he will pour out his Spirit (2:28).[115] Both outpourings constitute God's saving actions towards his people.[116] When the day of the Lord comes, including

---

111. Baker, *Joel, Obadiah, Malachi*, 28; Busenitz, *Joel & Obadiah*, 37.

112. Mohrmann notes that Joel takes a decisive turn at 2:18 from summons to repentance to prediction of future blessings ("Semantic Collisions," 161).

113. Peter cites this entire passage in his Pentecost sermon (Acts 2:16–21).

114. Barton argues that the phrase והיה אחרי־כן indicates secondary material added to a completed prophecy (*Joel and Obadiah*, 93–94). He admits, however, that such is hard to prove, and appeals to the general consensus of commentators. In response, later material does not mean that it was not authored by Joel himself (the author of the earlier material), nor that it was not intended to form a message consistent with the earlier material, and capable of chronological sequence.

115. Allen, *Joel, Obadiah, Jonah and Micah*, 98. Most commentators note that "pour out" communicates the idea of generosity (see HALOT, 1629).

116. Garrett, *Hosea, Joel*, 367. Hubbard notes, "The difference between the two stages is not that the first is material and the second spiritual but that the first is the restoration of old damage and the second is the inauguration of a new era in God's dealings with his people" (*Joel and Amos*, 72). Allen and Garrett note that the outpouring of the Spirit answers Moses' prayer in Num 11:29 (*Joel, Obadiah, Jonah, and Micah*, 99 and *Hosea, Joel*, 368, respectively).

cataclysmic signs in the heavens and on the earth (3:3–4), Israel can safely escape God's judgment by calling upon him for salvation (3:5).[117] The outpouring of the Spirit will prepare them for that critical moment (3:1–2).[118]

Joel 3:5 in Intertestamental Jewish Literature

The use of Joel 3:5 in intertestamental Jewish literature does not have many significant occurrences. Toews suggests that the translation of מלט with σῴζω creates verbal connections with texts such as 2 Sam 22:4; Ps 17:4; Jon 1:6.[119] The *Psalms of Solomon* contain two verses with verbal similarities. *Ps. Sol.* 6:1 reads, "Happy is the man whose heart is ready to call on the name of the Lord; when he remembers the name of the Lord, he will be saved."[120] The verbal allusions are clear, but Toews notes that the thematic ties such as the day of the Lord, the outpouring of the Spirit, locusts, and the end-time judgment are absent.[121] Similarly, *Ps. Sol.* 15:1 reads, "When I was persecuted I called on the Lord's name; I expected the help of Jacob's God and I was saved. For you, O God, are the hope and refuge of the poor."[122] Here Toews notes conceptual parallels with Joel (salvation and destruction on the day of the Lord's judgment) and Rom 10 (confessing the Lord's name, the heart, "the one who does these things will never be shaken" [*Ps. Sol.* 15:4], righteousness and salvation).[123] Finally, the Targumim renders Joel 3:5 as "everyone who *prays in* the name of the Lord shall be delivered."[124] These texts do not add any interpretive information to the verse that is not present in the original context.

---

117. Allen, *Joel, Obadiah, Jonah, and Micah*, 102.

118. Toews, "Law," 166. David Hubbard notes that while Joel does not explicitly identify these blessings as eschatological, the references to "in those days" (3:2) and "in those days and at that time" (4:1) give the passage an eschatological touch (*Joel and Amos*, 72). Peter's citation of 3:1 reads ταῖς ἐσχάταις ἡμέραις (Acts 2:17). VanGemeren also refers 2:18–27 to eschatology and argues that 2:18–27 are fulfilled when 3:1–5 are fulfilled ("Spirit," 89).

119. Toews, "Law," 166.

120. Charlesworth, *Old Testament Pseudepigrapha*, 2:657.

121. Toews, "Law," 167.

122. Charlesworth, *Old Testament Pseudepigrapha*, 2:664.

123. Toews, "Law," 167–68.

124. Cathcart and Gordon, *Targum*, 71.

Textual Factors

The LXX renders Joel 3:5 in a formal manner (καὶ ἔσται πᾶς ὃς ἂν ἐπικαλέσηται τὸ ὄνομα κυρίου σωθήσεται), and Paul's citation is almost verbatim (πᾶς γὰρ ὃς ἂν ἐπικαλέσηται τὸ ὄνομα κυρίου σωθήσεται). He omits καὶ ἔσται, probably for rhetorical or stylistic reasons.[125] Interestingly, Paul does not use a citation formula in Rom 10:13 as he does with most of the OT citations in Rom 9–11.[126]

Paul's Hermeneutic and Theological Point

Two issues arise from Paul's use of Joel 3:5. The first involves the application of this text to gentiles when Joel's immediate audience is Israel. The second involves Paul's application of this text to his day when Joel appears to be describing events immediately prior to the advent of YHWH and his judgment of the nations.

Several commentators argue that Joel 3:5 cannot legitimately be applied to gentiles. Allen writes, "Since the nations are represented in ch. 3 as destroyed, and aliens are to be debarred from Jerusalem (3:17), no substantial inclusion of Gentiles can be inferred from the oracle in its primary sense . . . He [Paul] is obviously extending the bounds of the original force of Joel's message. Those commentators who scan it for universalistic hints are in danger of misrepresenting its primary meaning."[127] While Calvin does not deny the legitimacy of Paul's application of Joel to gentiles, he notes the apparent tension in doing so: "Paul appears to misapply the Prophet's words; for Joel no doubt addresses here the people, to whom he was appointed as a teacher and prophet."[128]

In light of Paul's application, some have argued that Paul is guilty of bad exegesis. Bewer writes, "he [Joel] did not predict the event of Pentecost nor 'the new order of things of which Pentecost was the first example' (Dav.). He did not predict the enjoyment of the fuller illumination on the part of all, which had been the prerogative of the prophets and the hope of Nu. 11:30 and Je. 31:33f. and which later became the ideal of the Christian

---

125. Rowe, "Name," 152n55.

126. Block, "Romans 10:13," 181. Capes and Lindars note that Joel 2:26 contains elements of both OT citations in Rom 10:9–13: οὐ μὴ καταισχυνθῇ (Isa 28:16) and τὸ ὄνομα κυρίου (Joel 2:32 ["YHWH," 134 and "Old Testament," 521, respectively).

127. Allen, *Joel, Obadiah, Jonah, and Micah*, 101n24, 104. Also Crenshaw, *Joel*, 172; Mohrmann, "Semantic Collisions," 163. Wolf writes that Joel had no more intended a universal referent for "all" than he had known the name of Jesus (*Commentary*, 70).

128. Calvin, *Minor Prophets*, 106–7.

church."[129] However, this does not cohere with Paul's careful use of the OT which is evident throughout Rom 9:30–10:11.

Others explain Paul's usage without offering any justification. Allen argues that Paul is trying to theologically rationalize the existence of the Jewish-gentile Christian church.[130] Busenitz argues that Joel was referring only to Israelites,[131] but that "Paul utilizes the phrase in a broadened sense to include all peoples who call on the Lord, regardless of nationality (so also Acts 2:21). His use of it there [Rom 10:13] is heavily dependent on the theological framework erected in Romans 4."[132] However, apostolic use does not justify questionable hermeneutics. Apostles are not given the right to create meaning where there is none.

In light of that, Dillard appeals to a *sensus plenior* hermeneutic. Paul does not create meaning, but discerns an additional divinely-intended meaning. Dillard writes, "There can be little doubt in this context that Joel intends *all flesh* to refer to Israel alone—the phrase *all flesh* is explicated as *your* sons and daughters, slaves, young and old; the fortunes of Judah are contrasted to those of the Gentiles (4:1–17 [3:1–17]). Yet Paul understands that Joel spoke better than he knew."[133] However, the biblical evidence to support this hermeneutic is insufficient.

Robert Chisolm appeals to an analogical usage: "In Romans 10:13 Paul related this passage [Joel 2:32] to Gentile (as well as Jewish) salvation, but he was suggesting a mere analogy, not a strict fulfillment of Joel 2:32, which pertains to Israel."[134] Chisolm's solution does solve the tension of respecting the original OT meaning while affirming the legitimacy of Paul's application of the text. However, mere analogy with a scriptural situation or teaching does not give Paul the right to cite a verse in support of his situation or teaching. The application of the OT to NT situations requires stronger justification.

The best defense of Paul's use of Joel 3:5 argues that the original context hints at gentile salvation. Joel 3:5 refers to two groups of people who call upon YHWH and are saved: (1) those in Mount Zion and Jerusalem who escape, and (2) those among the survivors whom YHWH calls. If the second group refers to Israelites, then it does not add any information to

---

129. Bewer, *Obadiah and Joel*, 125.
130. Allen, *Joel, Obadiah, Jonah, and Micah*, 104.
131. Busenitz, *Joel and Obadiah*, 181.
132. Busenitz, *Joel and Obadiah*, 187n89.
133. Dillard, "Joel," 295.
134. Chisholm, "Joel," 1420–21. Northrup argues that Peter employs the passage in Acts 2:16–21 in a similar manner, that is, to illustrate what was happening at Pentecost, and to point out to the Jews that the signs of Pentecost were similar in character to those which would precede the Second Coming ("Joel's Concept," 198–200).

the verse. Rather, the second group refers to survivors of God's judgment upon the nations who experience salvation.[135] Furthermore, the eschatology of the OT teaches that gentiles will participate in the kingdom. Israel was created for the purpose of being a blessing to the nations. Paul's application of the text recognizes this wider vision of OT salvation.[136]

The second issue to address in Paul's use of Joel 3:5 concerns Paul's application of this text his day. While Paul does not cite any of the verses pertaining to the outpouring of the Spirit or cataclysmic signs as Peter does in Acts 2:16–21, Paul is likely still alluding to the larger context and story of that verse (the restoration of Israel in the Last Days).[137] As Wright notes, "when Paul quotes Joel 2:32 (lxx 3:5) in 10:13 he intends a reference to the whole passage, in which the promise of the spirit is prominent as one of the key features of the coming eschaton."[138]

Paul uses this text in Rom 10:13 because he believes that the time prophesied by Joel has begun with the resurrection of Christ. The outpouring of the Spirit, like the death and resurrection of Christ, is an objective, redemptive-historical act that fulfills OT prophecy and advances salvation history. The outpouring of the Spirit signifies that the era of the fulfillment of God's covenantal promises has begun.[139] Therefore, the promises of Joel 3:5 are available to all Jews and gentiles who call upon the name of the Lord.[140] Jesus is Lord of all (Rom 10:12), and his Spirit has been poured out on all flesh (Acts 2:17–18). Therefore, all who call upon the name of the Lord will be saved (Rom 10:11, 13).[141]

---

135. Keil and Delitzsch, *Commentary*, 10:143; Stuart, *Hosea–Jonah*, 262.

136. Calvin, *Minor Prophets*, 106–7; Garrett, *Hosea, Joel*, 375.

137. A methodology similar to that advocated by Dodd, *According*, 126–27.

138. Wright, *Paul*, 1166.

139. Keil and Delitzsch, *Commentary*, 10:143; Schreiner, *Romans*, 562; Wright, *Paul*, 1166.

140. The work of the Spirit among gentiles such as Cornelius (Acts 10) further justifies the idea that Joel 3:1–5 has reference to Jews and gentiles.

141. Köstenberger and Patterson cite Joel 3:1–5 as an example of a passage that has experienced fulfillment without consummation (*Invitation*, 355–56). The availability of the blessings of Joel 3:1–2, 5 does not mean that the cataclysmic signs of Joel 3:3–4 will not be literally fulfilled (though, as Allen notes, the fact that Joel 2:1–11 uses symbolic language to describe the locust plague may indicate that 3:1–5 also involves symbolic language [*Joel, Obadiah, Jonah, and Micah*, 100]).

CONCLUSION

The final paragraph of Rom 9:30—10:13 highlights the universal availability of righteousness by faith. Having critiqued Israel's pursuit of righteousness by obedience to the law (9:30–10:8), Paul gives sustained attention to the solution to Israel's plight: the confession of faith in Jesus, the resurrected Lord, which leads to righteousness and salvation (10:9–13). This attention to faith indicates that Paul's critique in the previous sections is indeed against attempts to earn righteousness by obeying the law—such efforts are the natural antithesis to faith in Christ. This final paragraph also reveals again that Paul respects the original meaning of the OT, and that he expected Israel to discern from their Scriptures that salvation comes through faith not works. That message was first preached by Isa 28:16 and Joel 3:5. Lastly, this paragraph teaches that the Pauline conception of faith involved trust in Jesus, the resurrected Messiah and divine Son of God.

Chapter 7

Conclusion

THE ARGUMENT OF ROM 9:30—10:13

This dissertation examines Paul's exegetical and theological argument in Rom 9:30—10:13, with special attention to his use of the Old Testament. In this passage, Paul addresses from the human standpoint why Israel has not obtained a right standing with God. Paul gives two reasons: (1) their lack of faith in Jesus as Messiah (9:30, 32b–33; 10:4, 9–13), and (2) their error with reference to the law (9:31–32a; 10:2–3, 5–8). Scholars offer three interpretations of Israel's error with reference to the law: (1) misunderstanding (Israel essentially misunderstood the true demand of the law [faith] and sought to fulfill it in the wrong way [works]; (2) nationalism (Israel limited the expression of righteousness to their nationalistic symbols, and thought that righteousness was available only for Jews); (3) legalism (Israel tried [and failed] to keep the law in order to attain righteousness by works instead of by faith). We have argued that Paul criticizes Israel for pursuing a right standing with God by obeying the Mosaic law when they should have discerned within their own Scriptures both humanity's inability to keep the Mosaic law and the necessity of salvation by faith alone. We now summarize our findings from each paragraph.

In the first paragraph (9:30–33), Paul establishes the main idea that he develops in the subsequent verses (10:1–13). He argues that Israel was trying to keep the law in order to obtain a right standing with God, but due to human inability, they fell short of their goal (9:31–32a). Blinded by such a pursuit, they rejected Jesus as Messiah and the salvation he offers (9:32b–33).

The second paragraph (10:1–4) continues the argument by developing and expanding the main ideas of 9:30–33. Israel needs salvation in Christ (Rom 10:1) because they zealously try to keep the law but not in an informed manner (Rom 10:2). More specifically, Israel is ignorant of God's way of providing righteousness, and tries instead to establish (earn) their own right standing with God (Rom 10:3a). Because of this, they do not submit to the righteousness God provides to those who have faith (Rom 10:3b). Israel should submit to God in faith because Christ ends using the law to obtain a right standing with God for those who believe (Rom 10:4).

Romans 10:5–8 contains OT citations which support Paul's theological argument in Rom 10:1–4. In Rom 10:5, Paul cites Lev 18:5 to demonstrate the negative side of Rom 10:4, namely, that Christ ends all attempts to use the law to obtain a right standing with God. Lev 18:5 represents the theological principle embedded in the law that eternal life comes to those who keep the law's demands. Paul utilizes the verse to argue that contemporary Israelites should cease trying to keep the law in order to earn a right standing with God.

In Rom 10:6–8, Paul cites Deut 8:17a; 9:4a; and 30:12–14 to develop the positive side of Rom 10:4, namely, that Christ brings righteousness to those who believe. Paul cites these passages because they articulate the same principle as the gospel: just as the Israelites in the OT did not need to do any works to find God's commandment, so there is no need for Paul's contemporary Israelites to do any works to find Christ. The only thing they need to do is seek a right standing with God by faith in him.

The final section of Rom 9:30—10:13 (10:9–13) picks up the earlier strands of 9:30–10:8 and ties them together into a powerful conclusion. While previous paragraphs emphasized Paul's critique of Israel's pursuit of righteousness by means of works, in the final paragraph Paul emphasizes the universal availability of righteousness by faith. Paul does this in order to present the solution to Israel's plight: faith in Jesus, the resurrected Lord.

These findings demonstrate the thesis that Paul criticizes Israel for pursuing a right standing with God by obeying the Mosaic law when they should have discerned within their own Scriptures both humanity's inability to keep the Mosaic law and the necessity of salvation by faith alone. Against the idea that Israel misunderstood the true demand of the law stand Paul's statements that the object of the law is righteousness (Rom 9:31), and that a person who does the law will have righteousness (Rom 10:5). Also, Paul does not contrast different approaches to the law, but different approaches to righteousness, namely, obedience to the works of the law versus faith in Christ (Rom 10:4–13). Israel did not misunderstand the message of the law, but rather the message of the OT as a whole which presents faith as the only means of salvation (Rom 9:33; 10:6–8, 11, 13).

Against the idea that Israel limited the availability of righteousness to those who adopted their nationalistic symbols stand several Pauline ideas. First, Paul describes Israel's error in terms of pursuing righteousness by works instead of by faith (9:31–32a; 10:2–3). He does not refer to the limitation of righteousness but to the attainment of righteousness. Furthermore, he does not mention any specific, nationalistic works such as circumcision, food laws, or Sabbath observance, but instead uses general terms for works (Rom 9:31) and zeal (10:2). Second, Paul builds his argument on a contrast between righteousness by works and righteousness by faith (9:31—10:3 contrasts with 10:9–13; 10:4 introduces the contrast between 10:5 and 10:6–8). This direct contrast between works and faith makes better sense of Paul's antitheses than the indirect contrast of exclusivism and faith.

CONTRIBUTION OF THE STUDY

Romans 9:30—10:13 is central to discussions on Paul and the law. Many have addressed the passage, and three previous dissertations provide a detailed exegesis of the passage with attention to Paul's use of the OT.[1] However, those dissertations take a different approach to Paul's use of the OT, the relationship between faith and the law, the validity of the new perspective on Paul, and the identification of Paul's main critique of Israel. Toews argues exegetically that the law essentially demands faith. Pattee proposes a network of texts with which Paul's direct citations interact, and argues that this network critiques Israel for hypocritically failing to include the gentiles in the people of God. Mohrmann argues that Paul often subverts the meaning of the OT texts he cites, and gives a new perspective interpretation to the passage. In contrast, we found that Paul respects the meaning of his OT citations, that the law essentially demands perfect obedience, and that Israel's error with reference to the law did not involve primarily her relationship with gentiles but her pursuit of righteousness by works instead of by faith. This dissertation demonstrates that a traditional law-gospel (Lutheran) approach to Paul is defensible within one of Paul's most important discussions of the law.[2]

---

1. Mohrmann, "Semantic Collisions"; Pattee, "Stumbling Stone"; Toews, "Law."

2. Paul's argument in Rom 9:30—10:13 also contributes to the biblical-theological discussion on the relationships between the law and the gospel and the Mosaic and

AREAS OF FURTHER RESEARCH

We conclude by highlighting three areas that deserve further study. First, the meaning and significance of νόμον δικαιοσύνης in Rom 9:31. Paul employs this unusual construction at the very beginning of his theological argument and uses it to communicate a major idea about the connection between law and righteousness. Research into the reason for this particular construction, parallel constructions, and the nature of the connection between the law and righteousness would add significant color to Paul's argument in this foundational paragraph.

Second, further investigation into the rationale behind Paul's selection of texts may enhance our understanding of how intertestamental Jews read their scriptures. Were they "pillar texts" in theological discussions? Were they cited together as *testamonia*?

Third, if this approach to the law is central to Paul, then it should emerge in his other discussions of the law and the gospel. Sustained work on similar texts such as Gal 3:1–29, as well as passages where Paul makes positive statements about the law (e.g., Rom 3:21–31) would reveal whether the interpretation proposed here coheres with Paul's wider picture of the law.

New Covenants as well as the systematic topic of covenant theology. The argument here reflects the theological position that the Mosaic covenant was a gracious covenant, not a republication of the pre-fall covenant made with Adam. Israel was not supposed to try to obey the Mosaic law and obtain a right standing with God; the terms of salvation under the Mosaic covenant were faith alone. However, the Mosaic covenant reflects humanity's obligation to perfectly obey God; Israel fixated upon that and did not focus on the presentation of a savior in the prescribed sacrifices. With the advent of Jesus, God has accomplished the work of redemption and introduced the New Covenant which makes the clearest presentation of God's grace and the necessity of faith alone in the administration of God's covenants. Two of the primary differences between the old (Mosaic) and new covenants are anticipation versus accomplishment, and a focus upon the requirement for obedience versus the necessity of faith alone.

Bibliography

Aageson, James. "Typology, Correspondence, and the Application of Scripture in Romans 9-11." *Journal for the Study of the New Testament* 31 (1987) 51-72.
Achtemeier, Paul. *Romans*. Interpretation. Atlanta: John Knox, 1985.
Aletti, Jean-Noël. "Romans." In *The International Bible Commentary: A Catholic and Ecumenical Commentary for the Twenty-First Century*, edited by William Farmer, 1553-600. Collegeville, MN: Liturgical, 1998.
Allen, Leslie. *The Books of Joel, Obadiah, Jonah, and Micah*. New International Commentary on the Old Testament. Grand Rapids: Eerdmans, 1976.
Aquinas, Thomas. *Commentary on the Letter of Saint Paul to the Romans*. Translated by F. R. Larchrer. Lander, WY: The Aquinas Institute for the Study of Sacred Doctrine, 2012.
Aune, David. "Romans as a *Logos Protreptikos*." In *The Romans Debate*, edited by Karl Donfried, 278-96. Rev. ed. Peabody, MA: Hendrickson, 1991.
Avemarie, Friedrich. "Paul and the Claim of the Law according to the Scripture: Leviticus 18:5 in Galatians 3:12 and Romans 10:5." In *The Beginnings of Christianity: A Collection of Articles*, edited by Jack Pastor et al., 125-48. Jerusalem: Yad Izhak Ben-Zvi, 2005.
Badenas, Robert. *Christ the End of the Law: Romans 10.4 in Pauline Perspective*. Journal for the Study of the New Testament Supplement Series. Sheffield, UK: JSOT, 1985.
Baker, David. *Joel, Obadiah, Malachi*. The New International Version Application Commentary. Grand Rapids: Zondervan, 2006.
Balentine, Samuel E. *Leviticus*. Interpretation. Louisville: John Knox, 2002.
Bandstra, Andrew John. *The Law and the Elements of the World: An Exegetical Study in Aspects of Paul's Teaching*. Kampen, NL: Kok, 1964.
Barclay, John. "Paul, Roman Religion, and the Emperor: Mapping the Point of Conflict." In *Pauline Churches and Diaspora Jews*, 345-62. Wissenschaftliche Untersuchungen zum Neuen Testament 1:275. Tübingen: Mohr-Siebeck, 2011.
———. "Why the Roman Empire was Insignificant to Paul." In *Pauline Churches and Diaspora Jews*, 363-87. Wissenschaftliche Untersuchungen zum Neuen Testament 1:275. Tübingen: Mohr-Siebeck, 2011.
Barker, Paul. "Contemporary Theological Interpretation of Deuteronomy." In *Interpreting Deuteronomy: Issues and Approches*, edited by David Firth et al., 60-90. Downers Grove, IL: InterVarsity, 2012.
———. *The Triumph of Grace in Deuteronomy: Faithless Israel, Faithful Yahweh in Deuteronomy*. Paternoster Biblical Monographs. Eugene, OR: Wipf & Stock, 2004.

Barnett, Paul. *Romans: The Revelation of God's Righteousness*. Geanies House, UK: Christian Focus, 2007.

Barrett, C. K. *A Commentary on the Epistle to the Romans*. Black's New Testament Commentaries. London: A. & C. Black, 1973.

———. "Romans 9.30–10:21: Fall and Responsibility of Israel." In *Die Israelfrage nach Rom 9–11*, edited by L. D. Lorenzi, 99–121. Rome: St Paul van den Mauern, 1977.

———. "Romans 9.30–10:21: Fall and Responsibility of Israel." In *Essays on Paul*, 132–53. Philadelphia: Westminster, 1982.

Barth, Karl. *Church Dogmatics*. Edited and translated by Geoffrey Bromiley et al. Edinburgh: T. & T. Clark, 2004.

———. *The Epistle to the Romans*. Translated by Edwyn Hoskeyns. New York: Oxford University Press, 1968.

———. *A Shorter Commentary on Romans*. Translated by D. H. van Daalen. Richmond, VA: John Knox, 1959.

Barth, Markus. *The People of God*. Eugene, OR: Wipf & Stock, 1983.

Barton, John. *Joel and Obadiah: A Commentary*. Old Testament Library. Louisville: Westminster John Knox, 2001.

Beale, G. K. *The Book of Revelation*. The New International Greek Testament Commentary. Grand Rapids: Eerdmans, 1999.

Beale, G. K., and D. A. Carson, eds. *Commentary on the New Testament Use of the Old Testament*. Grand Rapids: Baker, 2007.

Bechtler, Steven Richard. "Christ, the Τέλος of the Law: The Goal of Romans 10:4." *Catholic Biblical Quarterly* 56 (1994) 288–308.

Beker, J. Christiaan. *Paul the Apostle: The Triumph of God in Life and Thought*. Minneapolis: Fortress, 1984.

Bekken, Per Jarle. *The Word Is Near You: A Study of Deuteronomy 30:12–14 in Paul's Letter to the Romans in a Jewish Context*. Beihefte zur Zeitschrift für die neutestamentliche Wissenschaft. New York: Walter de Gruyter, 2007.

Bell, Richard. *Provoked to Jealousy: The Origin and Purpose of the Jealousy Motif in Romans 9–11*. Wissenschaftliche Untersuchungen zum Neuen Testament 2:63. Tübingen: Mohr-Siebeck, 1994.

Bellinger, W. H., Jr. *Leviticus and Numbers*. New International Biblical Commentary on the Old Testament. Peabody, MA: Hendrickson, 2001.

Beuken, Willem A. M. *Isaiah*. Vol. 2, *Chapters 28–39*. Translated by Brian Doyle. Historical Commentary on the Old Testament. Leuven, BE: Peeters, 2000.

Bewer, Julius. *A Critical and Exegetical Commentary on Obadiah and Joel*. The International Critical Commentary. New York: Scribner's, 1911.

Bird, Michael, and Preston Sprinkle, eds. *The Faith of Jesus Christ: Exegetical, Biblical, and Theological Studies*. Peabody, MA: Hendrickson, 2009.

Black, Matthew. "The Christological Use of the Old Testament in the New Testament." *New Testament Studies* 18 (1971) 1–14.

———. *Romans*. 2nd ed. The New Century Bible Commentary. Grand Rapids: Eerdmans, 1989.

Blass, F., and A. Debrunner. *A Greek Grammar of the New Testament and Other Early Christian Literature*. Translated and Revised by Robert Funk. Chicago: The University of Chicago Press, 1961.

Blenkinsopp, Joseph. *Isaiah 1–39*. The Anchor Bible. New Haven: Yale University Press, 2000.

Bibliography

Block, Daniel. *The Book of Ezekiel, Chapters 1–24*. New International Commentary on the Old Testament. Grand Rapids: Eerdmans, 1997.

———. "Who Do Commentators Say 'The Lord' Is? The Scandalous Rock of Romans 10:13." In *On the Writing of New Testament Commentaries: Festschrift for Grant R. Osborne on the Occasion of his 70th Birthday*, edited by Stanley Porter et al., 173–92. Boston: Brill, 2013.

Bock, Darrell. "Single Meaning, Multiple Contexts and Referents: The New Testament's Legitimate, Accurate, and Multifaceted Use of the Old." In *Three Views on the New Testament Use of the Old Testament*, edited by Kenneth Berding et al., 105–51. Grand Rapids: Zondervan, 2008.

Bockmuehl, Markus. *Revelation and Mystery in Ancient Judaism and Pauline Christianity*. Wissenschaftliche Untersuchungen zum Neuen Testament 2:36. Eugene, OR: Wipf & Stock, 2009.

Bonar, Andrew. *A Commentary on Leviticus*. Geneva Series of Commentaries. Carlisle, PA: The Banner of Truth Trust, 1998.

Boor, Werner de. *Der Brief des Paulus an die Römer*. Wuppertaler Studienbibel. Wuppertal, DEU: Brockhaus, 1973.

Bray, Gerald, ed. *Romans*. Rev. ed. Ancient Christian Commentary on Scripture. Downers Grove, IL: InterVarsity, 1998.

Bring, Ragnar. "Paul and the Old Testament: A Study of the Ideas of Faith, Election, and Law in Paul, with Special Reference to Rom. 9:30–10:13." *Studia Theologica* 25 (1971) 21–60.

Bruce, F. F. *The Letter of Paul the Apostle to the Romans*. Rev ed. The Tyndale New Testament Commentaries. Grand Rapids: Eerdmans, 1985.

———. *Paul: Apostle of the Free Spirit*. Milton Keynes, UK: Paternoster, 1977.

Brueggemann, Walter. *Deuteronomy*, Abingdon Old Testament Commentaries. Nashville: Abingdon, 2001.

Bryan, Christopher. *A Preface to Romans: Notes on the Epistle in its Literary and Culture Setting*. New York: Oxford University Press, 2000.

Bultmann, Rudolf. "Christ the End of the Law." In *Essays Philosophical and Theological*, 36–66. Translated by James Greig. New York: Macmillan, 1955.

———. *Theology of the New Testament*. Vol. 1. Translated by Kendrick Grobel. New York: Scribner's, 1951.

Burk, Denny. "Is Paul's Gospel Counterimperial? Evaluating the Prospects of the 'Fresh Perspective' for Evangelical Theology." *Journal of the Evangelical Theological Society* 51.2 (2008) 315–19.

Busenitz, Irvin. *Joel & Obadiah*. Geanies House, UK: Christian Focus, 2010.

Buswell, James Oliver. *A Systematic Theology of the Christian Religion*. Grand Rapids: Zondervan, 1962.

Byrne, Brendan. *Romans*. Sacra Pagina. Collegeville, MN: Liturgical, 1996.

Calvin, John. *Commentaries on the Epistle of Paul the Apostle to the Romans*. Translated and edited by John Owen. Calvin's Commentaries. Grand Rapids: Baker, 2010.

———. *Commentaries on the Four Last Books of Moses Arranged in the Form of a Harmony*. Vol. 1. Translated by Charles William Bingham. Calvin's Commentaries. Grand Rapids: Baker, 2005.

———. *Commentaries on the Twelve Minor Prophets*. Vol. 2, *Joel, Amos, Obadiah*. Translated by John Owen. Calvin's Commentaries. Grand Rapids: Baker, 2005.

---. *Commentary on the Prophet Isaiah*. Vol. 1. Translated by William Pringle. Calvin's Commentaries. Grand Rapids: Baker, 2005.

---. *Institutes of the Christian Religion*. Edited by John McNeill. Translated by Ford Lewis Battles. Louisville: John Knox, 2006.

Campbell, Douglas. *The Deliverance of God: An Apocalyptic Rereading of Justification in Paul*. Grand Rapids: Eerdmans, 2013.

---. *The Rhetoric of Righteousness in Romans 3.21–26*. Journal for the Study of the New Testament Supplement Series. Sheffield, UK: Sheffield Academic Press, 1992.

Campbell, W. S. "Christ the End of the Law: Romans 10:4." In *Studia Biblica 1978, 3: Papers on Paul and Other New Testament Authors*, edited by E. A. Livingstone, 73–81. Journal for the Study of the New Testament Supplement Series. Sheffield, UK: Sheffield Academic Press, 1980.

Capes, David. "YHWH and His Messiah: Pauline Exegesis and the Divine Christ." *Horizons in Biblical Theology* 16.2 (1994) 121–43.

Carson, D. A. "Atonement in Romans 3.21–26." In *The Glory of the Atonement*, edited by Charles Hill and Frank James, 119–39. Downers Grove, IL: InterVarsity, 1990.

---. *The Gospel According to John*. Pillar New Testament Commentary. Grand Rapids: Eerdmans, 1991.

---. "Mystery and Fulfillment: Toward a More Comprehensive Paradigm of Paul's Understanding of the Old and New." In *Justification and Variegated Nomism: The Paradoxes of Paul*, edited by D. A. Carson et al., 2:393–436. Wissenschaftliche Untersuchungen zum Neuen Testament 2:181. Grand Rapids: Baker, 2004.

Cathcart, Kevin, and Robert Gordon. *The Targum of the Minor Prophets: Translated, with a Critical Introduction, Apparatus, and Notes*. The Aramaic Bible 14. Wilmington, DE: Glazier, 1989.

Chalmers, Thomas. *Lectures on the Epistle of Paul the Apostle to the Romans*. New York: Carter, 1844.

Charlesworth, James, ed. *The Old Testament Pseudepigrapha*. 2 vols. Peabody, MA: Hendrickson, 1983.

Childs, Brevard. *Introduction to the Old Testament as Scripture*. Philadelphia: Fortress, 1979.

Chilton, Bruce. *The Isaiah Targum: Introduction, Translation, Apparatus and Notes*. The Aramaic Bible 11. Wilmington, DE: Glazier, 1987.

Chisolm, Robert. "Joel." In *The Bible Knowledge Commentary: Old Testament*, edited by John Walvoord et al., 1409–24. Colorado Springs: Cook, 1983.

Christensen, Duane L. *Deuteronomy 21:10–34:12*. Word Biblical Commentary 6B. Dallas, TX: Word, 2002.

Chrysostom, John. *Homilies on the Acts of the Apostles and the Epistle to the Romans*. Vol. 11 of *A Select Library of the Nicene and Post-Nicene Fathers of the Christian Church*. Edited by Philip Schaff. Grand Rapids: Eerdmans, 1975.

Ciampa, Roy. "Deuteronomy in Galatians and Romans." In *Deuteronomy in the New Testament*, edited by Maarten Menken et al., 99–117. Library of New Testament Studies. New York: T. & T. Clark, 2008.

Colson, F. H., and G. H. Whitaker, trans. *Philo*. 10 vols. Loeb Classical Library. Cambridge: Harvard University Press, 1929–62.

Coxhead, Steven. "Deuteronomy 30:11–14 as a Prophecy of the New Covenant in Christ." *Westminster Theological Journal* 68 (2006) 305–20.

Craigie, Peter C. *The Book of Deuteronomy.* New International Commentary on the Old Testament. Grand Rapids: Eerdmans, 1976.

Cranfield, C. E. B. *A Critical and Exegetical Commentary on the Epistle to the Romans.* International Critical Commentary, new series. 2 vols. Edinburgh: T. & T. Clark, 2011.

———. "Some Notes on Romans 9:30–33." In *Jesus und Paulus: Festschrift für Werner Georg Kümmel zum 70. Geburtstag,* edited by E. Earle Ellis et al., 35–43. Göttingen: Vandenhoeck & Ruprecht, 1975.

———. "St. Paul and the Law." *Scottish Journal of Theology* 17 (1964) 43–68.

———. "St. Paul and the Law." In *New Testament Issues,* edited by Richard Batey, 148–72. New York: Harper & Row, 1970.

———. "'The Works of the Law' in the Epistle to the Romans." *Journal for the Study of the New Testament* 43 (1991) 89–101.

Crenshaw, James. *Joel: A New Translation with Introduction and Commentary.* Anchor Bible. New York: Doubleday, 1995.

Das, A. Andrew. *Paul and the Jews.* Library of Pauline Studies. Peabody, MA: Hendrickson, 2003.

———. *Paul, the Law, and the Covenant.* Peabody, MA: Hendrickson, 2001.

Davies, Glenn. *Faith and Obedience in Romans: A Study in Romans 1–4.* Journal for the Study of the New Testament Supplement. Sheffield, UK: JSOT, 1990.

Delling, Gerhard. "τέλος." In *Theological Dictionary of the New Testament,* edited by Gerhard Kittel et al., 8:49–57.Translated by Geoffrey Bromiley. Grand Rapids: Eerdmans, 1972.

Denney, James. "St. Paul's Epistle to the Romans." In *The Expositor's Greek Testament,* edited by W. Robertson Nicoll, 2:555–725. Grand Rapids: Eerdmans, 1967.

Dennis, Lane, ed. *The ESV Study Bible.* Wheaton, IL: Crossway Bibles, 2008.

Dillard, Raymond. "Joel." In *The Minor Prophets,* edited by Thomas McComiskey, 239–313. Grand Rapids: Baker, 1998.

Dodd, C. H. *According to the Scriptures: The Sub-structure of New Testament Theology.* Digswell Place, UK: Nisbet, 1961.

———. *The Epistle of Paul to the Romans.* The Moffatt New Testament Commentary. New York: Harper, 1932.

Donfried, Karl P., ed. *The Romans Debate.* Rev. ed. Grand Rapids: Baker Academic, 2001.

Driver, S. R. *A Critical and Exegetical Commentary on Deuteronomy.* The International Critical Commentary. New York: Scribner's, 1916.

Dülmen, Andrea van. *Die Theologie das Gesetzes bei Paulus.* Stuttgart, DEU: Katholisches Bibelwerk, 1968.

Dumbrell, William. "Paul and Salvation History in Romans 9:30—10:4." In *Out of Egypt: Biblical Theology and Biblical Interpretation,* edited by Craig Bartholomew et al., 286–312. Scripture and Hermeneutics. Grand Rapids: Zondervan, 2004.

———. *Romans: A New Covenant Commentary.* Eugene, OR: Wipf & Stock, 2005.

Dunn, James. "4QMMT and Galatians." In *The New Perspective on Paul,* 339–45. Rev. ed. Grand Rapids: Eerdmans, 2008.

———. "Letter to the Romans." In *Dictionary of Paul and His Letters,* edited by Gerald Hawthorne et al., 838–50. Downers Grove, IL: InterVarsity, 1993.

———. "'Righteousness from the Law' and 'Righteousness from Faith': Paul's Interpretation of Scripture in Romans 10:1–10." In *Tradition and Interpretation in the New Testament: Essays in Honor of E. Earle Ellis for His 60th Birthday*, edited by Gerald Hawthorne et al., 216–28. Grand Rapids: Eerdmans, 1988.

———. *Romans*. 2 vols. Word Biblical Commentary 38A–B. Nashville: Nelson, 1988.

———. *The Theology of Paul the Apostle*. Grand Rapids: Eerdmans, 1998.

———. "Yet Once More—'The Works of the Law': A Response." In *The New Perspective on Paul*, 213–26. Rev. ed. Grand Rapids: Eerdmans, 2008.

Edwards, James. *Romans*. New International Biblical Commentary. Peabody, MA: Hendrickson, 1992.

Eisenbaum, Pamela. *Paul Was Not a Christian: The Original Message of a Misunderstood Apostle*. New York: Harper, 2009.

Elliot, Neil. "The Anti-Imperial Message of the Cross." In *Paul and Empire: Religion and Power in Roman Imperial Society*, edited by Richard Horsley, 167–83. Harrisburg, PA: Trinity, 1997.

Ellis, E. Earle. *Paul's Use of the Old Testament*. Grand Rapids: Eerdmans, 1957.

Estelle, Bryan D. "Leviticus 18:5 and Deuteronomy 30:1–14 in Biblical Theological Development: Entitlement to Heaven Foreclosed and Proffered." In *The Law is Not of Faith: Essays on Works and Grace in the Mosaic Covenant*, edited by Bryan D. Estelle et al., 109–46. Phillipsburg, NJ: P&R, 2009.

Estes, Daniel. "Calling on the Name of the Lord: The Meaning and Significance of ἐπικαλέω in Romans 10:13." *Themelios* 41.1 (2016) 20–36.

Evans, Craig A. *Ancient Texts for New Testament Studies: A Guide to the Background Literature*. Peabody, MA: Hendrickson, 2005.

Evans, Robert. *Pelagius: Inquiries and Reappraisals*. New York: Seabury, 1968.

Feldman, Louis, trans. *Josephus*. 9 vols. Loeb Classical Library. Cambridge: Harvard University Press, 1926–65.

Fitzmyer, Joseph. *Romans: A New Translation with Introduction and Commentary*. Anchor Bible. New York: Doubleday, 1993.

———. "The Semitic Background of the New Testament *Kyrios*-Title." In *A Wandering Aramean: Collected Aramaic Essays*, 115–42. Society of Biblical Literature Monograph Series. Missoula, MO: Scholars, 1979.

Flückiger, Felix. "Christus, das Gesetzes τέλος." *Theologische Zeitschrift* 11.2 (1955) 153–57.

Fuller, Daniel. *Gospel and Law: Contrast or Continuum? The Hermeneutics of Dispensationalism and Covenant Theology*. Grand Rapids: Eerdmans, 1980.

———. "Paul and 'The Works of the Law.'" *Westminster Theological Journal* 38.1 (1975) 28–42.

Gager, John. *The Origins of Anti-Semitism: Attitudes Toward Judaism in Pagan and Christian Antiquity*. New York: Oxford University Press, 1983.

Garrett, Duane. *Hosea, Joel*. The New American Commentary. Nashville: Broadman and Holman, 1997,

Gaston, Lloyd. *Paul and the Torah*. Eugene, OR: Wipf & Stock, 2006.

Gathercole, Simon. "Justified by Faith, Justified by his Blood: The Evidence of Romans 3:21–4:25." In *Justification and Variegated Nomism: The Paradoxes of Paul*, edited by D. A. Carson et al., 2:147–84. Wissenschaftliche Untersuchungen zum Neuen Testament 2:181. Grand Rapids: Baker, 2004.

———. "Torah, Life, and Salvation: Leviticus 18:5 in Early Judaism and the New Testament." In *From Prophecy to Testament: The Function of the Old Testament in the New Testament*, edited by Craig A. Evans, 126–45. Peabody, MA: Hendrickson, 2004.

Bibliography

Getty, Mary Ann. "An Apocalyptic Perspective on Rom 10:4." *Horizons in Biblical Theology* 4.1 (1982) 79–131.

———. "Paul and the Salvation of Israel: A Perspective on Romans 9–11." *Catholic Biblical Quarterly* 50 (1988) 456–69.

Gifford, E. H. *The Epistle of St. Paul to the Romans*. London: Murray, 1886.

Gignac, Alain. "Le Christ, τέλος de la Loi (Rm 10,4), une Lecture en Termes de Continuité et de Discontinuité, dans le Cadre du Paradigme Paulinien de L'élection." *Science et Esprit* 46.1 (1994) 55–81.

Gill, John. *Exposition of the Old and New Testaments*. Vol. 8, *John to Galatians*. The Baptist Commentary Series. Paris, AR: Baptist Standard Bearer, 1989.

Gordon, T. David. "Why Israel Did Not Obtain Torah-Righteousness: A Translation Note on Rom 9:32." *Westminster Theological Journal* 54 (1992) 163–66.

Grieb, A. Katherine. *The Story of Romans: A Narrative Defense of God's Righteousness*. Louisville: Westminster John Knox, 2002.

Grogan, Geoffrey. "Isaiah." In *The Expositor's Bible Commentary*, edited by Frank Gaebelein, 6:3–354. Grand Rapids: Zondervan, 1986.

Gundry, Robert. "The Inferiority of the New Perspective on Paul." In *The Old is Better: New Testament Essays in Support of Traditional Interpretations*, 195–224. Wissenschaftliche Untersuchungen zum Neuen Testament 1:178. Tübingen: Mohr-Siebeck, 2005.

Gutbrod, Walter. "νόμος." In *Theological Dictionary of the New Testament*, edited by Gerhard Kittel et al. and translated by Geoffrey Bromiley, 4:1022–84. Grand Rapids: Eerdmans, 1967.

Haacker, Klaus. *Der Brief des Paulus an die Römer*. Theologischer Handkommentar zum Neuen Testament. Leipzig: Evangelisches Verlagsanstalt, 1999.

Haldane, Robert. *Exposition of the Epistle to the Romans*. Reprint, Carlisle, PA: The Banner of Truth Trust, 1996.

Hall, G. H. *Deuteronomy*. The College Press NIV Commentary. Joplin, MO: College Press, 2000.

Hamilton, Victor. *Handbook on the Pentateuch*. 2nd ed. Grand Rapids: Baker Academic, 2005.

Harris, R. Laird. "Leviticus." In *The Expositor's Bible Commentary*, edited by Frank Gaebelein, 2:499–654. Grand Rapids: Zondervan, 1990.

Harrison, Everett. "Romans." In *The Expositor's Bible Commentary*, edited by Frank Gaebelein, 10:1–171. Grand Rapids: Zondervan, 1976.

Harrison, R. K. *Leviticus: An Introduction and Commentary*. Tyndale Old Testament Commentaries. Downers Grove, IL: InterVarsity, 1980.

Hartley, John. *Leviticus*. Word Biblical Commentary 4. Dallas, TX: Word, 1992.

Hays, Richard. *Echoes of Scripture in the Letters of Paul*. New Haven: Yale University Press, 1989.

Heil, John Paul. "Christ, the Termination of the Law (Romans 9:30–10:8)." *Catholic Biblical Quarterly* 63.3 (2001) 484–98.

———. *Paul's Letter to the Romans: A Reader-Response Commentary*. Eugene, OR: Wipf & Stock, 1987.

———. *Romans: Paul's Letter of Hope*. Analecta Biblica. Rome: Biblical Institute, 1987.

Hendriksen, William. *Exposition of Paul's Epistle to the Romans*. New Testament Commentary. Grand Rapids: Baker, 2007.

Hodge, Charles. *Romans*. Wheaton, IL: Crossway, 1993.

Holland, Tom. *Romans: The Divine Marriage*. Eugene, OR: Pickwick, 2011.
House, Paul. *Old Testament Theology*. Downers Grove, IL: InterVarsity, 1998.
Howard, George. "Christ the End of the Law: The Meaning of Romans 10:4ff." *Journal of Biblical Literature* 88 (1969) 331–37.
———. "The Tetragram and the New Testament." *Journal of Biblical Literature* 96.1 (1977) 63–83.
Hubbard, David. *Joel and Amos*. Tyndale Old Testament Commentaries. Downers Grove, IL: InterVarsity, 1989,
Hübner, Hans. *Law in Paul's Thought: A Contribution to the Development of Pauline Theology*. Translated by James Greig. Edinburgh: T. & T. Clark, 1986.
Huby, Joseph. *Saint Paul: Épître Aux Romains*. Edited by Stanislas Lyonnet. 2nd ed. Verbum Salutis. Paris: Beauchesne, 1957.
Hultgren, Arland. "Paul and the Law." In *The Blackwell Companion to Paul*, edited by Stephen Westerholm, 202–15. Malden, MA: Wiley-Blackwell, 2011.
———. *Paul's Letter to the Romans: A Commentary*. Grand Rapids: Eerdmans, 2011.
Humphrey, Edith. "Why Bring the Word Down? The Rhetoric of Demonstration and Disclosure in Romans 9:30–10:21." In *Romans and the People of God: Essays in Honor of Gordon D. Fee on the Occasion of His 65th Birthday*, edited by Sven Soderlund et al., 129–48. Grand Rapids: Eerdmans, 1999.
Hurtado, Larry. *Lord Jesus Christ: Devotion to Jesus in Earliest Christianity*. Grand Rapids: Eerdmans, 2003.
Jeremias, Joachim. "λίθος." In *Theological Dictionary of the New Testament*, edited by Gerhard Kittel et al. and translated by Geoffrey Bromiley, 4:268–80. Grand Rapids: Eerdmans, 1967.
Jewett, Robert. *Romans*. Hermeneia. Minneapolis: Fortress, 2007.
Johnson, E. Elizabeth. *The Function of Apocalyptic and Wisdom Traditions in Romans 9–11*. Society of Biblical Literature Dissertation Series. Atlanta: Scholars, 1989.
———. "Romans 9–11: The Faithfulness and Impartiality of God." In *Pauline Theology, Volume III: Romans*, edited by David M. Hay et al., 211–39. Minneapolis: Fortress, 1995.
Johnson, Luke Timothy. *Reading Romans: a Literary and Theological Commentary*. Macon, GA: Smyth & Helwys, 2001.
Jolivet, Ira. "Christ the τελος in Romans 10:4 as both Fulfillment and Termination of the Law." *Restoration Quarterly* 51.1 (2009) 13–30.
Kaiser, Walter. "The Law as God's Gracious Guidance for the Promotion of Holiness." In *Five Views on Law and Gospel*, edited by Wayne G. Strickland, 177–99. Counterpoints. Zondervan: Grand Rapids, 1999.
———. "Leviticus 18:5 and Paul: Do This and You Shall Live (Eternally?)." *Journal of the Evangelical Theological Society* 14 (1971) 19–28.
Kalland, Earl. "Deuteronomy." In *The Expositor's Bible Commentary*, edited by Frank Gaebelein, 3:1–235. Grand Rapids: Zondervan, 1992.
Käsemann, Ernst. *Commentary on Romans*. Translated and edited by Geoffrey W. Bromiley. Grand Rapids: Eerdmans, 1980.
Kautzsch, E., ed. *Gesenius' Hebrew Grammar*. 2nd ed. Oxford: Clarendon, 1910.
Kaylor, R. David. *Paul's Covenant Community: Jew and Gentile in Romans*. Atlanta: John Knox, 1988.
Keck, Leander. *Romans*. Abingdon New Testament Commentaries. Nashville: Abingdon, 2005.

Keener, Craig S. *Romans: A New Covenant Commentary*. New Covenant Commentary Series. Eugene, OR: Cascade, 2009.

Keil, C. F., and F. Delitzsch. *Commentary on the Old Testament*. 10 vols. Peabody, MA: Hendrickson, 2006.

Kim, Seyoon. *Christ and Caesar: The Gospel and the Roman Empire in the Writings of Paul and Luke*. Grand Rapids: Eerdmans, 2008.

Kirk, K. E. *The Epistle to the Romans*. The Clarendon Bible. Oxford: Clarendon, 1955.

Koch, Dietrich-Alex. *Die Schrift als Zeuge des Evangeliums: Untersuchungen zur Verwendung und zum Verständnis der Schrift bei Paulus*. Beiträge zur Historischen Theologie. Tübingen: Mohr-Siebeck, 1986.

Köstenberger, Andreas, and Richard Patterson. *Invitation to Biblical Interpretation: Exploring the Hermeneutical Triad of History, Literature, and Theology*. Invitation to Theological Studies. Grand Rapids: Kregel, 2011.

Kuss, Otto. *Der Römerbrief*. 3 vols. 2nd ed. Regensburg, DEU: Pustet, 1963.

Kruse, Colin. *Paul's Letter to the Romans*. Pillar New Testament Commentary. Grand Rapids: Eerdmans, 2012.

Ladd, G. E. *A Theology of the New Testament*. Rev. ed. Grand Rapids: Eerdmans, 1993.

Lagrange, Marie-Joseph. *Saint Paul: Épître aux Romains*. Etudes bibliques. Paris: Gabalda, 1950.

Lambrecht, Jan. "The Caesura Between Romans 9.30–3 and 10.1–4." *New Testament Studies* 45 (1999) 141–47.

Lange, J. P., and F. R. Fay. *The Epistle of Paul to the Romans*. Translated by J. F. Hurst. Bellingham, WA: Logos Bible Software, 2008.

Leitzmann, Hans. *An Die Römer*. Handbuch zum Neuen Testament. Tübingen: Mohr-Siebeck, 1928.

Lenski, R. C. H. *The Interpretation of St. Paul's Epistle to the Romans*. Columbus, OH: Lutheran Book Concern, 1936.

Levine, Baruch. *Leviticus*. The JPS Torah Commentary. New York: Jewish Publication Society, 2003.

Liddell, Henry George, and Robert Scott. *A Greek-English Lexicon*. Oxford: Clarendon, 1996.

Lindars, Barnabas. "The Old Testament and Universalism." *Bulletin of the John Rylands University Library of Manchester* 69 (1987) 511–27.

Linss, Wilhelm. "Exegesis of Telos in Romans 10:4." *Biblical Research* 23 (1988) 5–12.

Lodge, John G. *Romans 9–11: A Reader-Response Analysis*. International Studies in Formative Christianity and Judaism. Atlanta: Scholars, 1996.

Lohse, Eduard. *Der Brief an die Römer*. 15th ed. Kritisch-exegetischer Kommentar über das Neue Testament. Göttingen: Vandenhoeck & Ruprecht, 2003.

Longenecker, Bruce. *Eschatology and the Covenant: A Comparison of 4 Ezra and Romans 1–11*. Journal for the Study of the New Testament Supplement. Sheffield, UK: JSOT, 1991.

Longenecker, Bruce, and Todd Still. *Thinking Through Paul: A Survey of His Life, Letters, and Theology*. Grand Rapids: Zondervan, 2014.

Longenecker, Richard. *Biblical Exegesis in the Apostolic Period*. 2nd ed. Grand Rapids: Eerdmans, 1999.

———. *The Epistle to the Romans: A Commentary on the Greek Text*. The New International Greek Testament Commentary. Grand Rapids: Eerdmans, 2016.

———. *Paul: Apostle of Liberty*. Grand Rapids: Baker, 1964.

Lowery, David. "Christ, the End of the Law in Romans 10:4." In *Dispensationalism, Israel, and the Church: The Search for Definition*, edited by Craig Blaising et al., 230–47. Grand Rapids: Zondervan, 1992.

Lust, Johan, et al. *A Greek-English Lexicon of the Septuagint*. Rev. ed. Stuttgart: Deutsche Bibelgesellschaft, 2003. Electronic edition.

Luther, Martin. *Commentary on Romans*. Translated by J. Theodore Mueller. Grand Rapids: Kregel, 1976.

———. *Lectures on Isaiah: Chapters 1–39*. Luther's Works. Edited by Jaroslav Pelikan. Translated by Herbert J. A. Bouman. St. Louis: Concordia, 1969.

———. *Lectures on Romans: Glosses and Scholia*. Edited by Hilton C. Oswald. Luther's Works. St. Louis: Concordia, 1972.

Marshall, I. Howard. *New Testament Theology: Many Witnesses, One Gospel*. Downers Grove, IL: InterVarsity, 2004.

Martin, Brice. "Paul on Christ and the Law." *Journal of the Evangelical Theological Society* 26.3 (1983) 271–82.

Martínez, Florentino García. *The Dead Sea Scrolls Translated: The Qumran Texts in English*. 2nd ed. Translated by Wilfred G. E. Watson. Grand Rapids: Eerdmans, 1992.

McConville, J. G. *Deuteronomy*. Apollos Old Testament Commentary. Downers Grove, IL: InterVarsity, 2002.

———. *Grace in the End: A Study in Deuteronomic Theology*. Studies in Old Testament Biblical Theology. Grand Rapids: Zondervan, 1993.

McCormick, Micah. "The Active Obedience of Jesus Christ." PhD diss., The Southern Baptist Theological Seminary, 2010.

McCune, Rolland. *A Systematic Theology of Biblical Christianity: The Doctrines of Salvation, the Church, and Last Things*. Allen Park, MI: Detroit Baptist Theological Seminary, 2010.

McNamara, Martin, trans. *Targum Neofiti 1: Deuteronomy*. The Aramaic Bible 5A. Collegeville, MN: Liturgical, 1997.

Merrill, Eugene. *Deuteronomy*. The New American Commentary. Nashville: Broadman and Holman, 1994.

Metzger, Bruce. *A Textual Commentary on the Greek New Testament*. New York: United Bible Societies, 1975.

———. *A Textual Commentary on the Greek New Testament*. 2nd ed. Stuttgart: Deutsche Bibelgesellschaft, 2002.

Meyer, Jason. *The End of the Law: Mosaic Covenant in Pauline Theology*. NAC Studies in Bible and Theology. Nashville: B&H Publishing Group, 2009.

Meyer, Paul. "Romans 10:4 and the 'End' of the Law." In *The Divine Helmsman: Studies on God's Control of Human Events, Presented to Lou H. Silberman*, edited by James Crenshaw et al., 59–78. New York: KTAV, 1980.

Michel, Otto. *Der Brief an die Römer*. 5th ed. Kritisch-exegetischer Kommentar über das Neue Testament. Göttingen: Vandenhoeck & Ruprecht, 1978.

———. "ὁμολογέω." In *Theological Dictionary of the New Testament*, edited by Gerhard Kittel et al. and translated by Geoffrey Bromiley, 5:200–219. Grand Rapids: Eerdmans, 1968.

Milgrom, Jacob. *Leviticus 17–22: A New Translation with Introduction and Commentary*. The Anchor Yale Bible. New Haven: Yale University Press, 2000.

Millar, J. Gary. *Now Choose Life: Theology and Ethics in Deuteronomy*. New Studies in Biblical Theology. Grand Rapids: Eerdmans, 1999.

Miller, Patrick. *Deuteronomy*. Interpretation. Louisville: John Knox, 1990.

Mohrmann, Doug. "Making Sense of Sex: A Study of Leviticus 18." *Journal for the Study of the Old Testament* 29 (2004) 57–79.

———. "Semantic Collisions at the Intertextual Crossroads: A Diachronic and Synchronic Study of Romans 9:30–10:13." PhD diss., Durham University, 2001. http://etheses.dur.ac.uk/3829/.

Moo, Douglas. *Encountering the Book of Romans: A Theological Survey*. Encountering Biblical Studies. Grand Rapids: Baker Academic, 2002.

———. *The Epistle to the Romans*. New International Commentary on the New Testament. Grand Rapids: Eerdmans, 1996.

———. "Israel and the Law in Romans 5–11: Interaction with the New Perspective." In *Justification and Variegated Nomism: The Paradoxes of Paul*, edited by D. A. Carson et al., 2:185–216. Wissenschaftliche Untersuchungen zum Neuen Testament 2:181. Grand Rapids: Baker, 2004.

———. "'Law,' 'Works of the Law,' and Legalism in Paul." *Westminster Theological Journal* 45 (1983) 73–100.

———. "Paul and the Law in the Last Ten Years." *Scottish Journal of Theology* 40 (1987) 287–307.

———. "Paul's Reading of Deuteronomy: Law and Grace." In *For Our Good Always: Studies on the Message and Influence of Deuteronomy in Honor of Daniel I. Block*, edited by Jason DeRouchie et al., 389–412. Winona Lake, IN: Eisenbrauns, 2013.

———. *Romans*. New International Version Application Commentary. Grand Rapids: Zondervan, 2000.

———. "The Theology of Romans 9–11: A Response to E. Elizabeth Johnson." In *Pauline Theology: Romans*, edited by David Hay et al., 3:240–58. Minneapolis: Fortress, 1995.

Moo, Douglas J., and Andrew David Naselli. "The Problem of the New Testament's Use of the Old Testament." In *The Enduring Authority of the Christian Scriptures*, edited by D. A. Carson, 702–46. Grand Rapids: Eerdmans, 2016.

Morris, Leon. *The Epistle to the Romans*. Pillar New Testament Commentary. Grand Rapids: Eerdmans, 1988.

Motyer, J. Alec. *Isaiah*. Tyndale Old Testament Commentaries. Downers Grove, IL: InterVarsity, 2009.

Moule, C. F. D. "Obligation in the Ethic of Paul." In *Christian History and Interpretation: Studies Presented to John Knox*, edited by W. R. Farmer et al., 389–406. Cambridge: Cambridge University Press, 1967.

Mounce, Robert. *Romans*. New American Commentary. Nashville: Broadman and Holman, 1995.

Moyise, Steve. *Paul and Scripture: Studying the New Testament Use of the Old Testament*. Grand Rapids: Baker, 2010.

Munck, Johannes. *Christ and Israel: An Interpretation of Romans 9–11*. Philadelphia: Fortress, 1967.

Muraoka, T. *A Greek-English Lexicon of the Septuagint*. Walpole, MA: Peeters, 2009.

Murray, John. *The Epistle to the Romans*. 2 vols. New International Commentary on the New Testament, old series. Grand Rapids: Eerdmans, 1965.

Naselli, Andrew David. "Paul's Use of Isaiah 40:13 and John 41:3a (Eng. 41:11a) in Romans 11:34–35." PhD diss., Trinity Evangelical Divinity School, 2010.

Nestingen, James. "Christ the End of the Law: Romans 10:4 as an Historical Exegetical-Theological Problem." PhD diss., University of Toronto, 1984.

Neufeld, Vernon. *The Earliest Christian Confessions*. New Testament Tools and Studies. Grand Rapids: Eerdmans, 1963.

Northrup, Bernard. "Joel's Concept of the Day of the Lord." PhD diss., Dallas Theological Seminary, 1961.

Nygren, Anders. *Commentary on Romans*. Translated by Carl C. Rasmussen. Philadelphia: Muhlenberg, 1949.

Origen. *Commentary on the Epistle to the Romans, Books 6–10*. Translated by Thomas Scheck. The Fathers of the Church. Washington, DC: The Catholic University of America, 2002.

Oropeza, B. J. *Jews, Gentiles, and the Opponents of Paul: The Pauline Letters*. Apostasy in the New Testament Communities 2. Eugene, OR: Cascade, 2012.

Ortlund, Dane. "The Insanity of Faith: Paul's Theological Use of Isaiah in Romans 9:33." *Trinity Journal* 30 (2009) 269–88.

———. "Zeal Without Knowledge: An Inquiry into Paul's Use of ΖΗΛΟΣ in Romans 10, Galatians 1 and Philippians 3." PhD diss., Wheaton College, 2010.

Osborne, Grant R. *Romans*. The IVP New Testament Commentary Series. Downers Grove, IL: InterVarsity, 2004.

Oss, Douglas. "The Interpretation of the 'Stone' Passages by Peter and Paul: A Comparative Study." *Journal of the Evangelical Theological Society* 32.2 (1989) 181–200.

Oswalt, John. *The Book of Isaiah, Chapters 1–39*. The New International Commentary on the Old Testament. Grand Rapids: Eerdmans, 1986.

Owen, John. *Faith and Its Evidences*. Vol. 5 of *The Works of John Owen*, edited by William Goold. Carlisle, PA: Banner of Truth, 1990.

Pattee, Stephen Bowser. "Stumbling Stone or Conterstone? The Structure and Meaning of Paul's Argument in Romans 9:30–10:13." PhD diss, Marquette University, 1991.

Pauli, C. W. H., trans. *The Chaldee Paraphrase on the Prophet Isaiah*. London: London's Society House, 1871.

Pelagius. *Pelagius's Commentary on St Paul's Epistle to the Romans*. Translated by Theodore de Bruyn. Oxford: Clarendon, 2002.

Pesch, Rudolf. *Römerbrief*. Die neue Echter Bibel. Würzburg: Echter, 1983.

Piper, John. *The Justification of God: An Exegetical and Theological Study of Romans 9:1–23*. 2nd ed. Grand Rapids: Baker, 1993.

Porter, Stanley. *The Letter to the Romans: A Lingusitic and Literary Commentary*. Sheffield, UK: Sheffield Phoenix, 2015.

———. *Verbal Aspect in the Greek of the New Testament, with Reference to Tense and Mood*. Studies in Biblical Greek. New York: Lang, 1993.

Pratt, Jonathan. "The Relationship Between Justification and Sanctification in Romans 5–8." PhD diss., Dallas Theological Seminary, 1999.

———. "The Relationship Between Justification and Spiritual Fruit in Romans 5–8." *Themelios* 34.2 (2009) 162–78.

Rad, Gerhard von. *Deuteronomy: A Commentary*. The Old Testament Library. Philadelphia: Westminster, 1966.

———. *Old Testament Theology*. Vol. 1, *The Theology of Israel's Historical Traditions*. Translated by D. M. G. Stalker. Peabody, MA: Prince, 2005.
Räisänen, Heiki. *Paul and the Law*. 2nd ed. Wissenschaftliche Untersuchungen zum Neuen Testament 1:29. Tübingen: Mohr-Siebeck, 1987.
Refoulé, François. "Note sur Romains IX, 30–33." *Revue Biblique* 92 (1985) 161–86.
———. "Romains, x, 4. Encore une Fois." *Revue Biblique* 91 (1984) 321–50.
Reumann, John. *Righteousness in the New Testament*. Philadelphia: Fortress, 1982.
Rhyne, C. Thomas. *Faith Establishes the Law*. Society of Biblical Literature Dissertation Series. Chico, CA: Scholars, 1981.
———. "*Nomos Dikaiosynēs* and the Meaning of Romans 10:4." *The Catholic Biblical Quarterly* 47 (1985) 486–99.
Ridderbos, Herman. *Aan De Romeinen*. Commentaar op het Nieuwe Testament. Kampen, NL: Kok, 1959.
———. *Paul: An Outline of His Theology*. Translated by John Richard de Witt. Grand Rapids: Eerdmans, 1975.
Ridderbos, J. *Deuteronomy*. Translated by Ed M. van der Maas. Bible Student's Commentary. Grand Rapids: Zondervan, 1984.
Roberts, J. J. M. "Yahweh's Foundation in Zion (Isa 28:16)." *Journal of Biblical Literature* 106 (1987) 27–45.
Robertson, O. Palmer. *Understanding the Land of the Bible: A Biblical-Theological Guide*. Phillipsburg, NJ: P&R, 1996.
Robinson, James, ed. *The Nag Hammadi Library*. 3rd ed. San Francisco: HarperCollins, 1988.
Rooker, Mark F. *Leviticus*. New American Commentary. Nashville: Broadman & Holman, 2000.
Rosner, Brian. *Paul and the Law: Keeping the Commandments of God*. New Studies in Biblical Theology. Downers Grove, IL: InterVarsity, 2013.
Rowe, C. Kavin. "Romans 10:13: What is the Name of the Lord?" *Horizons in Biblical Theology* 22 (2000) 135–73.
Royster, Dmitri. *Saint Paul's Epistle to the Romans: A Pastoral Commentary*. Crestwood, NY: St. Vladimir's, 2008.
Sailhamer, John. *The Pentateuch as Narrative: A Biblical-Theological Commentary*. Library of Biblical Interpretation. Grand Rapids: Zondervan, 1992.
Sanday, William, and Arthur C. Headlam. *A Critical and Exegetical Commentary on the Epistle to the Romans*. International Critical Commentary, old series. Edinburgh: T. & T. Clark, 1902.
Sanders, E. P. *Paul, the Law, and the Jewish People*. Minneapolis: Fortress, 1985.
———. *Paul and Palestinian Judaism: A Comparison of Patterns of Religion*. Minneapolis: Fortress, 1977.
Schlatter, Adolf. *Romans: The Righteousness of God*. Translated by Siegfried Schatzmann. Peabody, MA: Hendrickson, 1995.
Schoeps, H. J. *Paul: The Theology of the Apostle in the Light of Jewish Religious History*. Translated by Harold Knight. Philadelphia: Westminster, 1961.
Schreiner, Thomas. *40 Questions about Christians and Biblical Law*. Grand Rapids: Kregel, 2010.
———. "Israel's Failure to Attain Righteousness in Romans 9.30–10.3." *Trinity Journal* 12 (1991) 209–20.

———. "Paul's View of the Law in Romans 10:4–5." *Westminster Theological Journal* 55 (1993) 113–35.

———. *Romans*. Baker Exegetical Commentary on the New Testament. Grand Rapids: Baker, 1998.

———. "'Works of Law' in Paul." *Novum Testamentum* 33 (1991) 217–44.

Schweitzer, Albert. *The Mysticism of Paul the Apostle*. New York: Seabury, 1968.

Seifrid, Mark. *Christ, Our Righteousness: Paul's Theology of Justification*. New Studies in Biblical Theology. Downers Grove, IL: InterVarsity, 2000.

———. "Paul's Approach to the Old Testament in Rom 10:6–8." *Trinity Journal* 6 (1985) 3–37.

———. "Paul's Use of Righteousness Language against Its Hellenistic Background." In *Justification and Variegated Nomism: The Paradoxes of Paul*, edited by D. A. Carson et al., 2:39–74. Wissenschaftliche Untersuchungen zum Neuen Testament 2:181. Grand Rapids: Baker Academic, 2004.

———. "Righteousness Language in the Hebrew Scriptures and Early Judaism." In *Justification and Variegated Nomism: The Complexities of Second Temple Judaism*, edited by D. A. Carson et al., 1:415–442. Wissenschaftliche Untersuchungen zum Neuen Testament 2:140. Grand Rapids: Baker Academic, 2001.

———. "Romans." In *Commentary on the New Testament Use of the Old Testament*, edited by G. K. Beale et al., 607–94. Grand Rapids: Baker, 2007.

———. "Unrighteous By Faith: Apostolic Proclamation in Romans 1:18–3:20." In *Justification and Variegated Nomism: The Paradoxes of Paul*, edited by D. A. Carson et al., 2:105–45. Wissenschaftliche Untersuchungen zum Neuen Testament 2:181. Grand Rapids: Baker, 2004.

Shum, Shiu-Lun. *Paul's Use of Isaiah: A Comparative Study of Paul's Letter to the Romans and the Sibylline and Qumran Sectarian Texts*. Wissenschaftliche Untersuchungen zum Neuen Testament 2:156. Tübingen: Mohr-Siebeck, 2002.

Silva, Moisés. "The New Testament Use of the Old Testament: Text Form and Authority." In *Scripture and Truth*, edited by D. A. Carson and John D. Woodbridge, 147–65. Grand Rapids: Zondervan, 1992.

Smiles, Vincent. "The Concept of 'Zeal' in Second-Temple Judaism and Paul's Critique of It in Romans 10:2." *Catholic Biblical Quarterly* 64 (2002) 282–99.

Smith, Gary. *Isaiah 1–39*. The New American Commentary. Nashville: Broadman & Holman, 2007.

Snodgrass, Klyne. "The Christological Stone Testimonia in the New Testament." PhD diss., The University of St. Andrews, 1973.

Southall, David J. *Rediscovering Righteousness in Romans: Personified dikaiosynē within Metaphoric and Narratorial Settings*. Wissenschaftliche Untersuchungen zum Neuen Testament 2:240. Tübingen: Mohr-Siebeck, 2008.

Spanje, Teunis Erik van. *Inconsistency in Paul? A Critique of the Work of Heiki Räisänen*. Wissenschaftliche Untersuchungen zum Neuen Testament 2:130. Tübingen: Mohr-Siebeck, 1999.

Sprinkle, Preston. *Law and Life: The Interpretation of Leviticus 18:5 in Early Judaism and in Paul*. Wissenschaftliche Untersuchungen zum Neuen Testament 2:241. Tübingen: Mohr-Siebeck, 2008.

———. "The Use of Genesis 42:18 (not Leviticus 18:5) in Luke 10:28: Joseph and the Good Samaritan." *Bulletin for Biblical Research* 17.2 (2007) 193–205.

Stanley, Christopher. *Paul and the Language of Scripture: Citation Technique in the Pauline Epistles and Contemporary Literature*. Society for New Testament Studies Monograph Series. New York: Cambridge University Press, 1992.

Stendahl, Krister. *Paul Among Jews and Gentiles and Other Essays*. Philadelphia: Fortress, 1978.

Stowers, Stanley. *A Rereading of Romans: Justice, Jews, and Gentiles*. Ann Arbor, MI: Edwards, 1994.

Strack, Hermann L., and Paul Billerbeck. *Kommentar zum Neuen Testament aus Talmud und Midrasch*. 6 vols. Munich: Beck, 1922–61.

Strickland, Wayne G. "The Inauguration of the Law of Christ with the Gospel of Christ: A Dispensational View." In *Five Views on Law and Gospel*, edited by Wayne G. Strickland, 229–79. Counterpoints. Grand Rapids: Zondervan, 1999.

Stuart, Douglas. *Hosea–Jonah*. Word Biblical Commentary 31. Dallas, TX: Word, 2002.

Stuhlmacher, Peter. *Paul's Letter to the Romans: A Commentary*. Translated by Scott J. Hafemann. Louisville: Westminster John Knox, 1989.

———. "The Theme of Romans." In *The Romans Debate*, edited by Karl Donfried, 333–45. Peabody, MA: Hendrickson, 1991.

Suggs, M. Jack. "'The Word is Near You': Romans 10:6–10 Within the Purpose of the Letter." In *Christian History and Interpretation: Studies Presented to John Knox*, edited by W. R. Farmer et al., 289–312. Cambridge: Cambridge University Press, 1967.

Theobald, Michael. "Unterschiedliche Gottesbilder in Röm 9–11? Die Israel-Kapitel als Anfrage an die theologischen Diskurses bei Paulus." In *The Letter to the Romans*, edited by Udo Schnelle, 135–77. Bibliotheca Ephemeridum Theologicarum Levaniensium. Walpole, MA: Uitgeveru Peeters, 2009.

Thielman, Frank. *From Plight to Solution: A Jewish Framework for Understanding Paul's View of the Law in Galatians and Romans*. Supplements to Novum Testamentum. Eugene, OR: Wipf & Stock: 1989.

———. *The Law and the New Testament: The Question of Continuity*. Companions to the New Testament. St. Louis: Crossroad, 1999.

———. *Paul and the Law: A Contextual Approach*. Downers Grove, IL: InterVarsity, 1994.

———. *Theology of the New Testament: A Canonical and Synthetic Approach*. Grand Rapids: Zondervan, 2005.

———. "Unexpected Mercy: Echoes of a Biblical Motif in Romans 9–11." *Scottish Journal of Theology* 47.2 (1994) 169–81.

Thompson, J. A. *Deuteronomy*. Tyndale Old Testament Commentaries. Downers Grove IL: InterVarsity, 1974.

Tigay, Jeffrey. *Deuteronomy*. The JPS Torah Commentary. Philadelphia: Jewish Publication Society, 1996.

Toews, John. "The Law in Paul's Letter to the Romans: A Study of Rom. 9.30–10.13." PhD diss., Northwestern University, 1977.

———. *Romans*. Believers Church Bible Commentary. Scottdale, PA: Herald, 2004.

Trueman, Carl. *John Owen: Reformed Catholic, Renaissance Man*. New York: Routledge, 2016.

VanGemeren, Willem A. "The Law is the Perfection of Righteousness in Jesus Christ." In *Five Views on Law and Gospel*, edited by Wayne Strickland, 13–58. Counterpoints. Grand Rapids: Zondervan, 1999.

———. "Response to Wayne G. Strickland." In *Five Views on Law and Gospel*, edited by Wayne G. Strickland, 280–89. Counterpoints. Grand Rapids: Zondervan, 1999.

———. "The Spirit of Restoration." *Westminster Theological Journal* 50 (1988) 81–102.

Venema, Cornelis. "The Law of Moses: Not a Disguised Covenant of Works, A Response to F. V. Fesko's 'The Republication of the Covenant of Works.'" *The Confessional Presbyterian* 9 (2013) 212–27.

Viard, André. *Saint Paul Épitre aux Romains*. Sources bibliques. Paris: Gabalda, 1975.

Vincent, Rafael. "Derash Homiletico en Romans 9–11." *Salesianum* 42 (1980) 751–88.

Vos, Geerhardus. "The Continuity of the Kyrios-Title in the New Testament." *Princeton Theological Review* 13 (1915) 161–89.

Vos, J. S. "Die Hermeneutische Antinomie bie Paulus (Galater 3.11–12; Römer 10.5–10)." *New Testament Studies* 38 (1992) 254–70.

Wagner, J. Ross. *Heralds of the Good News: Isaiah and Paul in Concert in the Letter to the Romans*. Supplements to Novum Testamentum. Leiden, NL: Koninklijke Brill NV, 2002.

Wallace, Daniel B. *Greek Grammar Beyond the Basics: An Exegetical Syntax of the New Testament*. Grand Rapids: Zondervan, 1996.

———. "The Semantics and Exegetical Significance of the Object-Complement Construction in the New Testament." *Grace Theological Journal* 6.1 (1985) 91–112.

Walvoord, John. "Law in the Book of Romans." *Bibliotheca Sacra* 94 (1937) 281–95.

Waters, Guy. "Romans 10:5 and the Covenant of Works." In *The Law is Not of Faith: Essays on Works and Grace in the Mosaic Covenant*, edited by Bryan D. Estelle et al., 210–39. Phillipsburg, NJ: P&R, 2009.

Watson, Francis. *Paul and the Hermeneutics of Faith*. New York: T. & T. Clark, 2004.

———. *Paul, Judaism and the Gentiles: A Sociological Approach*. Cambridge: Cambridge University Press, 1986.

———. *Paul, Judaism and the Gentiles: Beyond the New Perspective*. Rev. ed. Grand Rapids: Eerdmans, 2007.

Watts, John D. W. *Isaiah 1–33*. Rev. ed. Word Biblical Commentary 24. Nashville: Nelson, 2005.

Webb, Barry. *The Message of Isaiah: On Eagles' Wings*. The Bible Speaks Today. Downers Grove, IL: InterVarsity, 1996.

Wells, Tom, and Fred Zaspel. *New Covenant Theology: Description, Definition, Defense*. Frederick, MD: New Covenant Media, 2002.

Wenham, Gordon. *The Book of Leviticus*. New International Commentary on the Old Testament. Grand Rapids: Eerdmans, 1979.

Westerholm, Stephen. *Justification Reconsidered: Rethinking a Pauline Theme*. Grand Rapids: Eerdmans, 2013.

———. "Law in the NT." In *The New Interpreter's Dictionary of the Bible: I–Ma*, edited by Katharine Sakenfeld, 3:594–602. Nashville: Abingdon, 2008.

———. "The 'New Perspective' at Twenty-Five." In *Justification and Variegated Nomism: The Paradoxes of Paul*, edited by D. A. Carson et al., 2:1–38. Wissenschaftliche Untersuchungen zum Neuen Testament 2:181. Grand Rapids: Baker, 2004.

———. "Paul and the Law in Romans 9–11." In *Paul and the Mosaic Law*, edited by James D. G. Dunn, 215–37. Wissenschatfliche Untersuchungen zum Neuen Testament 1:89. Grand Rapids: Eerdmans, 2001.

———. *Perspectives Old and New on Paul: The "Lutheran" Paul and His Critics*. Grand Rapids: Eerdmans, 2004.

White, R. Fowler, and E. Calvin Beisner. "Covenant, Inheritance, and Typology: Understanding the Principles at Work in God's Covenants." In *By Faith Alone*, edited Gary L. W. Johnson et al., 147–70. Wheaton, IL: Crossway, 2006.

Wilckens, Ulrich. *Der Brief an die Römer*. 3 vols. Studienausgabe. Evangelisch-Katholischer zum Neuen Testament. Neukirchen, DEU: Neukirchener, 2010.

Williams, Ronald. *Williams' Hebrew Syntax*. 3rd ed. Revised and expanded by John Beckman. Toronto: University of Toronto Press, 2007.

Williams, Sam. "The 'Righteousness of God' in Romans." *Journal of Biblical Literature* 99 (1980) 241–90.

Winger, Michael. *By What Law? The Meaning of Νόμος in the Letters of Paul*. Society of Biblical Literature Dissertation Series. Atlanta: Scholars, 1992.

Wise, Michael, et al. *The Dead Sea Scrolls: A New Translation*. San Francisco: HarperCollins, 1996.

Witherington, Ben. *Romans: A Socio-Rhetorical Commentary*. Grand Rapids: Eerdmans, 2004.

Wolf, Hans Walter, *A Commentary on the Books of the Prophets Joel and Amos*. Translated by Waldemar Janzen, S. Dean McBridge, and Charles Meunchow. Edited by S. Dean McBride. Hermeneia. Minneapolis: Fortress, 1977.

Woodbridge, Paul. "Did Paul Change His Mind? An Examination of Some Aspects of Pauline Eschatology." *Themelios* 28:3 (2003) 5–18.

Wrede, W. *Paul*. Translated by Edward Lummis. London: Philip Green, 1907.

Wright, N. T. *The Climax of the Covenant: Christ and the Law in Pauline Theology*. Minneapolis: Fortress, 1991.

———. *Justification: God's Plan and Paul's Vision*. Downers Grove, IL: InterVarsity, 2009.

———. *The Kingdom New Testament: A Contemporary Translation*. New York: Harper Collins, 2011.

———. "The Messiah and the People of God: A Study in Pauline Theology with Particular Reference to the Argument of the Epistle to the Romans." PhD diss., University of Oxford, 1980.

———. "Paul and Caesar: A New Reading of Romans." In *A Royal Priesthood: The Use of the Bible Ethically and Politically*, edited by Craig Bartholomew, 173–93. Carlisle, PA: Paternoster, 2002.

———. *Paul and the Faithfulness of God*. Christian Origins and the Question of God 4. Minneapolis: Fortress, 2013.

———. *The Resurrection of the Son of God*. Christian Origins and the Question of God 3. Minneapolis: Fortress, 2003.

———. *Romans*. In *The New Interpreter's Bible: Acts; Introduction to Epistolary Literature; Romans; 1 Corinthians*, edited by Leander E. Keck, 10:395–795. Nashville: Abingdon, 2002.

Young, E. J. *Isaiah*. 3 vols. Grand Rapids: Eerdmans, 1965–72.

Ziegler, Joseph, ed. *Isaias*. Göttingen Septuagint 14. Göttingen: Vandenhoeck & Ruprecht, 1939.

www.ingramcontent.com/pod-product-compliance
Lightning Source LLC
Chambersburg PA
CBHW062043220426
43662CB00010B/1631